The
Baby & Child
Medical
Handbook

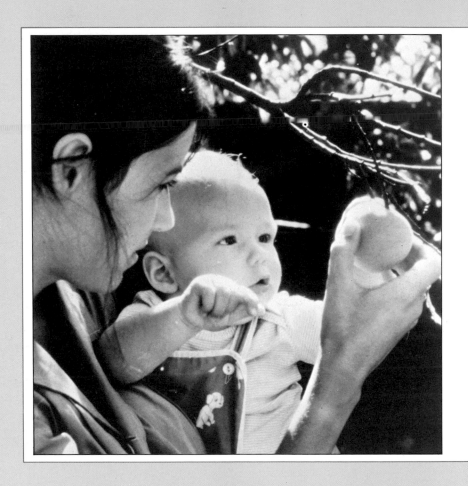

Miriam Stoppard MD MRCP

The Baby & Child Medical Handbook

DK

DORLING KINDERSLEY · LONDON

For Diana and Scott

Senior editor
Fiona MacIntyre
Editors
Charyn Jones
Jemima Dunne
Designers
Mark Evans
Roger Priddy

Senior art editor
Anne-Marie Bulat
Managing editor
Daphne Razazan

First published in Great Britain in 1986
by Dorling Kindersley Publishers Limited,
9 Henrietta Street,
London WC2E 8PS
Second impression 1986
Third impression 1987
Fourth impression 1988

British Library Cataloguing in
Publication Data

Stoppard, Miriam
    The baby & child medical handbook.
    1. Children—Diseases—Dictionaries
    I. Title
    618.92'00240431   RJ61
    ISBN 0-86318-108-2

Printed in Italy by
Arnoldo Mondadori, Verona

Contents

Note: we use the masculine pronoun "he" when referring to the baby or child. This is for convenience and clarity and does not reflect a preference for either sex.

Preface

It seems odd that so few books have been written for parents which are devoted entirely to children's illnesses. Many baby books have a section on common childhood complaints, some going so far as to include specific illnesses and their treatments; others approach the subject in a dictionary form, relying heavily on definitions without giving much background information and practical help to parents; very few, indeed, treat the subject with the kind of detail, explanations and guidelines that we have come·to expect from books on adult diseases. There seemed to be a gap, a need to be filled, hence this book.

The A-Z of common childhood complaints is the mainstay of the book. All the information is given in simple terms which are easy to understand. Parents are directed to possible courses of action in a clear, logical way, and advice is given step-by-step. Emphasis on speed is always made when time is of the essence and a doctor should be contacted immediately or an ambulance sought.

It can be difficult to tell exactly what is wrong with a child from the various symptoms—fever, pain, redness, swelling, vomiting—and on most occasions it requires a doctor to come to accurate diagnosis. However, to help the parent

Preface

narrow down the possible causes of the complaint, a section is devoted to the analysis of symptoms.

For some parents, having an ill child is not a transient event, but one which stretches into the future. Their responsibility is to cope with a chronically ill child. I have tried to cover the main conditions, giving information on causative factors, the expected course of the disease, how to make life easy on your child, yourself and the rest of the family. Long-term prognosing is always difficult, and sometimes dangerous, but I have attempted to indicate what the future might hold so that parents can make plans and get some idea of what to expect over the years. I apologize for those conditions which could not be included.

The Baby and Child Medical Handbook is full of illustrations—both drawings and photographs; in some chapters, the text is in the form of annotation to the illustrations. This is because one of my main aims is to give information in a readily accessible form, almost at a glance. There is, of course, ample opportunity to use the book as a straightforward reference book so that your knowledge gradually builds. But more than this, an anxious parent, faced with a sick child in the middle of the night, needs straight, uncomplicated information and advice and I have tried to arrange this in a way that I would like to see it if I found myself in that position as well.

I don't have any personal axes to grind, but the book is opinionated and I make no apologies for this. For instance, despite ongoing controversy in the United Kingdom, I hold strong views on the desirability of whooping cough immunization in the first year of an infant's life, and state them clearly. Where such an opinion is given, it is based on controlled research studies, or the lack of them, not on a purely personal basis. Throughout the book, however, the main aim remains the same: to give the parents enough clear, modern information, backed up by their own instincts, to know when to be their own family nurse or doctor and, on the other hand, to know when it is essential to get specialist medical help.

How to use this book

When your child is ill, you need to know what to do—whether to call the doctor, or whether you can safely treat your child at home yourself. You may also be unsure of what is wrong with him and need help in determining what the matter is.

If your child is ill and you think you know what is wrong
Turn straight to the relevant article in the A-Z of Common Complaints, pages 52 to 262. This is an alphabetical listing of the most common complaints affecting children—from bruises to bronchitis, stings to styes. There, you will find an explanation of the illness, with a list of the symptoms most likely to appear. The circumstances under which you should call the doctor are clearly defined, followed by the probable treatment. There is advice, too, on what you yourself can do to help your child (both treatment and nursing tips). There are special charts to aid diagnosis for diarrhoea, fever and vomiting.

If you are not sure what is wrong
If your child has an obvious symptom, but you are not sure which A-Z entry to look up, turn to the Visual Diagnosis Guides, pages 43 to 48. Although it is difficult to give a definitive diagnosis from only one or two symptoms, these guides should help to point you in the right direction.

If your child has had an accident
If your child has an accident, you must be prepared to deal with it. Where possible, this preparation should involve going on a first aid course, but you should frequently remind yourself of the basic life-saving techniques by referring to the First Aid section on pages 282 to 302.

How to use this book

If you are looking after a sick child
The section on pages 24 to 40 gives tips on caring for a sick child, and shows, with step-by-step illustrations, how to take a temperature and give medicines. It also provides practical advice on how to reduce fevers and make your child comfortable, how and what to feed him, how to keep him amused and, should the need arise, how to prepare him for a stay in hospital.

How to prevent accidents
The most sensible precautions for safeguarding your child inside and outside—at home and at play—are shown on pages 264 to 280. Road and car safety are also dealt with.

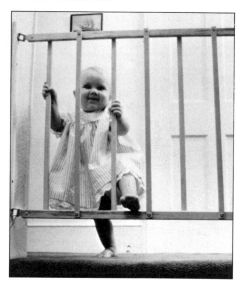

How your child's body works
An illustrated guide to the skeleton, muscles, organs and glands of your child's body is given on pages 12 to 22. This will help you to understand what the constituent parts of the body look like, where they are and how they function.

Understanding your child's body

Bones

The body is built on a framework of 206 bones called the skeleton. These bones act as levers for muscles to pull against, thus enabling movement, and they surround and protect the vital organs of the head, chest and abdomen.

How bones develop

Bones consist of a central shaft and two shaped ends. In a mature bone, the shaft and ends are hard structures, with a soft inner core of bone marrow (see below). In newborn babies, the bones are mostly made up of a soft, bendy material called cartilage, and, as your child develops, this cartilage is gradually converted to bone, a process known as *ossification*. In early childhood, the shaft is bone but the ends still consist largely of soft cartilage. By the time your child reaches adolescence, the bone formed in the ends joins the bone in the shaft and growth stops. Throughout childhood the bones are therefore fairly soft which is why so-called "greenstick fractures", where the bone bends rather than breaks, can occur (*see page 70*).

What happens when your child grows

Your child grows in height as his bones lengthen. This growth does not take place over the whole length of a bone, but at each end. Growth occurs gradually throughout childhood. At puberty, however, both girls and boys put on a rapid growth spurt. With girls this normally begins when they are about 11 years old and in boys, about a year later. Girls stop growing when they are about 18; boys continue growing for one or two years longer, which accounts, at least in part, for the greater average height in boys.

Joints

The separate bones of the skeleton are connected by joints, and these joints are held together by strong bands of fibrous tissue called ligaments. There are several different types of joint—fixed, partly movable and freely movable. *Fixed joints* allow no movement; *partly movable joints* allow slight movement; *freely movable joints* allow movement in several directions, and there are two different types—hinge joints and ball-and-socket joints.

How bone is constructed

Each bone consists of a shaft and two ends. When fully developed, the shaft is largely made up of hard (or compact) bone with a soft central core of bone marrow. Most of the blood cells are made in the bone marrow—particularly in the large bones such as the thigh bone. The ends are made up of spongy bone and capped with cartilage to cushion them against the next bone.

Adult's forearm

Child's forearm

Cross-section of mature bone

Cartilage
End
Compact bone
Shaft
Bone marrow
End
Spongy bone

Bone development The X-rays above show what happens to bones as they develop. The shape of each bone is present at birth. The bones in the child's arm are made up of areas of cartilage *(not visible on the X-ray) and bone (visible as solid white areas). As a child develops the cartilage is converted to bone. By adolescence, this conversion is complete and the bones are solid.*

Bones

Skull Made up of several bones fixed together to form a solid casing which protects the brain and other sensory organs in the head.

Collar bone (clavicle) A long, curved bone that joins the shoulder joint at one end and joins the breastbone at the other end.

Breastbone (sternum) The central bone to which most of the ribs are joined, so forming the rib cage.

Upper arm bone (humerus)

Lower arm bones

Radius

Ulna

Hip bone (pelvis) Large bone that forms part of the hip joint. The two hip bones are joined together at the front and to the spinal column at the back to form a bowl-like structure (pelvic girdle) which surrounds and protects the urinary system, bladder, and the reproductive organs in females.

Shoulder blade A large, flat bone which forms part of the shoulder joint.

Spinal column Made up of 33 bones, the spinal column surrounds and protects the delicate spinal cord—the major nerve "motorway" of the body.

Ribs Twelve pairs of ribs form a cage that houses the vital organs such as the heart, lungs and stomach.

Wrist bones (carpals)

Hand bones (metacarpals)

Finger bones (phalanges)

Thigh bone (femur)

Kneecap (patella)

Leg bones

Tibia

Fibula

Ankle bones (tarsals)

Foot bones (metatarsals)

Toe bones (phalanges)

Muscles

Muscles are made up of long bands of closely interlocking fibres that cause movement by contracting and relaxing. There are two main types of muscle in the body—involuntary and voluntary. *Involuntary muscles* operate all the time without conscious control and include the muscles of the heart and the digestive system. *Voluntary muscles,* also known as skeletal muscles, can be consciously controlled and it is these muscles that cause the visible movement of the limbs.

Some muscles are designed to relax and contract quickly to make specific movements, for example lifting an arm or kicking a ball, while others, such as the spinal muscles, are designed to remain in contraction for long periods of time. There are well over 600 named muscles in the body; illustrated opposite are some of the larger or most obvious ones.

How muscles grow

Although your baby can move quite vigorously at birth and all the muscles are present, they are not fully developed and will grow in length, breadth and thickness as your baby develops. The three most important factors affecting their development are the hormones present in the body, physical activity and diet. Before adolescence there is very little difference in the bulk and strength of boys' and girls' muscles. What difference there is is largely due to the tendency in boys to spend more time than girls on activities that require physical strength. After adolescence, however, the male hormones are important in the development of a boy's greater bulk and strength.

To develop properly, muscles must be used; if they are not used, they will actually decrease in size. A child who is encouraged to be active, and pursue physical activities requiring increasing stamina, will have larger, stronger and more well-coordinated muscles than a child who is lethargic and takes little exercise or one who is discouraged from doing so by over protective parents. Some children, however, have muscles that show great endurance while others seem to tire more easily, so try to let your child set his own limits. Don't expect your child to continue to the point of exhaustion; on the other hand, if he is full of energy, don't try to stop him continuing after other children have given up. Let him be the judge of his own limitations.

How muscles work

Muscles consist of a large central part known as the belly, which tapers at each end. The ends are attached to a bone, either directly, or by means of a narrow band of fibre called a tendon.

Most of the skeletal muscles work in pairs so that as one contracts, the other relaxes. To bend the elbow, the biceps muscle contracts and the triceps muscle relaxes; to straighten it, the triceps contracts and the biceps relaxes.

Muscles used to bend and straighten the elbow

Direction of movement

Biceps contracts

Triceps relaxes

Biceps relaxes

Direction of movement

Triceps contracts

Muscles

Facial muscles There are 67 different muscles in the face each with a different purpose; fewer are used to smile than to frown.

Chest muscles The large muscle across the top of the chest, the *pectoralis major,* helps to move the shoulder and is involved in deep breathing. The *intercostal muscles* between the ribs also help with breathing.

Pectoralis major

Intercostal muscles

Leg muscle The *tibialis anterior* at the front of the leg assists with walking and running.

Achilles tendon Attaching the calf muscle to the heel bone, this is one of the largest tendons in the body.

Neck muscles Some are concerned with swallowing, others support the neck and enable the head to turn and nod.

Upper arm muscles The *biceps* muscle in front bends the elbow; the *triceps* muscle at the back straightens the arm again.

Biceps

Triceps

Buttock muscles The *gluteus maximus* muscle of the buttocks helps with standing and climbing.

Thigh muscles The huge *hamstrings* at the back of the thighs move the hips and knees for kicking or running, the *sartorius* bends the knee and the *quadriceps* at the front straighten it again.

Quadriceps

Sartorius

Calf muscles The *gastrocnemius* and the *soleus* muscles at the back of the calf are concerned with walking, running and standing.

Gastrocnemius

Soleus

15

The head

The brain and the most important sensory organs of the body (the eyes, ears, nose and mouth) are situated in the head. They are surrounded and protected by the skull. The skull is made up of several bones which, in older children and adults, are fused together.

The brain

The brain is a very important and complex structure. It is the main control centre of the nervous system—the system comprising the brain, spinal cord and the nerves—which controls all bodily functions. The brain receives information from the outside world through the various sensory organs, including the skin, and acts on this information by sending out instructions to the different parts of the body. Some parts of the body receive their instructions from nerves directly connected to the brain, others, such as the arms and legs, receive their messages via nerves branching off the spinal cord.

The brain is divided into three main parts—the cerebral hemispheres, the cerebellum and the brain stem. Each part controls a different body function. The brain is protected by three membranes called the meninges, and it is cushioned by fluid called cerebro-spinal fluid. This fluid, which is produced in the centre of the brain, flows between the two innermost membranes, and also surrounds the spinal cord.

Teeth

Your child's first teeth, known as milk teeth, will probably begin to come through when he is about six or seven months old. The full set of 20 teeth should have come through by the time he is about three years old. The permanent adult teeth will begin to appear when your child is about six, but the full set of 32 teeth will not be complete until he is about 17. The first permanent teeth to come through are the first molars. The milk teeth become loose and fall out one at a time and are normally replaced immediately by the permanent teeth. Sometimes, however, a permanent tooth begins to come through before the milk tooth has fallen out. This can cause pain and the dentist may have to extract the milk tooth.

Milk teeth
Age of appearance

2-3 years

12 months

18 months

7 months

6 months

Upper set

Lower set

Permanent teeth
Age of appearance

17+ years

11-13 years

6-7 years

10-12 years

9-12 years

7-9 years

6-8 years

Upper set

Lower set

The head

Areas of control

Certain areas of the brain are responsible for controlling specific bodily functions: for example, the occipital lobe for vision and motor cortex for voluntary movement. Memory cannot be localized in the same way but is thought to be dealt with by the cerebral hemispheres as a whole.

Motor cortex The part of the brain concerned with initiating movement. Different areas are responsible for each part of the body, as follows: **A** toes, feet and legs; **B** thighs, abdomen and trunk; **C** shoulders and arms; **D** head, eyelids and cheeks; **E** jaws and lips.

Frontal lobes Emotions are controlled in this part of the brain.

Speech centre Speech is controlled in a small area of the frontal lobe. If your child is right-handed, the speech centre will be in the left cerebral hemisphere, as shown here; and vice versa if he is left-handed.

Sensory cortex All the sensations felt by the body are received and interpreted in this area.

Parietal lobe Involved with understanding speech, this area works with the occipital lobe to work out the size and shape of objects, and to read.

Occipital lobe Vision is controlled in this part of the brain

Temporal lobe Area responsible for controlling hearing.

Cerebellum Mainly concerned with balance and co-ordination of the muscles and joints.

Brain stem Controls the involuntary functions of the body such as heartbeat, breathing rate and temperature regulation.

Left cerebral hemisphere

Right cerebral hemisphere

Inside the brain

This cross-section of the brain shows the right cerebral hemisphere. It is joined to the left by a band of tissue called the corpus callosum. Each cerebral hemisphere is made up of two types of tissue: grey matter and white matter. Grey matter consists of the nerve cells, white matter consists of the nerve fibres. The hypothalamus is situated at the base of the brain and controls sleep and appetite. Under the central part of the brain is the pituitary gland, the gland that controls growth and development and ensures that all the glands in the endocrine system the hormone-producing glands, (*see page 21*) are functioning properly.

Cross-section of the brain

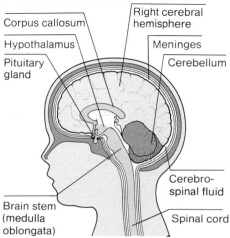

Corpus callosum

Hypothalamus

Pituitary gland

Right cerebral hemisphere

Meninges

Cerebellum

Cerebro-spinal fluid

Spinal cord

Brain stem (medulla oblongata)

The head

The sense organs

The most important sense organs of the body (the nose, mouth, eyes and ears) are all situated in the head. Between them, they give us a great deal of information about the outside world.

The nose and mouth

The nose is the organ of smell and also forms the main entrance to the respiratory system. Air is breathed in through the nose and passes down into the lungs via the windpipe (trachea). The nose is lined with a hair-covered membrane that filters, moistens and warms air as it is taken in to the body. The nose is also linked to the sinuses, which is why nasal infections can pass into the sinuses.

The mouth forms the entrance to the digestive system (*see page 21*); it is also involved (with the tongue, lips and larynx) in speech. The tongue is the organ of taste—different areas of the tongue distinguish the main types of flavour: salty, sweet, bitter and sour.

Cross-section of the nose and mouth.

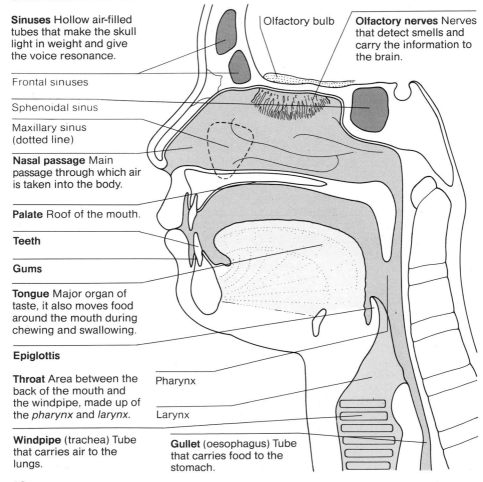

Sinuses Hollow air-filled tubes that make the skull light in weight and give the voice resonance.

Frontal sinuses

Sphenoidal sinus

Maxillary sinus (dotted line)

Nasal passage Main passage through which air is taken into the body.

Palate Roof of the mouth.

Teeth

Gums

Tongue Major organ of taste, it also moves food around the mouth during chewing and swallowing.

Epiglottis

Throat Area between the back of the mouth and the windpipe, made up of the *pharynx* and *larynx*.

Windpipe (trachea) Tube that carries air to the lungs.

Olfactory bulb

Olfactory nerves Nerves that detect smells and carry the information to the brain.

Pharynx

Larynx

Gullet (oesophagus) Tube that carries food to the stomach.

The head

The eye

The eye works by focusing rays of light through a lens on to a sensitive layer in the back of the eye called the retina. The information is then sent to the brain via the optic nerve to be interpreted. Each eye sees an object from a different angle. The brain co-ordinates the image picked up by each eye so that a solid, three-dimensional object is seen. The eye is held in place by six muscles, which allow it to swivel and see in many directions.

Cross-section of the eye

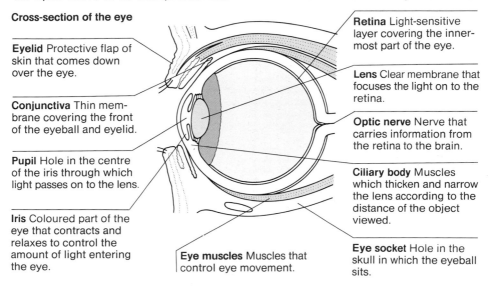

Eyelid Protective flap of skin that comes down over the eye.

Conjunctiva Thin membrane covering the front of the eyeball and eyelid.

Pupil Hole in the centre of the iris through which light passes on to the lens.

Iris Coloured part of the eye that contracts and relaxes to control the amount of light entering the eye.

Retina Light-sensitive layer covering the inner-most part of the eye.

Lens Clear membrane that focuses the light on to the retina.

Optic nerve Nerve that carries information from the retina to the brain.

Ciliary body Muscles which thicken and narrow the lens according to the distance of the object viewed.

Eye muscles Muscles that control eye movement.

Eye socket Hole in the skull in which the eyeball sits.

The ear

The ear is an important organ, not only for hearing, but also for balance. The ear consists of three parts: the outer, middle and inner ear. The part of the ear that you see is the outer ear. All three sections of the ear are involved with hearing; balance is controlled in the inner ear alone.

Cross-section of the ear

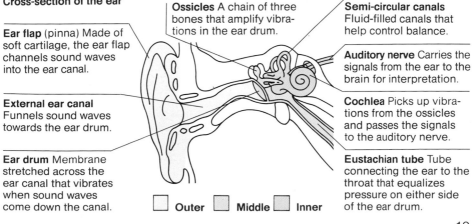

Ear flap (pinna) Made of soft cartilage, the ear flap channels sound waves into the ear canal.

External ear canal Funnels sound waves towards the ear drum.

Ear drum Membrane stretched across the ear canal that vibrates when sound waves come down the canal.

Ossicles A chain of three bones that amplify vibrations in the ear drum.

Semi-circular canals Fluid-filled canals that help control balance.

Auditory nerve Carries the signals from the ear to the brain for interpretation.

Cochlea Picks up vibrations from the ossicles and passes the signals to the auditory nerve.

Eustachian tube Tube connecting the ear to the throat that equalizes pressure on either side of the ear drum.

☐ **Outer** ☐ **Middle** ☐ **Inner**

19

Organs and glands

Housed in the centre of the body cavity are the organs that deal with digestion, breathing and blood circulation. The glands produce hormones, which control the functioning of the organs and growth and development.

Glands that swell

The glands that swell during an illness are not glands in the true sense because they do not secrete hormones. They are lymph nodes, part of the lymphatic system which is responsible for helping the body to fight infection. When infection occurs, more white cells are pro-duced all over the body and sent to the lymph nodes nearest the area of infection so that the germs can be destroyed. This causes the lymph nodes to swell and they may be slightly tender. Lymph nodes are sited all over the body; those in the neck are the most commonly activated by infection, but the other main sites are the armpit and groin.

Glands behind the ear These glands swell if your child has an ear infection.

Glands below the ear and the jaw These are the glands most commonly affec-ted by tonsillitis, for example.

Glands in the back of the neck. These swell if, for example, your child has German measles.

Circulatory system

The blood, which consists of red and white blood cells suspended in a fluid called plasma, is the body's main transport system. It carries oxygen from the lungs and nourishment from digested food around the body, and carries waste matter, such as carbon dioxide (a by-product of breathing) away from the body cells.

There are two parts to the circulatory system: the *systematic circulation* which carries blood to the tissues and the *pulmonary circulation* which carries blood from the heart to the lungs and back to the heart for oxygenation. Very simply, the circulatory system works as follows. Blood, bright red because it is loaded with oxygen, comes from the lungs into the left side of the heart. The heart pumps this blood out into the main artery, the aorta. This divides into two arteries, one to carry blood to the head, neck and arms, the other to carry it to the abdomen and legs. These then sub-divide into smaller and smaller arteries, ending in thin-walled capillaries in the body cells. It is in the capillaries that the nourishment and oxygen carried by the blood are passed into the cells, and waste matter, such as carbon dioxide, is picked up. The capillaries then join up to form veins which carry the blood, now darker red because it contains less oxygen, back to the heart. The veins join up to form larger and larger veins and finally form two large veins, the superior vena cava from the head, neck and arms, and the inferior vena cava from the abdomen and legs. These both carry blood into the right side of the heart. From here, the blood is pumped to the lungs, where the carbon dioxide is given up to be breathed out of the lungs and a fresh supply of oxygen is collected.

Organs and glands

Thyroid gland Regulates the general rate of growth and development of the body.

Oesophagus (gullet) Passage which carries food and drink from the mouth to the stomach.

Heart Muscular organ which pumps blood around the body at regular intervals.

Stomach Muscular organ where food is broken down by digestive juices.

Pancreas Produces digestive juices for use in the breakdown of food in the intestine. It also produces the hormone insulin which regulates the amount of sugar in the blood.

Liver Gland which secretes bile and regulates blood chemistry.

Small intestine Long, narrow tube, up to 6.7m (22ft) long in an adult, in which the digestion of food is completed and where nearly all the nutrients are absorbed.

Appendix Narrow, worm-like protrusion near the junction of the small and large intestine; its purpose is unknown.

Rectum Organ where faeces are stored before being expelled from the body.

Pituitary gland Controls the body's growth and development and ensures that all the glands in the endocrine system (the hormone-producing glands) function properly.

Windpipe (trachea) Passage which carries air from the nose and mouth to the lungs.

Lungs Two organs (one slightly larger than the other) which expand to take air into the body and relax to push the used air out.

Diaphragm A large dome-shaped sheet of muscle that separates the organs of the chest and the abdomen. It moves up and down to help breathing in conjunction with the intercostal muscles.

Spleen Destroys worn-out red blood cells and recycles the iron from them.

Adrenal gland

Kidney

Large intestine Wider and much shorter than the small intestine; water and undigested remains are passed into it from the small intestine. The water is re-absorbed but the undigested waste products pass on to the rectum as faeces.

21

Organs and glands

Organs of the lower abdomen

These include the two kidneys and the bladder (which, with the ureters and urethra, make up the urinary system), and the reproductive organs.

Male reproductive system

The male sex glands, the testes (testicles), are situated on the outside of the body in the scrotal sac. They produce sperm and testosterone, the hormone that controls the development of the sex organs and the secondary sexual characteristics such as broad shoulders and well-muscled arms and legs.

From puberty onwards, all the organs of the reproductive system enlarge. The testes then begin to manufacture sperm, first in small quantities, then increasingly larger amounts.

Prostate Small gland at the base of the bladder.

Vas deferens Tube connecting the penis and the testis along which sperm pass.

Penis Male sex organ.

Testes Glands where sperm are manufactured and which produce the male sex hormones.

Scrotal sac Pouch that surrounds the testes.

Kidneys These two organs filter the blood, removing any waste products from it. They also make urine.

Ureters Tubes connecting the kidneys and the bladder; there is one for each kidney.

Bladder Expandable bag in which liquid waste (urine) is stored before being excreted.

Urethra Passage that carries urine and fluid containing sperm (seminal fluid) out of the body.

Female reproductive system

At birth, the uterus is extremely small and it does not begin to grow until puberty. However, the ovaries already contain all the eggs that will ever be produced and released during a girl's fertile life. Female sex hormones, oestrogen and proges-terone, are manufactured by the ovaries. At puberty, their production begins to follow a monthly pattern, which stimulates the beginning of the menstrual cycle.

Uterus (womb) Organ in which developing fetus is carried.

Ovaries The organs where the female sex hormones are produced and the eggs are stored.

Fallopian tubes Tubes linking the uterus and the ovaries. These are the tubes into which the egg is released during the menstrual cycle.

Cervix Entrance to uterus

Kidneys These two organs filter the blood, removing any waste products from it. They also make urine.

Ureters Tubes connecting the kidneys and the bladder; there is one for each kidney.

Bladder Expandable bag in which liquid waste (urine) is stored before being excreted.

Vagina Female genital passage leading to the cervix.

Urethra Tube that carries urine out of the body.

Caring for
a sick child

Calling the doctor

Most parents know instinctively when their child is sickening for something: the child may not be as lively as usual; he may refuse his food; he may become clingy. However, the parent is not always able to diagnose exactly what is wrong, nor is he or she necessarily able to tell whether the child's symptoms are serious, or even potentially serious. An ill child is always distressing and the situation can be made even more tense if you cannot decide whether or not to call out the doctor.

There are some circumstances, after a serious injury, for example, when medical help must be sought immediately. For most parents, these situations are quite obvious. There are, however, many more situations where the seriousness isn't as clear-cut. This is where the worry comes in: "Are my child's symptoms quite normal or are they potentially serious?" What you must remember is that most doctors will not mind if you seek their advice. Always follow your instincts and, if you are ever in doubt, contact your doctor.

If your child is already undergoing treatment from your doctor and you are worried about his progress, call your doctor again. Don't take your child to a casualty department because the doctor in the casualty department will not be able to change your child's treatment without consulting your own doctor first.

You will almost certainly know when your child is sickening for something.

Calling the doctor

When to call your doctor

Listed below are the circumstances under which you should always call your doctor. The following are all important signs so never ignore them.

Temperature
● A raised temperature of over 39°C (102.2°F).
● A raised temperature of over 38°C (100.4°F), plus any other obvious signs of illness.
● A raised temperature accompanied by a convulsion or a raised temperature if your child has had convulsions in the past.
● A raised temperature accompanied by a stiff neck and headache.
● A temperature below 35°C (95°F). accompanied by a cold skin surface, drowsiness, quietness and listlessness.
● A temperature which drops and then rises again suddenly.
● A temperature of more than 38°C (100.4°F), for more than three days.

Diarrhoea
● If your baby has diarrhoea for more than six hours.
● If diarrhoea is accompanied by pain in the abdomen, a temperature or any other obvious signs of illness.

Vomiting
● If your baby has been vomiting for more than six hours.
● Prolonged, violent vomiting.
● Dizzy spells plus nausea and headaches.
● Nausea and vomiting accompanied by right-sided pain in the abdomen.

Loss of appetite
● If your baby goes off his food suddenly or is less than six months old and doesn't seem to be thriving.
● If your child usually has a hearty appetite, but refuses all food for a day and seems listless.

Pain and discomfort
● If your child has headaches and feels sick and dizzy.
● If your child complains of blurred vision, especially if he's recently had a bang on the head.
● If your child has severe griping pains, which occur at regular intervals.
● If your child has a pain in the right side of his abdomen and feels sick.

Breathing
● If your child's breathing is laboured and his ribs are being sharply drawn in with each breath.

Emergencies

Always get your child to the nearest casualty department by ambulance or car if you notice *any* of the following (*see also pages 282-302*):
● Your child has stopped breathing (*see page 283*).
● Your child is breathing with difficulty and his lips are going blue.
● Your child is unconscious (*see page 291*).
● Your child has a deep wound that is bleeding badly (*see page 292*).
● Your child has a serious burn (*see page 296*).
● Your child has a suspected broken bone (*see page 70*).
● Your child has a chemical in his
● eyes (*see page 131*).
● Your child's ear or eye has been pierced (*see pages 120 and 132*).
● Your child has been bitten by an animal or a snake (*see pages 65 and 219*).
● Your child has eaten a poisonous substance (*see page 299*).

Calling the doctor

What to tell your doctor

Your doctor will need to know the answers to specific questions, both to help him make a diagnosis and to gauge the severity of the illness or injury. The doctor needs as much information as possible. If necessary, write down everything that you think might be helpful on a piece of paper and have it with you when you are speaking to the doctor so that you do not forget. He will probably need to know the following:

● Your child's age.
● Whether your child has a temperature. If so, what is it; how long has he had it; have there been any fluctuations and, if so, what were they?
● If your child has a fever, did it come on quickly?
● Are your child's neck glands swollen?

● Has your child vomited?
● Has your child had diarrhoea?
● Has your child complained of any kind of pain and, if so, where is the pain?
● Has your child suffered from dizziness or blurred vision (particularly if he's recently had a knock on the head)?
● Has your child had a convulsion? If so, how long did it last?
● Has your child lost consciousness?
● Did your child eat the last meal offered and has he eaten within the past three hours?

What to expect from your doctor

Whether you take your child to the doctor's surgery or arrange for a home visit, there are certain things you should expect your doctor to do. Make sure he

Taking your child's pulse

The pulse is the wave of pressure that passes along each artery every time the heart beats. You can feel the pulse wherever an artery lies close to the skin. The most common site for taking the pulse is at the wrist (radial pulse). The pulse can also be taken in the neck (carotid pulse), although this is normally only done if you suspect that the heart has stopped beating altogether (see page 288).

The pulse rate will vary with age. It is normally faster after exercise and slower after resting. A young baby's heart will beat about 160 times a minute; by the time he is one year old it will beat about 100-120 times per minute and by the time he is about seven or eight years old, it will have slowed down to the adult rate of 80-90 beats per minute. A normal pulse is regular and strong; any abnormality, such as a fast, weak pulse or a slow pulse, may indicate that your child is ill.

If your child is under one, it is generally easier to place your hand on

his chest and count the actual heartbeat rather than trying to find one of his arteries because babies are generally quite chubby.

Taking the radial pulse

1 Support your child's wrist with your thumb and place two fingers in the hollow below the palm of his hand on the thumb side just below the wrist creases.

2 Count the number of beats you can feel in 15 seconds and multiply this figure by four to get the number of beats in a minute.

Calling the doctor

gives you an honest opinion of what he thinks is wrong with your child and that he answers all your questions fully.

Your doctor should give your child a thorough examination. If, for example, your child has an earache, the doctor should examine his ears. If he has abdominal pain then your doctor should examine his abdomen without his clothes on. If he has got a sore throat and a cough, your doctor should listen to his chest as well as examining the throat and feeling his neck glands. You should not accept a prescription for your child without an examination first.

Here is a list of things you should expect your doctor to do or tell you, or that you should remember to ask him.

Expect your doctor to:
● Examine your child thoroughly.
● Give you an honest opinion of what is wrong. If your doctor does not know what is wrong, you should expect him to tell you that further investigations are necessary in order to obtain a clear diagnosis.
● Tell you the implications of the illness or condition. If, for example, your child has an acute attack of sinusitis or a middle-ear infection, your doctor should tell you that your child may need several courses of antibiotics to eradicate it completely.
● Not give you medicine if he is sure that there is nothing wrong. He would be wrong to give you something simply because you have gone into the surgery expecting to be treated. Respect him for not being pressurized into giving you a prescription.
● Answer all your questions—be persistent until you are completely satisfied.
● Give you as much information as possible about the medicines prescribed for your child—whether to give them before or after a meal, whether there are any side-effects and whether there are any special precautions that you ought to take.

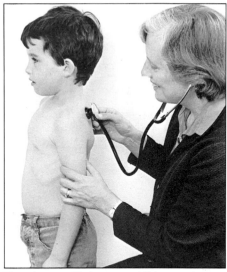

Your doctor will give your child a thorough examination.

● Warn you of any possible complications and tell you what danger signs to look out for.

Things to ask your doctor
● If your child has a recurrent condition such as cold sores or boils, ask your doctor what you can do if you notice the symptoms recurring.
● Ask your doctor for home nursing tips.
● If your child has a chronic condition, ask your doctor if there is anything that you can do yourself at home to help the condition. For example, if your child has infantile eczema, there's quite a lot you can do in terms of adding emollients to the bath water, using special soap, gently rubbing in moisturizing ointments and creams, even when the skin is clear.
● If your child has an infectious disease, ask your doctor about the incubation period (for the benefit of your friends whose children have come in contact with your child), the length of time your child will be infectious and how long he will have to stay off school.

Temperature

In children, normal body temperature ranges from 36°C (96.8°F) to 37°C (98.6°F). Any temperature over 37.7°C (100°F), taken orally, or 38°C (100.4°F), taken rectally, is classed as a fever. Hypothermia develops if the temperature falls below 35°C (95°F). Body temperature will vary according to how active your child has been and the time of day: it is lowest in the morning because there is little muscle activity during sleep, and highest in the late afternoon after a day's activity. It will also be high after your child has been running around.

An abnormally hot forehead may be the first indication that your child has a temperature. To be accurate, however, you must take your child's temperature with a thermometer (*see opposite* and *page 30*). Because the temperature control centre in the brain is primitive in young children, the temperature can shoot up more rapidly than in adults. When a fever is present, you should take your child's temperature again after 20 minutes, just in case it was only a transitory leap. Never regard a high temperature as an accurate reflection of your child's health; it is only one sign of illness. A child can be very ill without a temperature or quite healthy with one.

Thermometers

There are two main types of thermometer: mercury thermometers and liquid crystal, or forehead, thermometers. Mercury thermometers are the most accurate means of assessing a temperature. Made of glass, with a hollow tube running up the centre, they register temperature when the mercury expands and moves up the tube to a point on the scale. Try to buy one with a short reading time so that your child does not have a chance to get fidgety. (It is also useful to have a low-reading thermometer because babies and young children lose heat quickly and this can be dangerous, *see page 300*.) With a baby up to 1-1½ years you should use a rectal thermometer. From about then he'll tolerate his temperature being

Types of thermometers

Mercury thermometers

Oral thermometer

Normal reading

Rectal thermometer

Normal reading

Liquid crystal thermometers

Disc thermometer   Strip thermometer

°F 96.8 98.6 100.4 102.2 104
°C 36 37 38 39 40

Normal reading

Normal reading

Temperature

taken under his armpit. By the time your child is about six or seven you can probably take his temperature orally, as long as you are sure you can trust him not to bite the thermometer.

Liquid crystal thermometers are plastic thermometers with a heat-sensitive panel on one side and numbers and/or panels on the other side. When the sensitive side is placed on the forehead, the numbers or panels light up. Liquid crystal thermometers are not as accurate as mercury thermometers but they are quick, safe and easy to use.

Reading thermometers

The temperature registered on a liquid crystal thermometer is the number or panel that remains lit up. Mercury thermometers are more difficult to read. Hold the thermometer between your finger and thumb and turn it until you can see a thick silver line. The actual body temperature is the point on the scale reached by the mercury.

Tips for taking your child's temperature

● Never take your child's temperature if he has just stopped running about.
● Never leave your child alone with a thermometer in his mouth.
● If there is an accident and the thermometer breaks in your child's mouth, remove the pieces of glass quickly and carefully. The mercury is unlikely to spill from its tube but if it does, tell your child to spit out as much as he can and mop up the rest with a dry tissue. If your child swallows any mercury, call your doctor.
● Make sure there is no break in the mercury inside the thermometer—it will affect the reading.
● If your thermometer is cracked, throw it away immediately.
● Wash the thermometer after use with soap and cold water.
● Always store the thermometer in its own case.

Using forehead thermometers

There are several different types of forehead thermometer but they all work on the same principle. The two main ones are shown here. Always read the manufacturers instructions carefully.

Using the disc

Using the strip

2 Leave it for about 15 seconds. Numbers and coloured panels will light up in sequence, as left, before coming to rest at the reading for your child's temperature.

Place the disc in the centre of your child's forehead. Leave it for 15 seconds. Numbers will light up in sequence before coming to rest at the reading for your child's temperature.

1 Hold the strip against your child's forehead with both hands, keeping your fingers clear of the numbered panels. Make sure the strip is flat against your child's forehead.

Temperature

Using a mercury thermometer

Whether you are using a rectal or an oral thermometer, hold it by the top end and shake it down sharply until the mercury falls below the 35°C (95°F) mark. Always wash the thermometer in cold water after use. Never wash it with hot water because it can crack the glass.

Using a rectal thermometer

1 Lubricate the bulb of the thermometer with some baby cream or oil.

2 Lay your baby on his back and remove his nappy. Then grasp his heels, keeping your fingers between his ankles so that they do not rub together. Lift up his legs. Alternatively, lay him face down across your lap and place one hand over his back to prevent him wriggling.

3 Gently insert the thermometer into his rectum by about 2.5cm (1in) and hold it in place.

4 Leave the thermometer in place for two minutes (or according to manufacturer's instructions), then remove and read.

Using an oral thermometer

1 Ask your child to open his mouth and raise his tongue. Place the thermometer under his tongue.

2 Ask your child to place the tip of his tongue firmly behind his lower front teeth—this will hold the thermometer in place. Then ask him to close his lips—but not his teeth—over the thermometer so that the seal is airtight. Check to make sure he is not gripping the thermometer with his teeth.

3 Leave the thermometer in your child's mouth for two minutes (or according to the manufacturer's instructions) then remove and read.

Armpit method

1 Sit with your child on your lap, facing away from you. With the thermometer in your right hand, raise your child's left arm to expose the armpit.

2 Place the thermometer into the armpit and lower your child's arm over it. Hold the arm down for two minutes (or according to manufacturer's instructions), then remove and read.
Note The temperature reading when taken in the child's armpit will be about 0.6°C (1°F) lower than the child's actual body temperature.

Temperature

Treating a raised temperature

The raised temperature that accompanies an illness is the body's way of responding to infection, and is a sign that the body is marshalling its defences (*see page 134*). While this is a good sign it is also important not to let your child's temperature get to high. If he has a high temperature, he will be very uncomfortable and irritable; moreover, high temperature, particularly in young children, can lead to convulsions (*see page 95*). So it is important that you lower his temperature.

Removing bedclothes

Remove your child's clothes and any blankets so that his body cools down by radiation, then leave him covered by only a single cotton sheet. If his temperature rises over 39°C (102.2°F), he may be more comfortable left uncovered but wearing a short-sleeved cotton T-shirt and underpants or a vest and nappy.

Medicines

The most efficient way of reducing your child's fever is to give him medicine. Paracetamol is probably the best choice with children, as it has few side-effects. It also has the advantage that it is available in syrup, or elixir, form so is much easier to give to young children.

Paracetamol elixir can be bought at most chemists without a prescription and, as a child can develop a high temperature very quickly, it is a good idea to have a bottle in the medicine cabinet.

Whether you use junior paracetamol tablets or elixir, it is very important not to give your child more than the recommended dose—but don't give him less either—and do not give them to your child for longer than two days without consulting your doctor.

To make it more palatable to a child, paracetamol elixir is usually sweetened so, if at all possible, make sure your child brushes his teeth after taking it.

Tepid sponging

If your child's temperature is over 40°C (104°F) for longer than half an hour, and removing his bedclothes hasn't helped, try tepid sponging. Always use tepid water, never cold. Tepid water causes the blood vessels in the skin to dilate, therefore aiding heat loss; cold water causes the blood vessels to contract and retain heat.

1 Half fill a bucket with water that is comfortable to your elbow or the inside of your wrist and put several clean flannels or sponges in it. Place dry towels around your child so that the bed does not get wet.

2 Wring one of the flannels or sponges out slightly so that it is still dripping. Starting from the head, and using brisk but gentle strokes, sponge the whole of your child's body. Change the sponge when it feels warm.

3 Take your child's temperature after five or ten minutes. If it has dropped to 38°C (100.4°F), stop sponging. If his temperature has not dropped, keep sponging and take his temperature every five minutes. Stop when it has dropped.

4 Cover him with a cotton sheet, and watch him carefully. Be careful not to let him get too cold. Repeat tepid sponging if his temperature rises again. If his temperature does not drop, consult your doctor immediately.

Medicines

When you take your child to the doctor he may prescribe some form of medicine for your child. Ask your doctor to give you as much information as possible about the medicines: ask if there are likely to be any side-effects, or whether there are foods that should be avoided, or special precautions that should be taken while your child is taking the medication (*see page 27*).

Most medicines for young children are made up in a sweetened syrup to make them more palatable, and can be given with a spoon, tube or dropper. Droppers and tubes, are often more suitable for babies who haven't learnt to swallow from

a spoon. Some medicines for older children are supplied as tablets or capsules.

On most occasions your child will be co-operative but nearly everyone has been faced with the situation of trying to give medicine to a child who refuses to take it. It is very important that your child takes any medicine prescribed when he is ill. In fact, I think that this is one occasion when blackmail is justified. Be firm but never harsh, cruel or threatening and never punish your child for being difficult about taking the medicines. Very occasionally, a child will resist physically and in this case there is no alternative but for you to be forceful.

Giving medicines to a baby or young child

It can be more difficult to administer medicines to babies because they wriggle. You will need to enlist the help of another adult or older brother or sister. Position your baby so that he is slightly raised— never have your baby lying flat while giving him medicine because he may inhale the medicine into his lungs.

Using a spoon

1 If the baby is very young, sterilize the spoon by boiling it or placing it in a sterilizing solution. Hold your baby in the crook of your arm. If he won't open his mouth, open it by gently pulling down his chin; if necessary get someone to do this.

2 Place the spoon on his lower lip, raise the angle of the spoon and let the medicine run into his mouth.

Using a dropper

1 Hold your baby as described left and take up the specified amount of medicine into the glass tube.

2 Place the dropper in the corner of your baby's mouth and release the medicine gently.

Using a medicine tube

Pour the required dose into the tube. Hold your baby as described left. Place the mouthpiece on his lower lip and let the medicine run gently into his mouth.

Using your finger

If your baby will not take his medicine from a spoon or a dropper, measure the required dose into a container. Dip your little finger into it, then let your baby suck it off your finger.

Medicines

Giving medicines and tablets to older children

On the whole, children do not generally mind medicine too much and often want to pour medicine out for themselves rather than let you give it to them. I have listed a few tips, below, that may help if your child is difficult. For example, tablets can be crushed and mixed with jam and medicines can sometimes be mixed with a favourite drink. Capsules, however, should not be broken.

It is very important that your child takes his medicine exactly as prescribed.

Tips for giving medicines

Giving medicines to babies
● Get the help of another adult or older child.
● If you are on your own, wrap a blanket around your baby's arms so that you can stop him struggling and hold him steady.
● Only put a little of the medicine in his mouth at a time.
● If your baby spits the medicine out, get the other person to hold his mouth open while you pour the medicine into the back of his mouth and then, gently but firmly, close his mouth.

Giving medicines to older children
● Suggest that your child holds his nose while taking the medicine, so lessening the effect of the taste.
● Don't forcibly hold your child's nose as he may inhale some of the medicine.
● Mix liquid medicine with another syrup such as honey.
● Don't add liquid medicine to a drink as it will just sink to the bottom of the glass or stick to the sides and you won't be sure that your child has had the whole dose.
● Show your child that you have his favourite drink ready to wash the taste of the medicine away, even if you would not normally allow your child to have it very often.
● Help your child to clean his teeth after taking any liquid medicine to prevent syrup sticking to his teeth.
● Crush tablets between two spoons and mix the powder with honey, jam or ice-cream.

Medicines

Giving drops

Ear, nose or eye infections are generally treated with external drops. It is always easier to administer drops to a baby or young child if you lay him on a flat surface before you begin and enlist the help of another adult or an older child to keep him still and hold his head steady. An older child will probably be more co-operative and you will only need to ask him to tilt his head back or to the side, while you put the drops in.

Ear drops

1 Lay your baby on his side with the affected ear uppermost. Let the drops fall into the centre of his ear.

2 Hold your baby steady until the drops have run into the canal.

Nose drops

1 Tilt your baby's head back slightly and gently drop liquid into each nostril.

2 Count the number of drops as you put them in. Two or three drops at a time are normally sufficient; any more will run down his throat and cause him to cough and splutter.

Eye drops

1 Tilt your baby's head slightly so that his affected eye is lowermost. This way, no drops can run from the affected eye to the other. If this is difficult, get someone to hold him.

2 Very gently pull his lower eyelid down and let the drops fall between his eye and his lower lid.

Tips for giving drops

● Warm nose drops and ear drops by standing the container in warm, *not hot,* water for a few minutes, so that your child doesn't get a shock when they drop into his nose or ear.

● Do not let the dropper touch your child's nose, ear or eye, or you will transfer the germs back to the bottle. If the dropper does touch your child, wash it thoroughly before putting it back in the bottle.

● Proprietary drops should not be used for longer than three days without consulting a doctor—they can cause worse irritation and inflammation than the condition you were treating in the first place.

Medicines

Medicine chest

You should always keep some medicines in the house in case of emergency in the middle of the night when you may not be able to get to a chemist easily. Keep them somewhere obvious so that you can find them quickly when you need them. Never mix pills up in the same container and never keep unused prescription medicines. Keep all medicines out of reach of children in a locked cupboard, if necessary.

You should also have a first-aid kit. Keep all the equipment in a clean, dry, airtight box and put it somewhere it can be found in an emergency.

Medicines to avoid

The following items, commonly given as useful, should be avoided:
● Any proprietary product containing a local anaesthetic such as amethocaine or lignocaine because they can cause allergies. They are generally found in creams for mouth ulcers or insect stings.
● Any skin creams containing antihistamines—unless prescribed by your doctor—they can cause skin allergies.
● Proprietary products containing aspirin.
● Mouth washes, gargles, eye drops, nose drops and ear drops unless recommended by your doctor.

Medicine chest

1 Mercury thermometer—keep two in case one breaks.
2 Forehead thermometer.
3 Junior paracetamol tablets.
4 Paracetamol elixir.
5 Calamine lotion for soothing skin irritations, sunburn and stings.
6 Syrup of ipecac to make your child sick in case of non-corrosive poisoning (see page 299).

13 Surgical tape.
14 Crepe bandages for supporting sprains and strains.
15 Open-weave bandages.
16 Triangular bandage.
17 Blunt-ended tweezers, safety pins and scissors.

First-aid kit

7 Box of adhesive dressings.
8 Wound dressings—dressings that consist of a cotton wool and gauze pad already attached to a bandage.
9 Packet of skin closures.
10 Cotton wool.
11 Mild antiseptic cream.
12 Gauze dressings—keep dry and paraffin-coated ones.

Useful household items

● Packet of frozen peas, or ice cubes in plastic bags for cold compresses.
● Newspaper—when folded this makes an excellent splint.
● Elastic belt for supporting a strain or sprain.

● Bicarbonate of soda—this can be added to your child's bath to relieve itching.
● Salt—this can be added to your child's bath to cleanse wounds.
● Vinegar—mixed with water this can be used to soothe jellyfish stings.

Nursing a sick child

Very few parents escape being called upon to look after a sick child—all children fall ill at some time. Babies often become very clingy when they are ill and may cry more than normal because they do not understand what is happening to them. If a baby is being breast-fed he will probably want to be fed more often, as much for the comfort of being near you as anything else. Bottle-fed babies will also want to be cuddled, and will want smaller feeds more often. If your baby has recently given up his bottle, you may find that he wants it back again.

Older children also become rather insecure when they are ill and want to be with one of their parents all the time. Nursing a child does not require any special skills, just love. Few things can go wrong and if a child's condition takes a turn for the worse, most parents will spot it immediately. Simply use your common sense. If you are worried, take your child to your doctor or ask for a home visit (see pages 24-6). If any medicines are prescribed, make sure you give them exactly as directed (see page 27), and follow any nursing tips your doctor gives you. Try to be cheerful and optimistic because children are often frightened by being ill and will be quick to pick up any tension.

Should my child stay in bed?

Take your lead from your child. There's no need to keep a child with a fever in bed, though he should stay in a draught-free room where the temperature is fairly constant. The room does not have to be particularly hot—if it is comfortable for you, it should be warm enough for your child. If your child is really ill, he will probably want to stay still and will sleep a lot but when he is awake he will want to be with you—make up a bed for him in the room where you are working so that he can see and hear you. This will also be easier for you as you won't have to keep running backwards and forwards to his room. If your child wants to be out of bed and playing, let him do so in the corner of the room where you are working. Leave his bed straightened so that he can go there if he wants to. If he is very tired, it is better to put him to bed but remember to go and visit him regularly so that he does not feel left out.

Should I isolate my child?

It is now known that there is no point in keeping your child isolated if he has an infectious illness, such as chickenpox or measles, and the practice of sterilizing everything used by the child during his illness is out-of-date. This is because it has been shown that most infections are caught and passed on within 48 hours, although the symptoms may not appear in that time. Obviously, if your child has a more serious infection that does need isolation, such as hepatitis (see pages 159-60) or meningitis (see page 177), your doctor will arrange for your child to be admitted to hospital or advise you on the necessary precautions. Also, if

Tips for nursing your child

● Use cotton sheets—they are more comfortable for a child with a temperature.
● Change his sheets regularly, particularly if he has a fever—clean sheets feel better.
● Put a jumper and socks or slippers on over his pyjamas if he does not want to stay in bed all the time.
● Leave a box of tissues on his bedside table.
● Leave a bowl or bucket beside your child's bed if he is feeling sick so that he doesn't have to run to the toilet.
● If your child vomits, hold his head and comfort him while he is being sick, and give him a mint or strongly flavoured sweet, or help him clean his teeth, to take away the after-taste.

Nursing a sick child

your child has German measles (*see page 141*), you should warn any women you think may be pregnant—or who may come in contact with someone who is pregnant.

Feeding a sick child

Most children with a fever don't want to eat, so while you should offer food, you should never force your child to eat. As long as he is getting plenty of liquid, your child can survive perfectly well for two or three days on very little to eat. When the illness is over, your child's appetite will return. As soon as it does, take advantage of it and let your child eat as heartily as he wants to.

If he does want to eat, there is no particular food that is especially necessary when your child is ill, so forget the rules and spoil him a little by giving him

When your child has a fever it is important that she drinks as much as possible.

Nursing a sick child

his favourite foods until he is well again. I've always felt that there is no danger of a child slipping into bad habits as a result of special treatment while he is ill if he knows that the usual rules will be reinstituted as soon as he is well again.

Getting a sick child to drink

While your child can survive without much food when he is ill, it is very important that he drinks as much as possible to replace any fluid lost in sweating and vomiting or diarrhoea. A child with a fever needs to drink at least 100-150ml (3-5fl oz) liquid per kilo (2.2lb) of body weight per day. This should be increased to 200ml (7fl oz) per kilo (2.2lb) if he is vomiting or has diarrhoea (*see page 108*). Get your child to drink as

often as you can, even a little every half an hour while he's awake. Help an older child by leaving his favourite drink by the bed, and then remind him every so often to take a sip. Fizzy glucose drinks are not nutritious, nor are they necessary; I do not recommend them.

Occupying a sick child

When your child is ill you can legitimately spoil him. Let him play with games that previously have never been allowed in bed. Even messy activities like painting will not cause too much mess if you put a large sheet of polythene over the bed.

Be easy on yourself as well and relax all the rules on tidiness—you can always clear up later. Whatever you do, don't make a fuss and don't nag your child to

Feeding and drinking tips

Feeding your child
● Give your child small meals more often than you would normally.
● Don't scold your child for not eating —he will eat again as soon as he gets better.
● Give your child his favourite foods.

● If your child has a sore throat, give ice-cream or an ice lolly made with fruit juice or yogurt to soothe his throat.
● If your child is feeling slightly sick give him mashed potato.
● As soon as your child's appetite returns, take full advantage of it and let him eat as much as he can.

Making drinks more interesting
● Give your child a glass to drink out of which is normally reserved for adults.

● A sure ploy in our house is to offer drinks in a tiny glass or egg cup. It is more fun and makes the quantities look smaller.

● Give your child fresh fruit juices such as pear, apple, orange or water melon. Dilute them with fizzy mineral water to make them more interesting.
● Use an interesting straw such as a curly or bendy one.
● If your child does not like milk, make it more attractive by adding milkshake mixes or ice-cream.
● Vary the drinks as much as possible.
● With a young child or baby, get him to sip drinks from a teaspoon. Make it seem like a game by using a long-handled spoon.

Nursing a sick child

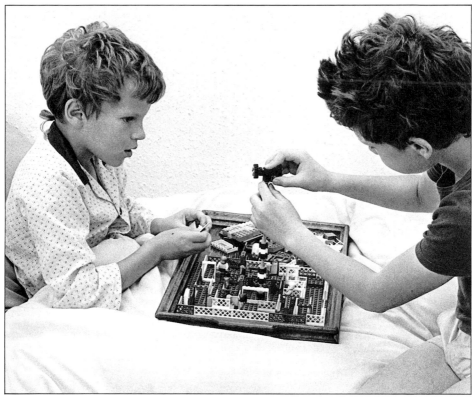

If your child is well enough, invite a friend over to play with him.

be tidy. Sit down and spend time with him, read him stories, play games or sing him songs, help him with his colouring, painting or building.

Let your child watch television or listen to the radio while he is ill—have the television in his room or in the room where you are both sitting. Buy him some new toys and give them to him one at a time. If he isn't feeling too ill, try wrapping them up and play a game with the parcel; ask him to guess what's in the packages and let him tear off the wrapping. Ask his friends to come and see him and let them play for a short time.

If your child is not in bed all the time, there's absolutely no reason to keep him indoors on a warm day, even if he has a mild fever, but don't let him exercise too strenuously. If he wants to stay outside for longer than a few minutes, he is probably getting better anyway.

Getting better

As your child gets better his appetite will start to come back and he will probably be more active. As soon as his temperature is back to normal in the morning and evening, he is probably ready to go back to school, although, if he has been suffering from an infectious illness it may be wise to check with your doctor first.

A young child may have regressed slightly while he was ill. For example, if he was just out of nappies you may have to start potty training again. Try not to worry about this too much.

Your child in hospital

You will be doing your child a great favour if you always encourage him to think about hospitals as friendly places. Try to take him with you if you are visiting a family friend or relative—provided the person does not mind and that the visiting regulations allow it.

Preparing your child for hospital

If your child has to go into hospital, for an operation, for example, and you are given several weeks or days warning, prepare him by discussing as many aspects of his stay as possible. Talk about it with the rest of the family as well and get him generally used to the idea.

Answer all his questions honestly. Don't make promises that you can't keep and don't tell lies. If he is having an operation he will probably ask you if there will be any pain or discomfort after the operation. If you say that nothing is going to hurt and it does, he will simply get a shock and will not trust you again in the future. Explain that there will be some discomfort but that it won't last long.

Another good way to prepare him for a hospital stay is to read him a book about someone who goes into hospital. You could also buy him a toy stethoscope and play doctors and nurses with him. Encourage him to be the doctor or nurse and suggest that he makes up a hospital bed for his favourite teddy bear or toy.

When your child is in hospital

Few children's wards are frightening places. However, it has been found that it is very important for parents to be with their children as much as possible while they are in hospital. Because of this, almost all hospitals now allow parents to stay in hospital with their child, particularly if he is very young. Many hospitals have sleeping facilities for parents with children up to the age of six.

When you are there, ask the ward sister and nurses how you can help with

What to take into hospital

If you can, you and your child should pack his case together a few days before he has to go in.
- Three pairs of pyjamas.
- Dressing gown and slippers.
- Three pairs of ankle socks.
- Hair brush and comb.
- Sponge bag with soap, flannel, toothbrush, toothpaste.
- Bedside clock.
- Portable radio or cassette player with headphones
- Favourite books and portable games.
- Favourite picture or photograph to put by his bedside.

the daily routine. You will probably be encouraged to bath and change your child and help with his feeding. You can read books and play games with him and any other children in the ward who want to join in. If the ward has a ward teacher, ask if you can help with your child's schoolwork. If your child is well enough and will be in hospital for a while, ask his own school teacher to give you the work he would normally be doing at school.

If you cannot be with your child all day, try to arrange a rota so that someone he knows well is with him all the time.

Back home from hospital

It's quite normal for a child to behave a little oddly when he comes out of hospital. Firstly, your child's sleeping and eating patterns may have changed. Hospital meals, and certainly bedtimes, tend to be earlier than you'd have them at home. Secondly, because your child has been away from his domestic discipline, you may find that he will make a fuss about small points like brushing his teeth. Don't be too hard on him at first, give him time to readjust to being at home before you insist that he fits in with the old routine.

Visual diagnosis guides

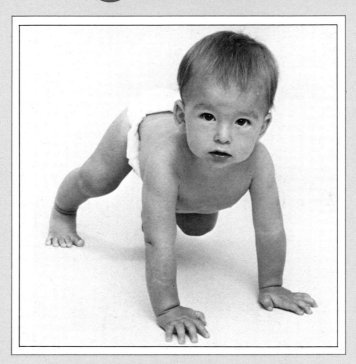

How to use this section

This section is designed to help if you don't know what has caused your child's symptoms, and are therefore unsure which A-Z entry to look up. Because it is impossible to give a definitive medical diagnosis from only one or two symptoms, this section instead helps you to make an educated guess as to the possible cause. For ease of reference, the body is illustrated in six sections (see below), and the symptoms relating to those parts are dealt with accordingly. To use the guide, turn to the page dealing with the affected part of the body and look for the symptom most similar to the one your child is suffering from (if your child has more than one symptom, look up the major one first). Then turn to the A-Z entry suggested as a possible cause for more detailed information. If you cannot find the symptom that you are looking for, turn to the major index on page 315 and either look up the symptom itself (for example, headache) or the part of the body affected (head).

Listed below are the parts of the body that may be affected, and the page on which you will find them. Problems affecting the skin in general, such as rashes, are also listed.

Eyes, mouth and scalp
page 43
Eyes
Hair
Head
Scalp
Lips
Mouth
Teeth
Gums
Cheeks

Ears, nose and throat
page 44
Ears
Nose
Throat
Neck
Cheeks

Abdomen, chest and back *page 45*
Chest
Lungs
Stomach
Groin
Abdomen
Shoulders
Back
Umbilicus (navel)

Genitals and bowels
page 46
Penis
Vagina
Bowels

Arms, hands, legs and feet *page 47*
Arms
Hands
Fingers
Fingernails
Legs
Knees
Feet
Toes
Toenails

The skin *page 48*
Rashes
Lumps
Swellings
Paleness
Coldness
Itchiness
Dryness

Eyes, mouth and scalp

Thick, yellow scales over part or all of your baby's scalp *possibly* Cradle cap, see page 99

White flakes on your child's scalp *possibly* Dandruff, see page 106

Bald patches of itchy, red or grey scaly rings *possibly* Ringworm, see page 208

Itchy head with tiny pearl-white eggs clinging to the hair roots *possibly* Lice, see page 174

Sore, watery eye *possibly* a Foreign body in the eye, see page 129

Weepy, sore, red eyes which may be gummed together in the morning *possibly* Conjunctivitis, see page 92

Weepy, red-rimmed, itchy eyes accompanied by sneezing *possibly* Hayfever, see page 151

One or both of your baby's eyes wander *possibly* Squint, see page 224

Pus oozing from the inner corner of your baby's eye *possibly* Sticky eye, see page 226

Severe headache and pain when neck is stretched *possibly* Meningitis, see page 177

Headache on one side of the forehead *possibly* Migraine, see page 178

Swollen, red area on your child's eyelid, nearly always the lower lid *possibly* Stye, see page 229

Red, scaly eyelids, with dandruff-like scales clinging to your child's eyelashes *possibly* Blepharitis, see page 66

Small, white, depressed ulcerated area inside the mouth *possibly* Aphthous mouth ulcer, see page 180

Large, red area with a yellow centre, usually inside the cheek *possibly* Traumatic mouth ulcer, see page 180

Creamy-yellow or white frothy patches inside your baby's mouth, which bleed when wiped *possibly* Oral thrush, see page 238

Tiny, itchy very painful blisters around the nostrils and lips *possibly* Cold sore, see page 87

Tiny blisters that ooze and crust over bright yellow *possibly* Impetigo, see page 165

Small cracks on the lips *possibly* Chapping, see page 81

Swollen red area on your baby's gum, accompanied by dribbling *possibly* Teething, see page 232

Painful, throbbing sensation in the tooth or gum in and older child *possibly* Toothache, see page 243 *Or* Gum boil, see page 148

Ear, nose and throat

Tiny white or yellow spots on and around a newborn baby's nose *possibly* Milia, see page 179

Nasal speech and mouth breathing *possibly* Adenoids, see page 241

Blotchy red rash that starts behind the ears and then spreads to the rest of the body, accompanied by swollen neck glands *possibly* German measles, see page 141

Brownish-red rash of small spots that starts behind the ears then spreads to the rest of the body, usually preceded by a runny nose and red, sore eyes *possibly* Measles, see page 176

Pain in and around the ear *possibly* Otitis media, see page 196 *Or* Toothache see page 243 *see also* Earache, page 121

Pussy discharge from the ear *possibly* Otitis media, see page 196

Pain inside the ear canal, made worse when the earlobe is pulled *possibly* Otitis externa, see page 194

Impaired hearing, accompanied by a sensation of fullness in the ear *possibly* Wax in ears, see page 258 *Or* Glue ear, see page 144 *Or* Foreign body in the ear, see page 120

Pain underneath the eyes *possibly* Sinusitis, see page 215

Sneezing, with a runny nose and itchy eyes *possibly* Hayfever, see page 151

A runny nose, often with a sore throat and fever *possibly* a Common cold, see page 90 *Or* Influenza, see page 166

Bleeding nose *possibly* Nosebleed, see page 190 *Or* Foreign body in the nose, see page 189

Swelling on either or both sides of the face *possibly* Mumps, see page 182

Hoarse cough or loss of voice *possibly* Croup, see page 100 *Or* Laryngitis, see page 172

Swollen neck glands with a sore throat which may be accompanied by a fever *possibly* Tonsillitis, see page 241 *Or* Glandular fever, see page 142 *Or* Scarlet fever, see page 211

Abdomen, chest and back

Rapid, difficult breathing in a baby under one year old, following a common cold
possibly Bronchiolitis, see page 72

Whooping sound during a coughing fit as air is breathed in
possibly Whooping cough, see page 259

Dry cough, with a fever and rapid laboured breathing over the age of one
possibly Bronchitis, see page 73

Painless bulge near the navel that increases in size when your child strains or coughs
possibly Umbilical hernia, see page 161

Weeping, umbilical cord stump in a newborn baby, which then crusts over
possibly Umbilical cord infection, see page 249

Flat, red or pink rash starting on the trunk and spreading to the neck and limbs, usually after a high fever
possibly Roseola infantum, see page 209

Intensely itchy, small blisters that appear in clusters on the trunk then spread to the rest of the body
possibly Chickenpox, see page 82

Nausea and vomiting while travelling
possibly Travel sickness, see page 246

Legs drawn up as if in pain to your baby's stomach, in the first three months with fits of crying
possibly Colic, see page 88

Projectile vomiting in a newborn baby where milk shoots out forcefully from the mouth after a feed
possibly Pyloric stenosis, see page 203

Severe spasmodic cramps in a baby under 12 months, with vomiting and red, jelly-like stools containing blood and mucus
possibly Intussusception, see page 169

Pain starting around the navel then moving to the lower right area of the groin in an older child
possibly Appendicitis, see page 53

Painless bulge in the groin that increases in size when your child coughs or strains
possibly Inguinal hernia, see page 161

Genitals and bowels

Persistent, involuntary soiling of the pants with loose bowel motions, in a child that has no other symptoms of illness and was previously toilet-trained *possibly* Encopresis, see page 126

Hard, pebble-like stools and pain in the lower abdomen *possibly* Constipation, see page 93

Loose, frequent bowel motions *possibly* Diarrhoea, see page 112

Red, jelly-like bowel motions containing blood and mucus, in a baby under one year, accompanied by severe abdominal pain *possibly* Intussusception, see page 169

Loose, frequent bowel motions accompanied by vomiting, shortly after eating *possibly* Food poisoning, see page 136

Foul-smelling, pale stools *possibly* Coeliac disease see page 85

Pimply red rash on area normally covered by your baby's nappy *possibly* Nappy rash, see page 185 *Or* Thrush, see page 238

Small, threadlike worms around the anus, with intense itchiness *possibly* Worms, see page 261

Red, swollen tip of penis *possibly* Balanitis, see page 62

Tight foreskin in a child over five years old *possibly* Phimosis, see page 199

Smoky, dark-coloured or reddish-brown urine *possibly* Hepatitis, see page 159 *Or* Nephritis, see page 187

Irritation of the vulva *possibly* Foreign body in the vagina, see page 251 *Or* Worms, see page 261

Frequent, painful passing of urine, accompanied by fever *possibly* Urinary tract infection, see page 250

Arms, hands, legs and feet

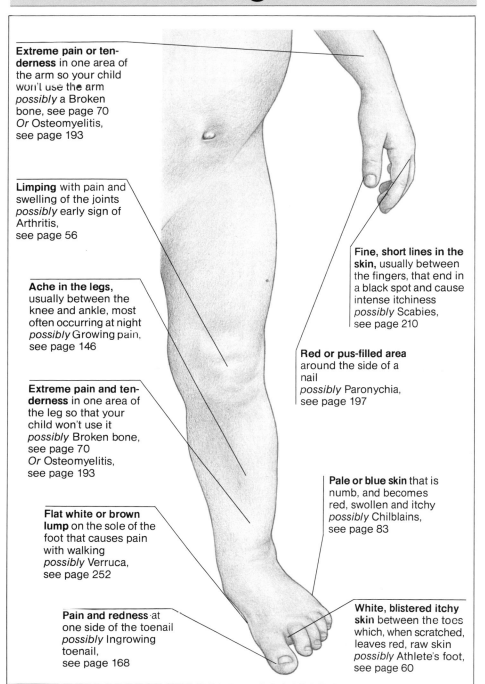

Extreme pain or tenderness in one area of the arm so your child won't use the arm *possibly* a Broken bone, see page 70 *Or* Osteomyelitis, see page 193

Limping with pain and swelling of the joints *possibly* early sign of Arthritis, see page 56

Ache in the legs, usually between the knee and ankle, most often occurring at night *possibly* Growing pain, see page 146

Extreme pain and tenderness in one area of the leg so that your child won't use it *possibly* Broken bone, see page 70 *Or* Osteomyelitis, see page 193

Flat white or brown lump on the sole of the foot that causes pain with walking *possibly* Verruca, see page 252

Pain and redness at one side of the toenail *possibly* Ingrowing toenail, see page 168

Fine, short lines in the skin, usually between the fingers, that end in a black spot and cause intense itchiness *possibly* Scabies, see page 210

Red or pus-filled area around the side of a nail *possibly* Paronychia, see page 197

Pale or blue skin that is numb, and becomes red, swollen and itchy *possibly* Chilblains, see page 83

White, blistered itchy skin between the toes which, when scratched, leaves red, raw skin *possibly* Athlete's foot, see page 60

The skin

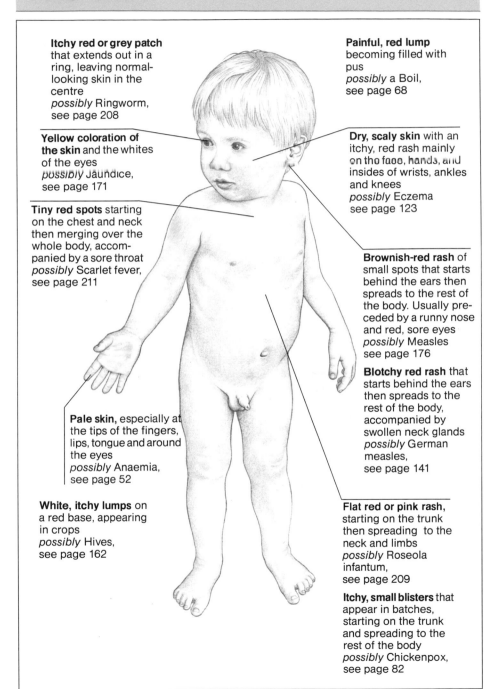

Itchy red or grey patch that extends out in a ring, leaving normal-looking skin in the centre *possibly* Ringworm, see page 208

Yellow coloration of the skin and the whites of the eyes *possibly* Jaundice, see page 171

Tiny red spots starting on the chest and neck then merging over the whole body, accompanied by a sore throat *possibly* Scarlet fever, see page 211

Pale skin, especially at the tips of the fingers, lips, tongue and around the eyes *possibly* Anaemia, see page 52

White, itchy lumps on a red base, appearing in crops *possibly* Hives, see page 162

Painful, red lump becoming filled with pus *possibly* a Boil, see page 68

Dry, scaly skin with an itchy, red rash mainly on the face, hands, and insides of wrists, ankles and knees *possibly* Eczema see page 123

Brownish-red rash of small spots that starts behind the ears then spreads to the rest of the body. Usually preceded by a runny nose and red, sore eyes *possibly* Measles see page 176

Blotchy red rash that starts behind the ears then spreads to the rest of the body, accompanied by swollen neck glands *possibly* German measles, see page 141

Flat red or pink rash, starting on the trunk then spreading to the neck and limbs *possibly* Roseola infantum, see page 209

Itchy, small blisters that appear in batches, starting on the trunk and spreading to the rest of the body *possibly* Chickenpox, see page 82

A-Z
of common
complaints

How to use this section

The A-Z of Common Complaints is the core of the book, covering all of the most common childhood complaints. The entries take two basic forms. In the majority, a detailed description of the illness is given, with a possible symptoms box for easy reference, a list of what to check for first, and treatments that might be given. In some cases, such as bed-wetting, no symptoms box is given as the symptom is the complaint's name.

Long-term complaints, such as cerebral palsy and spina bifida, are dealt with discursively. There is no check-list for What should I do first? nor do the headings Is it serious? or Should I call the doctor? appear. Instead, the treatments and procedures following diagnosis of a long-term ailment are given under the heading What can be done? An address to contact for help and advice is also given.

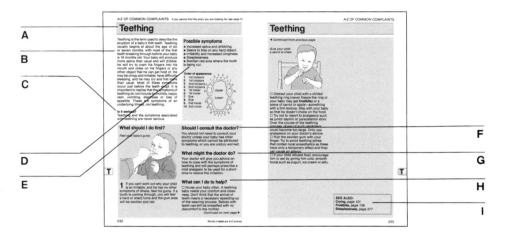

A Heading
Name by which the complaint is commonly known.

B Introduction
Gives a description of the complaint, explaining why it arises and how it is likely to develop.

C Is it serious?
States whether or not the complaint is serious, and the conditions under which it would become serious.

D Possible symptoms
Lists the symptoms that are likely to occur with the given complaint. Your child may have some or all of

them; he may or may not develop them in the order given, although that is the most likely sequence of appearance.

E What should I do first?
Details what you should do if you suspect your child has a certain complaint. This may involve action to determine whether your child definitely has the complaint (taking his temperature, checking for a rash); or may suggest home treatments which will provide immediate relief for your child while you contact the doctor (tepid sponging for fever, or calamine lotion for itchiness). If your child's

case is an emergency, the section will say so and will suggest that you call an ambulance or go straight to the nearest casualty department.

F Should I consult the doctor?
This will tell you the circumstances under which you should seek medical assistance. There are four levels of immediacy.
1 Emergency
In a life-threatening situation, you will be told to call an ambulance or go straight to the nearest casualty department.
2 Consult your doctor immediately
This means call your doctor

How to use this section

at once—even if it is the middle of the night or out of surgery hours—because your child needs medical attention as soon as possible. If the complaint is life-threatening and there is any risk of a delay in the doctor's arrival, the entry will tell you to call an ambulance or go straight to the nearest casualty department.

3 Consult your doctor as soon as possible
This means call your doctor to make an appointment at the earliest time possible. If your child's symptoms develop out of surgery hours, don't worry, but do ring as soon as the surgery opens.

4 Consult your doctor for advice
Your child has no serious problem, but it may be one which worries him or you. Make an appointment to talk to your doctor about it whenever it is convenient.

G What might the doctor do?
The treatment most likely to be given to your child is outlined.

H What can I do to help?
Makes suggestions as to what a parent can do to assist the doctor in the treatment of the child, as well as home treatment and nursing tips for the complaint itself.

I See also box
A cross-referencing system to other articles within the A-Z. The parent may be cross-referred to another complaint because it could be the possible cause of the child's symptoms, or it may be of background interest to the complaint in question.

Anaemia

Anaemia is a debilitating condition that is due either to a reduction in the number of normal red cells in the blood or in the amount of haemoglobin, the oxygen-carrying pigment derived from iron that gives the red cells their colour. This reduction can be caused by inadequate production of red cells in the bone marrow, by lack of iron and other blood-forming substances, by diseases such as **leukaemia, sickle cell anaemia** and **thalassaemia**, by excess blood loss, or by infection.

Is it serious?
Anaemia is serious because it may be a symptom of an underlying disease and therefore all cases must be investigated.

Possible symptoms
- Pale skin, especially at the tips of the fingers, the lips, around the eyes and the tongue.
- Fatigue, lethargy and weakness.
- Shortness of breath on exertion.
- Dizziness.
- Raised pulse rate.

What should I do first?

1 If your child seems listless and pale, and he is not eating well, check his eyes, mouth, fingertips and tongue for paleness.

2 Note whether your child is less active than his friends, if he is uncharacteristically breathless after a little exercise, or if he complains of **dizziness.**

Should I consult the doctor?

Consult your doctor immediately if you think your child is anaemic. Anaemia should always be investigated promptly and thoroughly by a doctor. You should never rely on home remedies.

What might the doctor do?

☐ Your doctor will first take blood samples and send them to a laboratory for analysis. If the diagnosis is confirmed, your child may have to go into hospital for a full investigation of the cause of the anaemia and possibly a blood transfusion if his condition is severe.

☐ If the anaemia is due to iron deficiency, your doctor will probably prescribe supplements of iron and may advise you to include more iron-rich foods in your child's diet. In addition, the cause of the iron deficiency should be tracked down by a paediatrician. Your child may need to attend a hospital clinic for tests.

What can I do to help?

☐ Make sure that your child is eating a properly balanced diet as set out by your doctor or dietician. Iron-rich foods include liver, egg yolk, dark green leafy vegetables and nuts. Vitamin C helps in the absorption of iron, so give your child a glass of orange juice with his egg, for example.

SEE ALSO:
Dizziness, *page 115*
Leukaemia, *page 173*
Sickle cell anaemia, *page 214*
Thalassaemia, *page 237*

Words in **bold** are A-Z entries

Appendicitis

Appendicitis occurs when infection causes the appendix to become inflamed and swollen. The appendix is a small tube—about 8cm (3in) long—that lies on the right side of the abdomen at the junction of the large and small intestines. The tube has one blind end and only a small opening at the other, and this opening may become partly or wholly blocked, leading to a build-up of bacteria. This can result in infection, which may necessitate surgical removal of the appendix (appendicectomy). Appendicitis is rare in babies under one year, but appendicectomy is the most common emergency operation among children.

Is it serious?

Appendicitis is not a serious condition as long as it is diagnosed early. However, if the symptoms are mistaken for something else, such as **constipation**, and there is any delay in treatment, the build-up of pus in the blocked appendix can cause the appendix to burst. This is known as peritonitis.

Possible symptoms

● Abdominal pain, starting around the navel, then moving down to the lower right abdomen.
● Slight temperature, rarely above 38°C (100.4°F).
● Loss of appetite.
● Vomiting.
● Diarrhoea or constipation.

Site of appendix

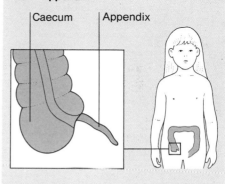

Caecum | Appendix

What should I do first?

Check abdomen for tenderness

1 If your child complains of an abdominal pain for more than a couple of hours, lay him flat on his back and examine his stomach. Press gently a few centimetres to the right of, and just below, the navel. Pain on gentle pressure, and a sharp pain when you suddenly remove your hands, are characteristic signs of appendicitis. Consult your doctor immediately.

2 If your child is constipated and you suspect appendicitis, don't give him laxatives. They can cause the appendix to burst if it is already inflamed.

3 Don't give your child anything to eat or drink. If an appendicectomy is necessary, it will be performed under a general anaesthetic and may be delayed if your child doesn't have an empty stomach.

Continued on next page ▶

Appendicitis

◀ Continued from previous page

Should I consult the doctor?

Consult your doctor immediately if you suspect appendicitis. Any delay could spread the infection to the rest of the intestines.

What might the doctor do?

☐ Your doctor will examine your child's abdomen and ask you when the pain started and what other symptoms there were. Diagnosis of this condition is difficult, and your doctor will probably arrange for the transfer of your child to hospital for confirmation of the diagnosis and for surgical removal of the appendix.

What can I do to help?

☐ Ask the hospital if you can stay with your child after the operation. Many hospitals now allow a parent to do so. Your presence will reassure your child and should speed his recovery.
☐ Encourage your child to rest and eat normally when he comes home from hospital, usually about five days after the operation. You will be advised by your doctor how to care for your child at home. Your child should be fit and well again in about two to three weeks.

SEE ALSO:
Constipation, *page 93*

Words in **bold** are A-Z entries

Appetite, loss of

A sick child will nearly always go off his food. Loss of appetite is a general sign of ill health and nearly always accompanies a fever. It is also a symptom of a problem in the stomach and intestines, such as **gastroenteritis**, or of a **sore throat** if it makes swallowing painful. Minor disorders such as **travel sickness** will usually cause your child to lose his appetite, but this will be only temporary. You should not worry about loss of appetite being a symptom of an underlying problem if your child has simply missed a meal due to tiredness or because you've had a battle of wills at mealtime. This is perfectly normal, and your child will make up for it in the following meals.

Is it serious?
If your child refuses to eat for 24 hours, and you can find no reason for the loss of appetite, this is a cause for concern.

What should I do first?

Hold down your child's tongue with the handle of a clean spoon

1 If your child refuses food for a day but he is taking plenty of fluids, check his temperature and examine his throat for possible inflammation of the tonsils. With the handle of a spoon, depress his tongue gently and ask him to say a long "aaah". He may be having difficulty in swallowing because of **tonsillitis.**

2 Check to see if your child is suffering from **earache.** An ear infection like **otitis media** could be painful enough to put him off his food.

3 Check for abdominal pain (*see page 53*). Pain in the lower right of the abdomen may mean **appendicitis.**

4 Check if there is any pain when your child passes urine. This could be a sign of a **urinary tract infection.**

5 If your child's temperature is normal, and you can find no evidence of illness, although he still refuses food, get him to drink plenty of fluids.

Should I consult the doctor?

Consult your doctor if the loss of appetite persists, even without any other symptoms, for 24 hours.

What might the doctor do?

☐ Your doctor will examine your child to see if there is any physical reason why he should be off food. If none can be found, your doctor will probably keep a check on your child's condition.

What can I do to help?

☐ Make sure your child gets plenty of nutrients by disguising them in drinks: for example, enrich a milk shake with egg yolk and wheatgerm.

SEE ALSO:
Appendicitis, *page 53*
Earache, *page 121*
Gastroenteritis, *page 139*
Otitis media, *page 196*
Sore throat, *page 220*
Tonsillitis, *page 241*
Travel sickness, *page 246*
Urinary tract infection, *page 250*

Arthritis

A

Arthritis is the inflammation of a joint. This is usually accompanied by swelling, pain, stiffness and tenderness. Arthritis may be caused by an injury to a joint, or by an infection in the joint, when it is called septic arthritis. In rare cases, it may be caused by **rheumatic fever**, or by a malfunctioning of the body's defence mechanism which leads the antibodies to attack the body's own tissues, causing inflammation and a fluctuating temperature. This is called Still's disease or juvenile rheumatoid arthritis. Still's disease starts between the ages of two and five and affects mainly girls.

If your child is ill with an infectious disease such as **influenza** or **measles**, he may have arthritic pains in his joints. These will, however, disappear once the infection has passed.

Is it serious?
Arthritis is a serious disorder that can lead to permanent deformity.

Possible symptoms
- Pain and swelling in a joint or several joints.
- Limping if hip or knee joints are affected.
- General aches and pains all round the body.
- A temperature of 40°C (104°F) or higher, or a temperature that fluctuates from normal to 39°C (102.2°F).
- Loss of appetite.

What should I do first?

1 Check to see if your child has a temperature. If it is as high as 40°C (104°F), and there is pain in the joints, treat this as an emergency. This could be septic arthritis. If his temperature fluctuates from normal to as high as 39°C (102·2°F), and he seems unwell, consult your doctor immediately. This could be Still's disease.

Check for swelling and tenderness

2 If you notice that your child is walking with a **limp**, check his

joints for swelling and tenderness by pressing on and around them.

3 If your child has had an injury to a joint and he complains of aches and pains, check the joint for tenderness and swelling.

4 If the pain is felt by your child between the joints and not on the joint itself, this could be a **growing pain**. Check the calf and thigh muscles for tenderness.

5 Don't give your child any pain-killing drugs until you have seen your doctor.

Should I consult the doctor?
Consult your doctor immediately if your child has a high, fluctuating temperature and a painful, swollen joint. Consult your doctor as soon as possible if you notice your child limping.

Continued on next page ▶

Words in **bold** are A-Z entries

Arthritis

◀ Continued from previous page

What might the doctor do?

☐ Your doctor will examine your child and ask about any other symptoms or illnesses your child may have had over previous months.

☐ If your doctor suspects arthritis, your child will probably be referred to a specialist for examination and blood tests to find a definite cause. Your child may have to stay in hospital to complete any necessary tests.

☐ If your child has septic arthritis, he will be given antibiotics intravenously to eradicate the infection in the joint.

☐ If your child has Still's disease, he may be prescribed paracetamol elixir and anti-inflammatory drugs. He will be taught a set of exercises to increase mobility in the affected joints.

What can I do to help?

Rest a hot-water bottle on the affected joint

☐ Wrap a hot-water bottle in a towel and rest it on the affected joint. Heat is sometimes soothing and can help to get the joint moving.

☐ Apply a cold compress to the joint if it is hot and swollen. Wrap a plastic bag filled with ice cubes in a piece of cloth and apply it directly to the joint.

☐ Make sure your child has plenty of rest and a protein-rich diet.

☐ Gently massage the joints. Sometimes this can relieve aches and pains.

☐ Take your child for regular 30-minute swimming sessions. Swimming in warm water is excellent exercise for arthritis sufferers. Check with your doctor before doing this.

☐ Practice the special exercises at home with your child if the physiotherapist agrees.

Pull gently on each finger to prevent the finger joints from stiffening

Support your child's arm, and ask him to do circles in the air with his hands. Hold his forearm steady so only the wrist joint is moved

SEE ALSO:
Growing pain, *page 147*
Influenza, *page 165*
Limp, *page 175*
Measles, *page 176*
Rheumatic fever, *page 209*

Asthma

A

Asthma is an allergic disease which affects the air passages (*bronchi*). When the allergic reaction takes place, the bronchi constrict and become clogged with mucus, making breathing difficult. An asthma attack can be very frightening for a child because the feeling of suffocation can cause panic, making breathing even more difficult. The initial cause of the allergic reaction, the allergen, is usually airborne—pollen or house dust, for example. Once asthma is established, emotional stress and exercise can also bring on an attack.

Asthma does not usually begin until a child is about two years of age. The condition tends to run in families and is unfortunately usually accompanied by other allergic diseases, such as **eczema** or **hayfever**. However, most children get better as they get older.

Many babies under one year wheeze if they suffer from **bronchiolitis**, when their small air passages become inflamed. These babies are not necessarily suffering from asthma; as they grow and their air passages widen, the wheezing will stop. Infection and not an allergic reaction is the usual cause of this wheezing.

Is it serious?
Asthma attacks can be frightening, but with medication and advice from your doctor, your child should suffer no serious complications.

Possible symptoms
● Laboured breathing: breathing out becomes difficult and the abdomen may be drawn inward with the effort of breathing in.
● Sensation of suffocation.
● Wheezing.
● Persistent cough.
● Blueness around the lips (cyanosis) because of lack of oxygen.

Area affected

Blocked bronchi

What should I do first?

1 Consult your doctor immediately if your child is having an asthma attack.

2 If the attack occurs when your child is in bed, sit him up, propped up with pillows. Otherwise, sit him on a chair with his arms braced against the back to take the weight off his chest; this allows the chest muscles to force air out more efficiently.

3 Stay calm; a show of anxiety would only make your child more fearful.

4 While waiting for the doctor, try to take your child's mind off the asthma attack. Sing to him, for example, to try to help him forget about the wheezing.

Continued on next page ▶

Words in **bold** are A-Z entries

Asthma

◀ Continued from previous page

Should I consult the doctor?

Consult your doctor immediately if your child has an asthma attack.

What might the doctor do?

A bronchodilator will ease breathing

☐ Your doctor will probably treat the attack with a bronchodilator drug, which opens up the bronchi by relaxing the muscles in the linings. This drug is inhaled directly into the bronchi and gets right to the site of the obstruction. A severe attack may require treatment in hospital, where bigger doses of bronchodilator drugs may be given by inhalant or by intravenous drip.

☐ If there is some evidence of a chest infection, antibiotics will be prescribed.

☐ Your doctor will discuss prevention of further attacks. He may try to determine the allergen, probably by performing skin tests for the most likely allergens, such as pollen and house dust. Your doctor will arrange for you to have a small supply of a bronchodilator drug, either in a liquid form or, more commonly, as capsules for insertion in an inhaler. This should be taken as soon as an attack begins. Your doctor will ask you to inform him if your child has a severe attack, or if an attack does not respond to two doses of the bronchodilator.

☐ Your doctor may prescribe a steroid drug if other simpler measures don't prevent further attacks. A small dose of steroid may be inhaled three or four times a day or, if this is not effective, a larger dose will be given in tablet form.

What can I do to help?

☐ If your doctor failed to pinpoint the allergen, try to track it down yourself. Notice when the attacks occur and at what time of the day or year. Avoid obvious allergens such as feather pillows and keep the dust down in your house by vacuuming floors rather than sweeping them.

☐ Many asthmatics are allergic to animals. If you have a pet, ask a friend to look after it for a couple of weeks and see if your child's asthma attacks are reduced.

☐ Make sure your child has the prescribed drugs nearby at all times. Inform his school about the possibility of attacks occurring.

☐ Ask to be referred to a physiotherapist so that your child can learn breathing exercises to help him to relax during an attack.

☐ Encourage your child to stand and sit up straight so that his lungs have more space. Don't let him get overweight as this will put an extra burden on his lungs.

☐ Moderate exercise can help his breathing, but too much can bring on an asthma attack. Swimming, however, can be especially helpful.

SEE ALSO:
Bronchiolitis, *page 72*
Eczema, *page 123*
Hayfever, *page 151*

Athlete's foot

A

This is a fungal infection that affects the soft area between and underneath the toes. In an advanced stage, it also affects the nails. It is contagious and is usually picked up by walking barefoot in communal areas, such as shower rooms, gymnasia and swimming pools, where infected feet have been. The infection is aggravated by sweaty feet because the fungus, *tinea,* which also causes **ringworm** elsewhere on the body, thrives in warm, moist conditions.

Is it serious?

Athlete's foot is a common condition, requiring simple treatment and good hygiene to cure it. However, as it is contagious, you should act quickly so that the infection is not spread.

Possible symptoms

Possible sites of blistered skin

- White, blistered skin between and underneath the toes. The area is itchy and, when scratched, splits and leaves raw, red skin underneath.
- Dry, peeling skin.
- Thick, yellow toenails.

What should I do first?

1 If your child has itchy feet, check the area between and underneath the toes for white blisters and redness.

2 Check underneath the foot for blisters and cracking.

3 Check the condition of the toenails.

4 Buy an antifungal foot powder or cream from your chemist, and, after washing and drying the feet thoroughly, apply the treatment, following the manufacturer's instructions.

5 Emphasize to your child that he must not go barefoot until the condition has cleared up.

6 Keep your child's towel and bathmat separate from those of the rest of the family and wash them every day.

Should I consult the doctor?

Consult your doctor as soon as possible if the underside of the foot is already affected, or if the nails are distorted or yellowing. Consult your doctor if the self-help measures fail to improve the condition within two or three weeks.

What might the doctor do?

☐ If the fungus has affected the toenails, your doctor will prescribe an antifungal medication that may need to be taken for as long as nine months.

☐ If you consulted your doctor because self-help measures failed, your doctor will prescribe another antifungal powder or cream and will advise you on the correct procedure for good foot hygiene.

What can I do to help?

☐ Make sure your child has clean socks every day, preferably made from natural fibres such as cotton or wool.

☐ Rotate your child's shoes, especially his running shoes, so they have a chance to dry out between wearings.

> **SEE ALSO:**
> **Ringworm,** *page 208*

Words in **bold** are A-Z entries

Autism

The word autism is used to define a behaviour pattern in which a child suffers from a profound inability to relate to other people, including his parents. The autistic child lives in curious isolation. For example, even though not deaf, he may not appear to hear what is being said to him and in many cases may never speak, or may speak in an unusual way. With hindsight, parents may remember that their autistic child was not a cuddly baby, he seldom if ever smiled, and that he never indicated a desire to be picked up by stretching out his arms.

There have been many theories about the cause of this rare disorder since it was first described in 1943, but it is now clear that it is not induced by parental behaviour and is not a reaction to environ- mental factors. Autism cannot usually be diagnosed until it is realized that speech has not developed at the normal time, if at all. By this time you will probably have noticed that your child is withdrawn and spends hours in solitary play. Quite often your child will adopt behaviour rituals such as touching certain objects in a set sequence or rocking backwards and forwards. Disruption of these routines can bring on severe temper tantrums. This behaviour reflects the child's need to surround himself with an environment that never varies. Some autistic children have a heightened sensitivity to certain objects and they may constantly look carefully at their own hand and finger movements or rub surfaces as if to appreciate the textures.

A

Possible symptoms

- Social withdrawal.
- Hearing abnormalities.
- Avoidance of eye contact.
- Speech disorders.
- Repetitive behaviour patterns.
- Indifference to pain.

What can be done?

Autistic children usually attend special schools from an early age, and if the parents cannot manage at home, treatment in a therapeutic residential setting may be advised. Many different therapies for autism have been tried out, but success in all of them has been limited. Intensive psychotherapy has been disappointing and medication with tranquillizers is useful only in controlling aggressive behaviour. Behaviour therapy and holding therapy (in which the parent is encouraged to hold the child close for as long as possible in order to build up physical and emotional contact) have been useful. But remember that all therapy needs to be prescribed and supervised by experts in this field.

FOR HELP AND ADVICE CONTACT:
National Autistic Society
276 Willesden Lane
London NW2 5RB
01-541 3844

Balanitis

Balanitis is the inflammation of the tip (*glans*) of the penis. It may be caused by **nappy rash**, by an allergic reaction to the soap powder in which your child's clothing is washed, or by a tight foreskin in boys over the age of five (**phimosis**). Up until this age, the foreskin is normally tight.

Is it serious?
The condition is not serious, though it is important for your child's comfort that you treat the condition promptly. If balanitis is recurrent, your son may need to be circumcised.

Possible symptoms

- Red, swollen tip to the penis.
- Pussy discharge from the tip.
- A foreskin that cannot be drawn back.
- If your child is still in nappies, a general inflammation around the buttocks and in the genital region.

What should I do first?

1 As soon as you notice any redness around the tip of the penis, carefully and gently try to draw back the foreskin. Don't force it, and leave it alone if your son is under five years of age. If the foreskin won't retract, leave it alone and consult your doctor as soon as possible.

2 If the foreskin will retract, wash and dry the penis thoroughly and apply an antiseptic ointment.

3 If the condition is part of nappy rash, change your child's nappies frequently, wash and dry the area thoroughly at every nappy change, and liberally apply a barrier cream over the area covered by the nappy, including the penis.

Should I consult the doctor?

Consult your doctor as soon as possible if your child complains of pain, if you cannot retract the foreskin, or if home treatment fails to relieve the swelling within 48 hours.

What might the doctor do?

☐ Your doctor may prescribe an antibiotic cream to relieve the inflammation.

☐ If the foreskin is tight, your doctor will keep a regular check on it; if the foreskin has failed to stretch by the time the boy is six, the condition may need to be corrected surgically with circumcision. Your doctor will refer you to a paediatrician who will assess your child to see if he really needs to be circumcised.

What can I do to help?

☐ Always change your child's nappies frequently to prevent the recurrence of nappy rash.

☐ Teach your child good personal hygiene from an early age. Up until the age of five, regular bathing will keep the penis adequately cleaned. After this age, encourage your child to draw back the foreskin and wash the area daily.

☐ If an allergic reaction has caused balanitis, try changing your washing powder, and make sure that your child's clothing is thoroughly rinsed.

SEE ALSO:
Nappy rash, *page 185*
Phimosis, *page 199*

Words in **bold** are A-Z entries

Bedwetting

B

Children master bladder control at different ages. Just as they develop skills at different rates, so their ability to hold urine for long periods varies. However, although one in ten normal boys still wets the bed at the age of five, most children become dry at night between the ages of three and four. A child should not be classified as a bedwetter while he is still training his bladder to last the 10-12 hours of night-time sleep.

A return to bedwetting once a child has gained bladder control is nearly always a sign of increased tension and anxiety.

This often happens as a result of an important occasion, such as the arrival of a new baby in the house, or starting school. A few children may have a physical reason for their incontinence, such as a **urinary tract infection** or some abnormality of the urinary system. If bedwetting is accompanied by increased thirst and frequent urination during the day, this could be a symptom of **diabetes**.

Is it serious?
Although irritating for parents, bedwetting is not a serious problem.

What should I do first?

1 Put a rubber sheet on the bed and cover it with a small top sheet that can be easily washed and dried every day if necessary.

2 Examine your own behaviour. You may be the source of the problem. You may be pushing your child too hard or creating a tense atmosphere.

3 Make sure your child empties his bladder before going to bed; if he wishes, leave a potty in his room so that he doesn't have to go any distance to the bathroom.

4 Check whether your child's urine has a fishy smell. This could indicate a urinary tract infection.

Should I consult the doctor?

Consult your doctor as soon as possible if both you and your child are becoming discouraged or if you suspect that there may be some physical cause of the problem such as a urinary tract infection, which causes the urine to have an unpleasantly fishy odour.

What might the doctor do?

☐ Your doctor will examine your child and take a urine sample to exclude the possibility of a urinary tract infection or a malformation of the urinary tract.
☐ Your doctor may recommend that you fit a special pad on your child's bed which lets off an alarm when moistened with urine. Your child can learn to react to this alarm and get up and go to the toilet. This system is of use only if your child is over six years old and doesn't object to it.

What can I do to help?

☐ Minimize the problem and make sure the rest of the household follows your lead. Don't scold your child and always make light of the subject, no matter how tiresome it becomes.
☐ Try giving your child a star for every dry night. He can place it on a calendar and watch his progress.
☐ Don't limit the amount of liquid you give your child before bedtime. This has no effect on his bedwetting.
☐ Don't try anything, such as the alarm pad, that your child objects to; it will only increase the tension.

SEE ALSO:
Diabetes mellitus, *page 110*
Urinary tract infection, *page 250*

Birthmark

B

A birthmark is a patch of discoloration in the skin, caused by a collection of small blood vessels or pigment just under the surface. The birthmark, which may be flat or raised, may be present at birth or may appear in the first months of life.

Brown birthmarks are circular and may have hair growing out of them. These are called moles and they are usually permanent and should not be interfered with by anyone but a specialist.

Storkbites are small, pink and spidery and appear on the back of the neck, the upper eyelids or the nose. They disappear within a few years.

A Mongolian spot looks like a blue bruise in the skin and is usually found among dark-skinned people. It occurs most often on the lower back or buttocks.

A strawberry naevus is a raised red mark with a bumpy surface which is sometimes shaped like a strawberry. It usually disappears by the time a child is five, but before it does, it enlarges alarmingly, growing darker or lighter, before gradually disappearing. It is most common in girls and can bleed spontaneously.

A port wine stain looks exactly like its name—a red patch on the skin. It can appear over much of the face and forehead or the limbs, and it is usually quite large. This is the most distressing birthmark because it does not disappear, though it can fade to a paler pink. It is more common among blond children.

Is it serious?

A birthmark is almost always harmless and, apart from a port wine stain, most will disappear by the age of five.

What should I do first?

1 The most important thing is not to rush at treatment because many birthmarks disappear spontaneously.

2 If a strawberry naevus bleeds, place a clean pad or handkerchief over the mark. It should stop bleeding after a minute or so.

Should I consult the doctor?

Consult your doctor for advice if you feel that the birthmark is disfiguring and that your child may suffer as a result in the future.

What might the doctor do?

☐ If the birthmark is very unsightly, your doctor may refer you to a plastic surgeon. Birthmarks can be treated with a wide variety of modern techniques, including tattooing and laser therapy. If you decide against cosmetic surgery for any reason, your doctor may prescribe special camouflage make-up for your child.

What can I do to help?

☐ If the mark is unsightly and disturbs you and your child, use the camouflage make-up.

☐ Try not to show your child that you are anxious about the birthmark.

Words in **bold** are A-Z entries

Bites

B

Most children love the company of animals, but because they are not always as gentle with them as they should be, bites do occur. The most common animal bites—from dogs and cats—leave puncture marks; humans leave teeth marks. Insect bites leave a weal resembling **hives**—a white centre on a red base. They are extremely itchy but the pain and localized reaction fade within three to four hours. The common flea, normally from a household pet, also bites to leave itchy weals.

Are they serious?
Animal, human and insect bites are rarely serious. If they are untreated, however, they could become infected.

What should I do first?

1 Reassure your child and calm him down. If he has been bitten by a dog or a horse, for example, it is important for him not to remain afraid of these animals throughout his childhood, so try to persuade him that it is an isolated incident.

Apply antiseptic cream

2 For animal and human bites, wash the wound with soap and water to remove any blood, saliva or dirt. Apply an antiseptic cream and put a clean dressing over the wound.

3 For insect bites, apply calamine lotion to relieve the irritation.

Should I consult the doctor?

Consult your doctor as soon as possible to check that an animal or human bite is not infected or deep enough to carry the risk of **tetanus**. Consult your doctor immediately if the wound is bleeding heavily or if, after 12 hours, the area looks red and swollen.

What might the doctor do?

☐ Your doctor will ask you when your child had his last tetanus inoculation and, if it was more than six months ago, he will give him a tetanus booster.
☐ If the wound is infected, your doctor will probably prescribe antibiotics.

What can I do to help?

☐ You must emphasize to your child the need to treat animals carefully and not to tease them. In most cases, if a pet caused the injury, it will be an isolated incident and you should not need to get rid of the animal.
☐ If you are travelling abroad, be prepared for any problems by carrying a first-aid pack and updating tetanus boosters before you go.
☐ You will need to clean the carpet, curtains and furniture if you suspect that your child has been bitten by fleas. A special flea powder to dust furnishings is available from veterinary surgeons. Take your pet along to the vet for treatment too.
☐ If your child is being bitten by mosquitoes, apply an insect repellent to his skin or clothes, and put an incense stick in his room at night, or spray the room with an insect repellent.

SEE ALSO:
Hives, *page 162*
Tetanus, *page 236*

Blepharitis

B

Blepharitis is an inflammation of the skin around the edges of the eyelids. It usually affects both eyes. Inflammation can become worse if the area is infected: **styes** may occur. Blepharitis is often accompanied by dandruff and may be part of a condition known as seborrhoeic **eczema**.

Is it serious?
Even though the condition may initially be only a minor irritant, it should be treated because it can recur.

Possible symptoms
● Red, scaly eyelids.
● Discharge of pus from the eyelids, which dries to look like dandruff clinging to the eyelashes.

What should I do first?

1 If you notice your child rubbing his eyelids, check to see if the area seems red and scaly, or if the eyelashes are matted together with pus.

Wipe from the nose outwards

2 Don't use any patent creams or eye lotions. Wash away the discharge morning and night with warm boiled water, to which you have added a little salt or bicarbonate of soda. Use a clean cotton-wool swab for each eye and wipe from the nose outwards.

3 Check for **cradle cap** or **dandruff** on the scalp.

Should I consult the doctor?

Consult your doctor if the washing treatment doesn't clear the scaliness and redness within one week.

What might the doctor do?

☐ Your doctor may prescribe a soothing, anti-inflammatory skin cream to damp down the inflammation.
☐ If your child has seborrhoeic eczema, your doctor may prescribe special shampoos and scalp lotions.
☐ If there is an infection, such as a stye, your doctor may prescribe antibiotic ointment or eye drops to remove the pussy discharge.

What can I do to help?

☐ Pay particular attention to hygiene. If your child's eyelids have become infected, the infection can be easily spread to other members of the family, so wash your hands thoroughly before and after you administer the treatment.
☐ Discourage your child from touching his eyes.
☐ Apply a thin smear of Vaseline to your child's eyelids at night. The scales will wash away easily in the morning.

SEE ALSO:
Cradle cap, *page 99*
Dandruff, *page 106*
Eczema, *page 123*
Stye, *page 229*

Words in **bold** are A-Z entries

Blister

A blister is a fluid-filled bubble of skin that forms as a result of **burns** or friction, or as a result of exposure to extremes of temperature. Blisters vary in size, depending on the cause, and their purpose is to form a cushion to protect the new layer of skin growing underneath. The fluid is eventually reabsorbed by the body and the outer surface dries out and peels away, leaving the healed skin behind. If the blister is broken before healing has taken place, there is a risk of infection.

Is it serious?
A blister is not usually serious.

Possible symptoms

● Raised surface of the skin, filled with fluid, which may be as large as several centimetres across.

What should I do first?

1 Don't prick a blister that has formed as a result of friction, burning or extremes of temperature; leave it intact.

Protect blister with a pad, taped in place

2 Protect blisters where friction may cause them to burst. For example, if the blister is as a result of ill-fitting shoes or wearing shoes without socks, change your child's shoes for the time being, put two pairs of socks on your child, or use special sponge pads or corn plasters to protect the blister.

3 If the blister bursts, keep it clean and dry and cover it with a gauze dressing.

Should I consult the doctor?

Consult your doctor as soon as possible if the blister is large or the result of a scald or **sunburn.** Consult your doctor as soon as possible if the area becomes infected, that is, if the blister becomes pussy, if red streaks extend outwards from it, if the skin surrounding it becomes red, tender or swollen, or if your child complains of pain.

What might the doctor do?

☐ If the blister is large, it may require bursting. Your doctor will do this.
☐ If the blister is infected, your doctor will prescribe antibiotics.

SEE ALSO:
Burn, *page 76*
Frostbite, *page 138*
Sunburn, *page 230*

Boil

A boil is a large, tender, red lump that results when a hair follicle becomes infected with bacteria (*staphylococci*). (If the infection occurs further up the hair follicle, near to the skin's surface, this is called a pimple.) The pus-filled lump gradually comes to a white or yellow head and bursts after about two or three days, or it may heal on its own without bursting and slowly disappear. Because the hair follicles are so close together, the bacteria can infect a wide area, causing more boils to occur. This is most likely to happen on the face. The boils usually appear on areas where there are pressure points, such as where a collar rubs or on the buttocks.

Is it serious?

Although unsightly, a boil is not serious. However, it can be extremely painful, especially if it develops over a bony area such as the jaw or forehead where the skin is stretched tight.

Possible symptoms

● Large, painful, red lump.
● Increasing tenderness and throbbing as pus builds up inside the lump. After a day or two, the red lump forms a white or yellow pus-filled centre, which may or may not burst.

Cross-section of skin

Epidermis

Dermis

Collection of pus | Hair follicle

What should I do first?

1 If your child complains of throbbing pain, stop him from scratching or touching the area.

Wash boil with surgical spirit

2 Wash the skin with surgical spirit or a solution of 5ml (one teaspoonful) of salt in a glass of warm water to prevent infection from spreading. Then put a sterile gauze dressing over the boil.

3 Do not squeeze the boil, even when it comes to a head. Squeezing will spread the infection to the surrounding area and make the outbreak much worse.

Should I consult the doctor?

Consult your doctor as soon as possible if the boil does not come to a head within five days, or if the boil is causing your child a lot of pain because it is situated over a bony area or in an awkward place, such as the armpit. Consult your doctor as soon as possible if you notice red streaks spreading out from the centre of the boil. This may mean that the infection is spreading.

Continued on next page ▶

Boil

◄ *Continued from previous page*

What might the doctor do?

☐ Your doctor will examine the boil and the surrounding area. If he can feel pus under the skin, your doctor will probably lance the boil with a small scalpel and drain the pus, thus reducing pain immediately.

☐ If there is an infection and it has spread to the surrounding area, or if your child has had a number of boils over the previous months, your doctor may prescribe an anti-infective cream to treat the skin's surface, or antibiotic tablets to prevent the internal spread of the infection.

☐ If there are crops of boils, your doctor may prescribe a special anti-septic to put in the bath water.

☐ If the boils are recurrent, your child will be referred to a dermatologist to find out the underlying cause.

What can I do to help?

Keep boil covered with a dressing

☐ Once the boil has burst, keep the area clean and covered with a dressing for a few days.

☐ Keep your child's towel and facecloth separate from those of the family.

☐ If the boil is in a place where clothing might rub it, put a thick pad over the dressing to prevent any friction.

☐ If your child has a boil on the buttocks and is still in nappies, try to leave nappies off as much as possible. Change them frequently and use an antiseptic cream around the site of the boil.

B

Broken bone

Children's bones are like young, bendy twigs on a tree; they do not snap as easily as the harder bones of an adult. A *greenstick fracture* is most common in children; the bone bends rather than breaks, and in this type of fracture, minimal damage occurs in the surrounding tissue. A *simple fracture* is one where the bone breaks in one place. In a *compound fracture,* the bone sticks through the skin and may damage the blood vessels and muscles. If the bone breaks through the skin or is exposed by a deep wound, this is also known as an *open fracture.*

Is it serious?

A broken bone should always be treated promptly by a doctor for a number of reasons. The bone has to be set correctly, and any damage to surrounding organs or tissues has to be repaired. There is also a risk of infection if the break is an open fracture and the bone is exposed to the air.

Possible symptoms

● Swelling around the site of the injury.
● Bruising around the site of the injury.
● Possible deformation of the affected area.
● Inability to move the affected area normally or without pain.
● Pain.

Types of fracture

Greenstick   Simple   Compound

What should I do first?

1 Call an ambulance if the bone is bent or curved, or if the bone is sticking through the skin. Otherwise, take your child to the nearest casualty department.

2 If the broken limb appears bent or curved, don't try to straighten it. Don't move your child unless you have to for his own safety. Any movement may increase internal damage and will cause more pain. If a bone has broken through the skin, or if there is a wound leading down to the fracture, drape a sterile dressing or gauze over the wound. Don't attempt any cleaning and don't touch the wound.

Tape broken fingers together

3 If there is no bone sticking through the skin, but your child cannot move the affected area without pain, immobilize the joints above and below the break to prevent worsening of the injury: for an arm, put it in a sling; for a leg, tie the knees and ankles together. Take your child to the nearest casualty department if you can, but call an ambulance if the legs are affected, because you will need a stretcher.

Continued on next page ▶

Words in **bold** are A-Z entries

Broken bone

◀ *Continued from previous page*

4 Don't give your child anything to eat and drink. He may need a general anaesthetic and this will be delayed if his stomach is not empty.

Immobilize the limb

5 Keep your child warm and as calm as possible while you get medical help. If possible, raise the affected part after immobilizing it.

Should I consult the doctor?

Call an ambulance if the limb is bent or curved, if the bone is sticking through the skin or if a leg is broken. Take your child to the nearest casualty department if you suspect your child has a broken bone.

What might the doctor do?

☐ The hospital doctor will X-ray your child to determine the extent of the damage. With a straightforward break, the bone will be immobilized by strapping with a tight bandage, or by setting it in a plaster of Paris cast.
☐ If the break is a compound fracture, the bones will be manipulated into position under a general anaesthetic before being immobilized in plaster.

☐ If there is an open wound with the broken bone, antibiotics will be given to prevent infection.
☐ If your child has a bad break in his leg, he may have to remain in hospital in traction. The damaged bone is pulled apart and held in the correct position for healing with a system of pulleys and weights.

What can I do to help?

☐ If your child has a plaster cast, make sure it stays dry and help your child to lead as normal a life as possible while the bone heals. Most broken bones in children heal within six to ten weeks, depending on the severity of the fracture.
☐ If your child has to remain in hospital in traction, make his stay as entertaining as possible by bringing in his favourite games and toys, as well as new books and perhaps a personal cassette machine. Try to stay with him if you can.

B

Bronchiolitis

B

Bronchiolitis is inflammation of the smallest airways in the lungs (*bronchioles*). It is usually caused by a virus and occurs in babies under one year old. The condition may start as a **cough** or **common cold**. The virus causes the lining of the small airways to swell and to fill with mucus. This results in breathing difficulty and the baby will have to struggle for breath.

Is it serious?

Bronchiolitis is serious because the condition can cause severe breathing difficulties.

Possible symptoms

- Rapid breathing—over 60 breaths per minute.
- Breathing difficulties.
- Raised temperature.
- Blueness of the lips and tongue.
- Drowsiness.

Area affected

Alveoli

Inflamed bronchiole

What should I do first?

1 If your baby is distressed because of difficulty with breathing, and he starts to turn blue around the lips, treat this as an emergency. Consult your doctor immediately or take your child to the nearest casualty department.

2 Try to soothe your baby; crying makes the breathing problem worse.

3 If you are breastfeeding, offer the breast frequently. This will help to keep your baby's fluid levels up. Offer your bottlefed baby frequent fluids, too.

4 Take your baby's temperature every six hours, and more often if he appears hot. If the temperature is over 38°C (100.4°F), give your baby paracetamol elixir to bring his temperature down.

Should I consult the doctor?

Consult your doctor immediately or take your baby to the nearest casualty department if he has obvious breathing problems or if there is any sign of blueness around his lips and on his tongue. Consult your doctor imme-

diately if you notice any deterioration in your baby's condition after he has had a cold or cough.

What might the doctor do?

☐ If your doctor is satisfied that your baby's infection is a mild one, he will advise you on nursing procedures so that you can look after your baby at home. However, most babies with this condition are usually admitted to hospital overnight for observation.

What can I do to help?

☐ If your baby is admitted to hospital, stay with him if the hospital will allow this.
☐ Try to keep your baby away from other children and adults who have coughs and colds.

SEE ALSO:
Common cold, *page 90*
Cough, *page 97*

Words in **bold** are A-Z entries

Bronchitis

Bronchitis is inflammation of the membranes that line the larger airways leading to the lungs. The condition may arise because a minor upper respiratory tract infection, such as a **common cold** or **sore throat**, reduces your child's resistance to infection. The infection, which may be viral or bacterial, causes the lining of the air passages to swell and mucus to build up, making breathing difficult. There is also a dry hacking **cough,** which, after one or two days, produces phlegm. If this is swallowed, the child may vomit it up.

Is it serious?
In children over a year old, bronchitis is not usually serious, but in rare cases wheezing and **vomiting** may be troublesome enough to require hospitalization.

Possible symptoms
- Raised temperature.
- Dry hacking cough, changing to a cough that produces green or yellow phlegm.
- Rapid breathing, over 40 breaths per minute, with wheezing.
- Breathing difficulties.
- Loss of appetite.
- Vomiting with the cough.
- Blueness of the lips and tongue.

What should I do first?

1 If your chid has recently had a cold, **sinusitis,** sore throat or an ear infection, and his condition worsens, take his temperature to see if he has a fever. If your child has a fever, take his temperature every four hours. If it is as high as 38°C (100.4°F), lower it with tepid sponging, (*see page 31),* or paracetamol elixir.

Pat your child's back

2 If your child is coughing persistently, check if there is any phlegm. If there is, encourage your child to

cough it up. Hold him over your lap if he cannot understand how to do this, and pat him on the back during the coughing attack.

3 Keep offering your child liquids; even if he won't eat, encourage him to take plenty of fluids to prevent the risk of **dehydration**.

4 Don't give him patent cough suppressants if there is phlegm, as this needs to be coughed up.

5 Keep your child calm, quiet and warm.

Should I consult the doctor?

Consult your doctor immediately or take your child to the nearest casualty department if your child is breathing with difficulty, drawing in his chest with every breath, or if there is any sign of blueness around his lips and on his tongue. This should be treated as an emergency. Consult your doctor as soon as possible if your child's upper respiratory tract infection gets worse.

Continued on next page ▶

Bronchitis

◀ *Continued from previous page*

B

What might the doctor do?

☐ If your child is in great distress because of breathing difficulties or vomiting, your doctor may admit him to hospital so that he can be given either oxygen to help with breathing or intravenous fluids to combat dehydration if your child has been vomiting as well.

☐ Your doctor will prescribe antibiotics if a bacterial infection is present. If your child's bronchitis is caused by a virus, your doctor will advise you on the nursing procedures for bronchitis because there will be no specific medication. Your doctor will show you how to help your child cough up the phlegm.

What can I do to help?

Prop your child up to ease breathing

☐ Prop your child up when he is sleeping so that he can breathe more easily.

☐ Keep your child quiet; running around and too much excitement may cause a coughing attack and vomiting.

SEE ALSO:
Common cold, *page 90*
Cough, *page 97*
Dehydration, *page 108*
Sinusitis, *page 215*
Sore throat, *page 220*
Vomiting, *page 256*

Words in **bold** are A-Z entries

Bruise

A bruise is a purplish-red stain in the skin, usually resulting from a blow or a knock that ruptures the small blood vessels near the skin's surface. Children with fair skin show a bruise more readily than children with olive skin. It usually takes 10-14 days for a bruise to disappear completely; as it fades, it changes colour to maroon, and then green or yellow as the blood pigments break down and are reabsorbed by the body.

Is it serious?
A bruise is rarely serious. If a bruise appears without reason, this may relate to uncommon but serious conditions such as **leukaemia** and **haemophilia**.

Possible symptoms

● Purplish-red mark on the skin which fades to maroon and then green or yellow.
● Tenderness for a day or two.
● Swelling if the bruise is over a bone.

What should I do first?

1 A minor bruise needs no treatment at all, just a cuddle and reassurance if your child is upset.

Apply a cold compress

2 If the bruise is large, apply a cold compress for half an hour or so. This will contain the bruising.

Should I consult the doctor?

Consult your doctor immediately if pain on the site of the bruise gets worse after 24 hours; an underlying bone could be broken. Consult your doctor immediately if a bruise appears spontaneously with no apparent cause.

What might the doctor do?

☐ Your doctor will examine your child to determine if there is a **broken bone** and refer you to a hospital casualty department for treatment if necessary.
☐ Your doctor will refer you to a specialist clinic if your child suffers from recurrent bruising or bruises that appear spontaneously. This could indicate haemophilia or leukaemia.

SEE ALSO:
Broken bone, *page 70*
Haemophilia, *page 149*
Leukaemia, *page 173*

Burn

A burn is an injury to the skin following exposure to heat from fires, hot liquids, chemicals, sun, or electric current. The severity of a burn will depend on the situation and the cause. In a *superficial burn* there may be just a reddened patch of skin or a fluid-filled **blister**; in a *deep burn* layers of skin may actually be removed. Only small, superficial burns should be treated at home—no matter how minor a burn may seem to be, or how painless, there will always be some damage to the underlying tissue (in deep burns there may not always be pain because nerve endings have been damaged). All burns ooze a colourless liquid (*plasma*), and if too much is lost, your child could go into a state of shock (*see page 293*).

Are they serious?

Apart from the most superficial burns, all burns should be treated seriously because of the possible scarring, risk of infection and shock. Electrical burns are serious because they may be deep but appear minor.

Possible symptoms

- Raw, red areas.
- Fluid-filled blisters.
- Small blackened area after an electric current has touched the skin.

What should I do first?

For small, superficial burns

Cool affected area

1 Cool the affected area by placing it under cold running water for 10-15 minutes, or as long as your child can tolerate it, or apply ice cubes if only a small area is affected.

2 Cover the burn with a sterile dressing or a clean, ironed handkerchief; the dressing should extend beyond the injured area. Don't apply any creams or lotions, certainly not butter or fat.

3 Give your child junior paracetamol tablets or elixir to relieve the pain.

4 Raise the affected part slightly so that blood flow to the area is slowed down. This will help to ease the pain.

Continued on next page ▶

Words in **bold** are A-Z entries

Burn

B

◀ *Continued from previous page*
For major, deep burns, or any electrical burn

1 If the burns were caused by liquids such as boiling water, oil or chemicals, put on a pair of rubber gloves or use a cloth or towel to prevent them from getting on to your skin, and remove your child's clothing. The clothes will continue to burn him until they are removed. Do not remove any clothing that is sticking to the skin.

2 If your child has suffered an electric shock, first break his contact with the electricity by turning off the current or knocking him away with a nonconducting material, such as wood (*see page 298*).

3 Cool the affected area by running cold water over the skin for as long as your child can tolerate it. If the burns cover a large area, put your child into a cool bath.

4 Cover the affected area with a sterile dressing or any clean, non-fluffy material, such as an ironed handkerchief or pillowcase. Don't apply any creams or lotions, certainly not butter or fat.

Raise your child's legs

5 Lay your child down with his legs raised and supported and his head turned to one side. This prevents shock by keeping the essential blood supply in the vital organs. Wrap him in a clean sheet to reduce the risk of infection.

6 Take your child to the nearest casualty department by ambulance or by car if someone else can drive you there.

Should I consult the doctor?

As only small, superficial burns should be treated at home, consult your doctor immediately or take your child to the nearest casualty department for all deep burns, burns on your child's face or any electric burn. Consult your doctor as soon as possible if a superficial burn does not heal in a week, or if the area becomes red and swollen and pus forms, indicating infection.

What might the doctor do?

☐ The hospital doctor will evaluate the burn and treat your child accordingly.
☐ If the burn has become infected, your doctor will cover the area with an antibiotic dressing. Your child may also be prescribed antibiotics to clear up the infection.

What can I do to help?

☐ Try to safeguard your child against hazards in the home by putting safety guards around the stove and fireplace and dummy plugs in unused electric sockets.
☐ Teach your child about the dangers of fire and burning as soon as he is old enough to understand.
☐ Check the labels when you buy clothing for your child to ensure that the fabric is non-flammable.

SEE ALSO:
Blister, *page 67*
First aid, *page 297*

Catarrh

Catarrh is an excess of mucus in the nose and throat. It may be the result of a **common cold**, it may occur with the onset of an infectious disease such as **measles**, or it may be a symptom of **influenza**. With catarrh, the mucus is clear and runny, though it may become thick and yellow before the underlying condition clears up. One of the most dramatic forms of acute catarrh occurs in **hayfever** sufferers, when the allergic reaction of a runny nose is accompanied by itchy, tearful eyes and sneezing.

Chronic catarrh may be caused by **sinusitis**. The mucus from the infected sinuses runs down the back of the throat, causing the child to cough, particularly when lying down. Breathing becomes difficult, and, if a great deal of mucus is swallowed, this unpleasant sensation may lead to vomiting. Occasionally there may be catarrh with a middle ear infection, enlarged adenoids or nasal polyps.

Is it serious?
Catarrh that accompanies a minor illness is not serious. However, chronic catarrh will require treatment.

Possible symptoms
- Nasal congestion.
- Runny nose with a clear discharge.
- Coughing, especially at night.
- Difficulty in feeding in small babies.
- Vomiting if the mucus is swallowed.

What should I do first?

1 Encourage your child to blow his nose frequently. The catarrh will probably not need any more treatment than this.

Give regular menthol inhalations

2 If your child is having difficulty breathing, apply a menthol rub to his chest, or drops to his clothing or pillow at night, or encourage him, if he is old enough, to inhale the fumes from menthol crystals dissolved in hot water. Put the bowl on a safe work surface and cover both the bowl and your child's head with a towel so that he gets the full effect of the menthol.

3 If your child is coughing at night, prop him up with pillows so that the mucus doesn't drip down his throat.

4 Never use nose drops without your doctor's advice.

Continued on next page ▶

Words in **bold** are A-Z entries

Catarrh

◀ Continued from previous page

Should I consult the doctor?

Consult your doctor as soon as possible if the catarrh is making feeding difficult for your baby. Consult your doctor as soon as possible if you think the catarrh may be the result of an allergic reaction, such as hayfever, or if it persists for no apparent reason.

What might the doctor do?

Give nose drops before a feed

☐ For a baby, your doctor may prescribe nose drops to relieve the congestion before a feed.
☐ If your doctor thinks the catarrh is caused by an allergy, he will probably give your child a series of tests to find the possible causes.
☐ If the catarrh is caused by chronic sinusitis or a middle ear infection (**otitis media**), antibiotics will be prescribed. If it is caused by enlarged adenoids or nasal polyps, surgical removal may be recommended.

What can I do to help?

☐ Never try to clear your child's nose with a cotton-wool swab; this will only push the mucus further back
☐ Unless your doctor recommends them, avoid using decongestant medicines, which can lead to a build-up of mucus; they dry up the mucus so efficiently that the body makes more in order to compensate.
☐ Teach your child to blow his nose properly by clearing out one nostril at a time.

> **SEE ALSO:**
> **Common cold,** *page 90*
> **Hayfever,** *page 151*
> **Influenza,** *page 166*
> **Measles,** *page 176*
> **Otitis media,** *page 196*
> **Sinusitis,** *page 215*

Cerebral palsy

Cerebral palsy is the name given to disorders of the brain that occur early in life and result in a lack of full control of physical movement. In some children, the damage occurs in pregnancy; in others, during a difficult labour, when the baby may suffer from a lack of oxygen. Cerebral palsy may also result if a premature baby has severe breathing problems, with bleeding in the brain and lack of oxygen both contributing to the condition. Other, less common, problems which may damage the parts of the brain controlling movement, thus giving rise to cerebral palsy, are serious head injury and meningitis.

Because the more sophisticated voluntary control centres of the brain do not function in the first months of life, cerebral palsy may not be apparent at birth. After nine months it may show itself if the child is slow to sit up, is generally unsteady, or cannot grasp and hold an object. Cerebral palsy may affect one side (the right arm and leg), both legs with the arms hardly affected at all, or all four limbs and the trunk. Walking is delayed but usually possible. If the limbs tend to be stiff and fixed in certain postures, the child is technically termed "spastic". If he is prone to frequent, purposeless, writhing movements, he is said to be "athetoid".

Cerebral palsy is not a progressive disease which steadily gets worse. Nor is it uncommon for children with cerebral palsy to have normal intelligence and normal social capabilities.

Possible symptoms

- Delayed sitting.
- Delayed walking.
- Stiffness in arms and legs.
- Persistent abnormal postures.

What can be done?

The treatment for cerebral palsy consists of trying to develop the child's physical, mental and social capabilities to the full. Therefore it is important that the child is fully assessed by a specialist and a physiotherapist so that he can be given treatment at an early age. Stretching exercises will prevent fixed deformity of the limbs; orthopaedic appliances such as calipers, and in some cases surgery, can improve mobility; and education, such as speech therapy, can compensate for the physical disability.

Where there is no mental handicap, the outlook for the child is extremely good. Children adjust quite well to severe lack of motor function as long as their intellectual capacity is good and they can make themselves understood. The reaction of the family is of great importance. Parents must guard against feeling sorry for the child. If there are other children in the family, the child must be treated as nearly as possible in the same way as they are, though this may be hard for parents. As with all disabled children, the emphasis should be on what the child can do rather than on what he cannot.

FOR HELP AND ADVICE CONTACT:
The Spastic Society
16 Fitzroy Square
London W1
01-387 9571

Chapping

Chaps are small cracks in the skin that can be painful if they are deep. In nearly all cases, chapping is preceded by drying out of the skin due to its exposure to cold air or to hot, dry air. Chapping is therefore most common in exposed parts of the body such as on the lips, fingers, hands and ears.

Is it serious?
Chapping is not serious.

Possible symptoms

● Small cracks in the skin, most commonly on the lips, fingers, hands and ears.
● Bleeding if the cracks are deep.

What should I do first?

1 Keep your child's skin well moisturized with cream.
2 Keep your child warm in cold weather, particularly his hands and ears.

Put lip salve or Vaseline on dry lips

3 If your child has dry lips, put lip salve or Vaseline on regularly throughout the day.
4 If the chap cracks, place a piece of surgical tape or adhesive tape over it, where possible, for about 12 hours, to stop it drying out and cracking even more.

Should I consult the doctor?

Consult your doctor as soon as possible if the chaps fail to heal or become infected, that is, if they are red, tender and pus-filled.

What might the doctor do?

☐ Your doctor will give you general advice on how to stop your child's skin from drying to the point of cracking and he may prescribe an emollient cream to keep the skin moist.
☐ If there is an infection, your doctor will prescribe antibiotics.

What can I do to help?

☐ Don't wash your child with soap too often during cold weather. Soap defats the skin and makes it rough. An emollient cream or baby lotion can be used instead of soap to clean the skin.

SEE ALSO:
Chilblains, *page 83*

Chickenpox

C

Chickenpox is a common, infectious, childhood disease. It has an incubation period of between 17 and 21 days and causes only mild symptoms. Some sufferers may have a headache and a fever, though the majority give no indication of illness at all except for the characteristic itchy chickenpox spots. The spots cover most parts of the body and can even appear in the mouth, anus, vagina or ears. They appear in crops every three to four days and quickly develop tiny **blisters** that leave a scab. Your child is infectious until the scabs have dropped off. The spots may leave shallow scars when they heal if the child scratches too vigorously.

Is it serious?

Chickenpox is not serious. However, in rare cases, the chickenpox virus may cause **encephalitis** or be complicated by a condition known as **Reye's syndrome.**

Possible symptoms

Sites of rash

Early site

Later sites

- Small blisters appearing in new batches every three to four days, usually starting on the trunk, then spreading to the face, arms and legs, and eventually scabbing over.
- Intense itchiness.
- Headache and fever.

What should I do first?

1 Damp down the itchiness by applying calamine lotion to the rash or giving your child warm baths in which you have dissolved a handful of bicarbonate of soda.

2 As far as possible, keep your child away from other children; don't send him to school or nursery until the scabs have all dropped off.

Should I consult the doctor?

Consult your doctor as soon as possible to confirm that your child has chickenpox. Consult your doctor as soon as possible if any of the spots develops a redness with swelling, which indicates infection, or if the child is unable to stop scratching the spots. Consult your doctor immediately if your child is feverish or complains of neckache when the spots have scabbed over and he should be feeling better.

What might the doctor do?

☐ Your doctor will prescribe an anti-infective cream if any of the spots is infected.

☐ If itchiness is causing your child sleepless nights, your doctor may prescribe a sedative.

What can I do to help?

☐ If your child is still in nappies, change them frequently and leave them off whenever possible to allow the spots to scab over.

☐ Cut your child's fingernails short and discourage him from scratching.

SEE ALSO:
Blister, *page 67*
Encephalitis, *page 125*
Itching, *page 170*
Reye's syndrome, *page 206*

Words in **bold** are A-Z entries

Chilblains

Chilblains are areas of red, itchy skin that are the result of a hypersensitivity to cold. When the skin of a cold-sensitive child is exposed to cold and damp, the blood vessels beneath the skin close up to conserve heat, causing the skin to become numb and pale. When the blood vessels dilate again, with warmth, the skin becomes red and itchy. Chilblains usually appear on the ankles, hands and feet, and on the back of the legs.

Are they serious?
Chilblains are not serious, but they are irritating.

Possible symptoms

● Pale, numb skin, particularly on the hands and feet.

Common sites

● Red, swollen and itchy skin when the area warms up.

What should I do first?

Dust over area with talc

1 If your child has been out in the cold without sufficient warm clothing and then complains of itchiness, dust the skin with talcum powder or cornflour to ease the irritation.

2 Stop your child from breaking the skin of the affected areas by covering them with clothing or putting mittens or gloves on your child.

Should I consult the doctor?

Consult your doctor as soon as possible if the chilblains give your child a great deal of discomfort.

What might the doctor do?

☐ Your doctor may prescribe a vaso-dilator cream to improve circulation.

What can I do to help?

☐ Keep all the susceptible parts on your child's body covered up and warm in damp and cold weather.
☐ Put thermal insoles in your child's shoes to keep his feet warm.

SEE ALSO:
Itching, *page 170*

Choking

Choking is the body's way of dislodging a foreign body—usually food or a plaything—which has entered the airway instead of the passage to the stomach. If there is enough air getting through to the lungs, your child will be able to cough to bring the object back up into his mouth.

Is it serious?
If your child is coughing very feebly or if he is gasping for breath or turning blue in the face, this is serious and should be treated as an emergency (*see page 294*). If the airway is totally blocked, your child will become unconscious.

Possible symptoms
- Spluttering or coughing.
- Gasping for breath.
- Blueness around the lips (cyanosis).
- Unconsciousness.

What should I do first?

Slap your baby gently on the back

1 With a baby, lay him along your forearm, with his head held firmly in your hand. His head should be below his chest. Give him four light slaps on his back with your other hand. With an older child, lay him across your knee with his head tipped forward, holding him firmly by the waist. Hit him sharply between the shoulder blades.

2 If the foreign body is coughed into the throat and you can see it, try to hook it out with a finger. Hold the child steady with your other hand to prevent him from re-inhaling the object. Be very careful not to push the object further into his throat.

Should I consult the doctor?

Call for an ambulance immediately and tell the operator if your child has turned blue or lost consciousness. While waiting for medical assistance, keep slapping your child on his back to try to dislodge the foreign body. If your child loses consciousness, lay him in the recovery position (*see page 285*) until help arrives. Stay with him and if he stops breathing, start giving mouth-to-mouth ventilation (*see page 286*).

What might the doctor do?

The ambulance attendant or the doctor will try to revive your child if necessary and remove the foreign body if it is still lodged in the throat.

What can I do to help?

☐ Make sure your child understands that he must not put any small toys in his mouth because of the risk of choking. Toys small enough to be swallowed should not be given to children under three years of age.
☐ Never leave a small child unattended when he is eating.
☐ Never give peanuts or other small foods to a child under three years old.

Words in **bold** are A-Z entries

Coeliac disease

Coeliac disease, or gluten sensitivity, is the result of an allergic reaction in the lining of the small intestine when the intestine comes into contact with gluten. (Gluten is a protein found in cereals and grains and is therefore difficult to avoid in a normal diet.) The lining of the intestine becomes smooth, preventing nutrients from being properly absorbed and metabolized. The child fails to thrive because valuable proteins, calories, vitamins and minerals pass out of his body in the stools. Symptoms of coeliac disease normally appear within a few weeks of cereals being introduced into the diet. Because of the dietary deficiencies, the child may appear unhappy and irritable.

If left undiagnosed and untreated by a change of diet, coeliac disease leads to a distended abdomen (because of wind), and to stick-like limbs. The buttocks in particular become flat, wasted and saggy.

Is it serious?
Coeliac disease is serious if undetected because it could permanently stunt your child's growth.

Possible symptoms

- Frequent, bulky, pale, foul-smelling stools which are difficult to flush away because they are so full of fat.
- Loss of appetite.
- Failure to thrive.
- Distended stomach because of wind.
- Stick-like limbs.
- Irritability and lethargy.
- Saggy, flat buttocks.

What should I do first?

1 If your baby has recently been weaned on to cereals, and his stools become foul-smelling and frequent, try to flush the motions down the lavatory to see if they float.

2 Don't put your child on to a gluten-free diet without medical advice. You may be unnecessarily reducing your child's protein intake and causing problems by restricting the diet without medical supervision.

Should I consult the doctor?

Consult your doctor as soon as possible if your child is not gaining weight and his bowel motions are frequent and foul-smelling.

What might the doctor do?

☐ To check for coeliac disease, your doctor will arrange blood and faeces tests for your child. If these indicate the likelihood of coeliac disease, your child will probably be admitted to hospital for a biopsy (removal under anaesthetic of a tiny piece of the intestine for testing).

☐ Once the diagnosis has been confirmed, your child will need to eat a gluten-free diet for life. Your doctor will refer you to a dietician for advice about the kind of foods your child should have. The reaction once the diet is begun is startling. Within days there is an improvement in mood, an increase in appetite and a return to normal bowel motions.

Continued on next page ▶

Coeliac disease

◄ Continued from previous page

What can I do to help?

☐ The best way to approach the special diet is to make gluten-free dishes for all the family so that your child does not feel different. Special gluten-free flours are available, and some cereals —for example, maize, rice, and buckwheat—don't contain gluten. There are also a number of cookery books on the market with gluten-free recipes.

Wholemeal bread

Ice cream

Muesli

Rye bread

Buckwheat spaghetti

Brown rice

Foods to avoid   **Foods to eat**

☐ Familiarize yourself, with the help of the hospital dietician, with foods to be avoided: non-dairy ice cream, muesli, cocoa powder, and mustard, for example, all contain gluten.
☐ When buying prepared dishes, scrutinize the labels to make sure they don't include ingredients containing gluten.
☐ As your child gets older, you will have to emphasize the need to be wary of all foods that you haven't prepared yourself or checked for gluten. School lunches, party foods and restaurants will present problems, but with planning you should be able to prevent your child from feeling abnormal.

SEE ALSO:
Diarrhoea, *page 112*

Words in **bold** are A-Z entries

Cold sores

Cold sores are tiny **blisters** that form around the nostrils and lips and elsewhere on the face. The blisters break open and weep before they crust over and disappear. Cold sores are caused by a virus (*Herpes simplex*) that lives permanently in the nerve endings of some adults and children. A rise in skin temperature—perhaps caused by a cold, or by going out in the sun—activates the virus. The first attack takes the form of painful **mouth ulcers.** Subsequent attacks, which tend to occur most often when children are run down, take the form of blisters.

Are they serious?

Cold sores are not serious unless they occur near the eye, where they may cause an ulcer to form on the front of the eyeball.

Possible symptoms

Common site

● Raised red area, usually around the nostrils and lips, which tingles and feels itchy. Tiny blisters then form on the spot.
● Weeping blisters which then crust over.

What should I do first?

1 Once blisters have formed, stop your child from touching the area. Keep his hands clean.

2 Apply surgical spirit to the cold sores to dry them up, or smear a soothing cream such as Vaseline on to them to keep them moist while the virus runs its course. One or the other treatment may give your child some relief.

Should I consult the doctor?

Consult your doctor as soon as possible if a cold sore is near your child's eye. Consult your doctor as soon as possible if the cold sores become redder and develop pussy centres. They will have become infected with bacteria. Ask your doctor's advice if your child suffers from recurrent cold sores.

What might the doctor do?

□ If the cold sores are infected, your doctor will prescribe an antibiotic ointment that lubricates the area and treats the infection.
□ Your doctor may prescribe an antiviral cream to spread over the affected area regularly to contain the attack.

What can I do to help?

□ Make sure that your child uses his own towel and facecloth.
□ Don't let your child kiss other children. The virus can be transmitted this way.
□ If your child tends to develop cold sores after exposure to sunlight, smear a sunblock on his lips or nose when he plays out in the sun.

> **SEE ALSO:**
> **Blister,** *page 67*
> **Mouth ulcer,** *page 180*
> **Sunburn,** *page 230*

Colic

Colic, as applied to a baby under four months of age, describes a crying spell, during which the baby's face becomes very red and both legs are drawn up to his stomach as if he is in great pain. This crying spell usually comes in the early evening; during the rest of the day the baby is generally contented. The crying can reach screaming pitch and last from one to three hours. It doesn't usually stop as a result of the proven methods of soothing. Colic is so common that it is regarded by paediatricians as normal, but for parents it can be difficult to endure. The cause of the apparent spasmodic pain is not known. It is often at its worst at three months of age but goes by four months.

Is it serious?
The fact that your baby is contented during the rest of the day means that this crying bout is not related to a serious physical problem. Colicky babies are usually healthy and thriving.

Possible symptoms

● Your baby cannot settle in the early evening and cries no matter what you do to calm him.

Classic colic spasm

● He becomes red-faced and draws his legs up into his stomach as if in pain.
● He may wake from a short sleep with a startled cry.

What should I do first?

1 Try all the methods of soothing your baby that you know work at other times of the day. This may mean you are constantly offering the breast or bottle; changing nappies; burping; nursing and rocking; walking with the baby held over your shoulder; putting the baby in a sling against your body; playing music to give a constant background noise; or walking him in a pram.

Continued on next page ▶

Methods of soothing

A relaxing bath

Hold your baby close to your body

Constant movement

Words in **bold** are A-Z entries

Colic

◀ *Continued from previous page*

Lay your baby on a hot-water bottle

2 Lay him on his tummy over a hot-water bottle wrapped in a towel.

3 Try using a pacifier: your baby may need to suck all the time.

4 Don't use any patent medicines without your doctor's advice.

5 Bath your baby at this difficult time of the day. A warm bath seems to relax most babies and this will pass the time when the crying seems worst.

Should I consult the doctor?

Consult your doctor as soon as possible if you find you cannot cope with the nightly crying sessions.

What might the doctor do?

☐ Your doctor will reassure you that your baby is healthy. Your doctor may discuss the use of *dicyclomine,* which relaxes the intestine and does relieve colic symptoms in older babies. It is not usually given to babies under three months.

☐ If you are being driven to breaking point, discuss with your doctor whether a mild sedative for yourself or for your baby might be advisable.

What can I do to help?

☐ Make sure you look after yourself. Sleep during the day, if you can, when the baby sleeps. You will be better able to cope with the evenings.

☐ Invite good friends in to share that time of the evening; a relaxed atmosphere may calm you and your baby.

☐ Talk to other parents who have had colicky babies. Once you realize you are not alone and that colic does pass, you may find it easier to bear.

C

> **SEE ALSO:**
> **Crying,** *page 101*

Common cold

The common cold is caused by a virus, and as we have no way of killing viral infections there is therefore no specific cure for a cold. The virus enters the body through the nasal passages and throat, causing inflammation of the mucous membranes lining these passages. This gives rise to the well-known symptoms of a runny nose and **sore throat.** It takes the body's defences up to ten days to overcome the virus.

Is it serious?
The common cold is not a serious illness, but because it lowers the body's resistance, complications such as **bronchitis** or **pneumonia** can arise. A common cold should be regarded more seriously in a baby because even minor cold symptoms, like a blocked nose, can cause feeding problems. There is also a greater chance of complications.

Possible symptoms
- Sneezing.
- Runny or blocked nose.
- Raised temperature.
- Coughing.
- Sore throat.
- Aching muscles.
- Irritability.
- Catarrh.

What should I do first?

1 If your child has any cold symptoms, take his temperature to check if he has a fever, too. If not, keep him warm and comfortable. He needn't be put to bed unless he wants to go. If he has a high temperature, around 38°C (100.4°F), and it does not subside within four to five hours, put him to bed and try to bring his temperature down (*page 31*).

2 Check if the nasal discharge is clear or yellow. If it turns yellow, there may be a secondary infection. If the discharge is clear, your child may have **hayfever.**

3 Don't give your child any patent cough medicines without your doctor's advice.

Should I consult the doctor?

Consult your doctor immediately if you think your child has developed another infection on top of the cold.

Consult your doctor as soon as possible if your baby isn't feeding well because of the cold or seems distressed, or if your child has a hacking cough that causes sleepless nights.

What might the doctor do?

☐ If there is another infection present, your doctor will treat it accordingly.

Insert drops

☐ Your doctor may prescribe nose drops to be given before a feed.

Continued on next page ▶

Words in **bold** are A-Z entries

Common cold

◀ *Continued from previous page*
They should never be used more frequently than your doctor suggests, or over long periods, as they can damage the lining of the nose.
☐ Your doctor may also prescribe a cough suppressant or an expectorant for a bad cough.

☐ Try sprinkling capsules of camphor on clothing or bedding; this may help your child's breathing during the night.
☐ To ease your child's sore throat and clear the nasal passages, give him a hot drink of freshly squeezed lemon juice and water before putting him to bed.

What can I do to help?

Raise the cot mattress

☐ With a baby, help him to breathe more easily by raising his head with a pillow under the cot mattress.
☐ Give your child plenty to drink. Even if he isn't hungry, make sure he keeps up his fluid intake.
☐ Help your child to blow his nose properly by blowing one nostril at a time.
☐ If possible, keep the air in your child's room humid so that the raw lining of his nose is not further irritated by a dry atmosphere.

Smear on Vaseline to prevent chafing

☐ If constant blowing has made your child's nose and upper lip sore, smear a little Vaseline on to prevent chafing.

SEE ALSO:
Bronchitis, *page 73*
Catarrh, *page 78*
Cough, *page 97*
Croup, *page 100*
Fever, *page 134*
Hayfever, *page 151*
Pneumonia, *page 200*
Sore throat, *page 220*

Conjunctivitis

Conjunctivitis is an inflammation of the *conjunctiva,* which is the membrane covering the eyeball and the inside of the eyelid. The inflammation may be caused by a viral or bacterial infection or by injury from a **foreign body** or chemicals, or it may be the result of an allergic reaction. The eyes become red and weepy, and they can be painful or extremely itchy and may be irritated by bright light. The condition, which may affect one or both eyes, can be contagious.

Is it serious?
Although conjunctivitis is not a serious eye infection, it should always be treated by a doctor.

Possible symptoms
● Weepy, red eye that feels sore or itchy.
● Intolerance of bright light.
● Discharge of pus causing eyelashes to stick together after a night's sleep.

Cross-section of the eye

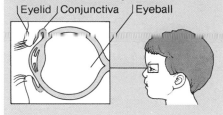

Eyelid | Conjunctiva | Eyeball

What should I do first?

1 Check to see if there is a foreign body in the eye; if possible remove it (*see page 129*).

2 As a temporary measure, before consulting your doctor, bathe each eye, whether both are affected or not, with a solution of 5ml (one teaspoonful) of salt in a glass of warm, previously boiled water. Using a new ball of cotton wool for each eye, begin at the inner corner of the eye and wipe outwards.

3 If only one eye is affected, reduce friction between the conjunctiva and other parts of the eye by keeping your child's eye closed. Tape a gauze pad or clean, ironed handkerchief over the area, and hold it in place with a lightly tied bandage.

4 To prevent the spread of infection, encourage your child to keep his hands clean and not to rub his eyes.

Should I consult the doctor?

Consult your doctor as soon as possible if you suspect conjunctivitis.

What might the doctor do?

☐ If the condition is caused by an infection, your doctor will prescribe antibiotic eye drops or ointment to clear it. If the infection does not respond to treatment within a few days, your doctor may refer you to an eye specialist.
☐ If the irritation is caused by an allergy, such as **hayfever**, your doctor will prescribe anti-inflammatory eye drops and antihistamine medication.
☐ If there is a foreign body in your child's eye, your doctor will remove it.

What can I do to help?

☐ Emphasize to your child that the infection can be spread by his hands. He should keep them clean and use a separate facecloth and towel.
☐ If your child suffers from hayfever, keep him away from freshly mown lawns during the worst hayfever months.

SEE ALSO:
Eye, foreign body in, *page 129*
Hayfever, *page 151*

Constipation

A child who is constipated passes hard, pebble-like stools and this may cause discomfort or actual pain when the stools are passed. Constipation is a word that is used to describe the consistency of stools and not the regularity or frequency of bowel movements. During babyhood, constipation is unlikely for either breast-fed or bottlefed babies. When they start on solid food, however, they can suffer from constipation if their diet doesn't contain enough fresh fruit and vegetables and liquids. By the age of two or three, constipation may become a problem for a different reason: some parents are so obsessed with the importance of "regularity" during the period when their child is learning bowel control that the child reacts by holding back the stools as a weapon in a battle of wills.

As a guiding rule, if your child is perfectly happy and healthy and shows no signs of discomfort when going to the toilet, and if his stools are not as hard as pebbles, he is not constipated. Furthermore, if your child's stools are hard and dry during a period when, because of illness, he is feverish or has been vomiting, this is not true constipation. The body compensates for loss of fluid from

Possible symptoms

- Hard pebble-like stools.
- Pain in the lower abdomen.
- Blood on nappy or underpants.

vomiting or fever by absorbing water from the stools, and bowel activity should return to normal when the illness has passed.

If your child involuntarily soils his underpants when he was previously toilet trained, you might think he has diarrhoea, but in fact this could be a condition known as **encopresis**, when chronic constipation leads to hard stools becoming impacted in the intestine and loose, watery motions leak out past the blockage.

Is it serious?
Occasional constipation is not serious and can be avoided by means of a diet rich in fibre. Chronic constipation can be a serious matter because it can cause problems in later life. Blood in the stools may indicate an underlying disorder and should always be cause for concern.

What should I do first?

1 If your child strains when passing stools and complains of pain, check the consistency of what he has passed.

Check for tenderness

2 If he complains of stomach pain, check the right side of his abdomen below his navel (*see page 53*), for possible **appendicitis**.

Should I consult the doctor?

Consult your doctor as soon as possible if your child complains of pain when moving his bowels. Consult your doctor immediately if you notice red blood on his nappy or underpants; the passing of a large, dry stool may have injured his anal passage. This is called an anal fissure and your child may be reluctant to pass any more stools for fear of the pain caused by this tiny crack. Consult your doctor immediately if you suspect appendicitis.

Continued on next page ▶

Constipation

◀ Continued from previous page

What might the doctor do?

☐ Your doctor will prescribe a very mild laxative, specially formulated for babies and children, which is safe to give your child for short periods. He will also give you advice about your child's diet.

☐ If your doctor suspects an anal fissure, he will examine your child's rectum and if there is a tiny crack he will gently lubricate the anal passage to help the skin to heal.

What can I do to help?

☐ Never use laxatives unless your doctor advises it. They encourage a lazy bowel.

☐ If your child has been prescribed a laxative, follow the manufacturer's instructions precisely.

☐ Make sure your child is getting plenty to drink.

Wholemeal bread

Bananas

Prunes

Corn

☐ Include as many natural, unprocessed foods in your child's diet as possible, with some dietary fibre in the form of whole grains—such as brown rice and wholemeal bread—and fresh fruit and vegetables. It is not a good idea just to scatter bran over your child's meals; this can deplete certain minerals in the diet. A few stewed prunes or dried figs, however, can produce a soft stool within 24 hours.

☐ Don't leave your child sitting on his potty for long periods of time. He may get the impression that he must either perform or lose your approval.

☐ Don't rush your school-age child when he is in the toilet. If the pace is hectic in the morning, make sure he has time to go to the toilet without the anxiety of having to rush off to school. Many children prefer to go to the toilet at home because they find the school facilities lack privacy.

> **SEE ALSO:**
> **Appendicitis,** *page 53*
> **Encopresis,** *page 126*

Words in **bold** are A-Z entries

Convulsion

A convulsion is a fit or seizure that occurs when the brain reacts abnormally. During the convulsion, your child loses consciousness, becomes rigid for some seconds while holding his breath, then rhythmically bends and straightens his arms and legs for some minutes. Your child may cry out at the beginning of the seizure. He may urinate and he may defecate. When the convulsion is over, your child will be in a confused state and he may want to sleep.

The most common cause of convulsions is a raised temperature that accompanies a viral infection such as **influenza**. This type of convulsion is known as a febrile convulsion and generally occurs between the ages of six months and six years. The tendency to suffer from febrile convulsions runs in families. Convulsions may also be caused by **meningitis**, **encephalitis** and, rarely, chemical abnormalities of the blood, such as a low level of glucose in diabetics. Sometimes no specific cause is found. **Epilepsy** is another cause of convulsions.

Is it serious?
Though dramatic and frightening, a convulsion is not life-threatening but it should be treated seriously.

Possible symptoms
- Sudden rise in temperature.
- Crying out and loss of consciousness.
- Rigid phase with the breath held.
- Rhythmic jerking of the limbs.
- Urination and/or defecation.
- Confusion and drowsiness.

What should I do first?

1 As soon as your child loses consciousness, remove any furniture from the area so that his jerking limbs don't knock against anything hard. With a baby or young child, put him over your knee as if to spank him. This ensures that his tongue does not fall backwards and obstruct the airway.

2 Don't leave your child alone for a moment.

3 Don't try to stop him from jerking his limbs; you may injure him.

4 Don't try to force anything into his mouth and never try to force the teeth apart if they are clenched.

Turn your child on his side

5 As soon as the violent movements have ceased, turn your child on to his side so that he will not inhale his tongue or saliva.

Continued on next page ▶

95

Convulsion

◀ *Continued from previous page*

Should I consult the doctor?

Consult your doctor immediately as soon as the convulsion has passed. If there is someone with you, ask him to call the doctor while you stay with your child. If the doctor hasn't arrived within 15 minutes or if the convulsion hasn't passed, take your child to the nearest casualty department. Any fit that continues for 20 minutes should be stopped with an anti-convulsant drug.

What might the doctor do?

☐ If the convulsion is continuing, your doctor will give your child an injection of an anti-convulsant drug.
☐ If your child is less than two years old when he has his first convulsion, your doctor will admit him to hospital immediately so that tests can be carried out to exclude any serious cause of convulsions such as meningitis.
☐ With an older child, your doctor will refer him to hospital if the cause of the convulsion is not clear. Tests will be carried out, and the paediatrician will advise whether or not anti-convulsant drug treatment is needed

in the event of your child contracting another infectious fever.
☐ Your doctor will give you advice on how to avoid a rapid rise in temperature in the future.

What can I do to help?

Sponge child to reduce temperature

☐ Once the convulsion is over, if your child is feverish and has a high temperature, remove his clothing and cool his skin by tepid sponging (*see page 31*). Cover him with a light sheet when he sleeps.
☐ Don't give him any patent medicines without your doctor's advice.
☐ Stay calm yourself.

SEE ALSO:
Encephalitis, *page 125*
Epilepsy, *page 127*
Fever, *page 134*
Influenza, *page 166*
Meningitis, *page 177*

Words in **bold** are A-Z entries

Cough

A cough is either a symptom of an illness or the body's way of reacting to an irritant in the throat or air passages. A cough may bring up phlegm from the chest and clear mucus from the air passages, for example, during an attack of **asthma** or **whooping cough** (this is known as a productive cough). A dry cough, which produces no phlegm, serves no useful purpose and its cause is not always obvious. The irritation provoking the cough may be mucus from chronically infected sinuses or nasal discharge from a common cold, both of which dribble down and tickle the back of the throat. A dry cough may also be the body's way of bringing up a foreign body stuck in the windpipe. Coughing may be caused by "passive smoking". If adults around your child smoke a lot, the smoke may irritate your child's throat and cause a cough. Children may also adopt a cough as an attention-seeking device, when it becomes a **tic** or mannerism.

Is it serious?

A cough is not usually serious, although it can be irritating. However, a cough which causes breathing difficulties such that your child turns blue around the lips and gasps for breath, is serious and should be treated as an emergency.

What should I do first?

1 If your child is coughing up phlegm, lay him over your lap as if you were going to spank him. Pat him gently on the back to help him bring up the phlegm.

2 Don't give your child cough-suppressant medicines for a cough that produces phlegm. The risk of infection increases if the phlegm is not coughed up.

3 If you think that your child has a foreign body in his throat, try to remove it (*see page 294*).

Prop up your child

4 If your child is coughing at night, prop up his head and shoulders with pillows. This will stop mucus or nasal discharge from dribbling down the throat.

5 To soothe your child's throat, give him a hot lemon drink sweetened with honey.

Should I consult the doctor?

Consult your doctor as soon as possible if your child's cough doesn't get better after three or four days, or if your child is not getting any sleep at night, or if you cannot remove the foreign body from your child's throat. Consult your doctor immediately if your baby develops a hacking cough or if your child's coughing is accompanied by rapid, laboured or wheezy breathing. This could be **croup** or asthma.

What might the doctor do?

☐ If your child's cough is part of an infection such as **otitis media**, **tonsillitis**, or croup, your doctor will prescribe antibiotics to clear up that infection.
☐ If your child is suffering from a viral infection, your doctor will advise you on how to relieve the symptoms and help your child to cough up the phlegm.

Continued on next page ▶

Cough

◀ *Continued from previous page*

☐ If the cough is part of an asthmatic condition, your doctor may prescribe bronchodilator drugs that help to widen the air passages.

☐ Your doctor may prescribe nose drops to administer sparingly to your child before he goes to bed. These drops ease congestion and prevent mucus from dribbling down the back of the throat.

☐ Your doctor may prescribe a cough medicine: either a cough suppressant (to soothe the throat and reduce irritation) or an expectorant (to encourage coughing up of phlegm).

What can I do to help?

☐ Keep your child quiet and warm so that any minor infection does not spread into the lungs and cause a more serious condition such as **bronchitis**.

☐ Don't let your child run around too much during the day. Breathlessness can bring on a coughing fit.

Lying on the stomach cuts down mucus irritation

☐ Encourage your child to lie on his stomach or his side at night so that mucus will not dribble into his throat.

☐ Keep the air in your child's room moist by leaving a window open. Don't overheat the room.

☐ Don't smoke at home and don't take your child into smoky atmospheres.

SEE ALSO:
Asthma, *page 58*
Bronchitis, *page 73*
Croup, *page 100*
Otitis media, *page 196*
Tic, *page 240*
Tonsillitis, *page 241*
Whooping cough, *page 260*

Words in **bold** are A-Z entries

Cradle cap

Cradle cap is a thick yellow encrustation on the scalp. It occurs mainly in babies, though children up to the age of three can have cradle cap. The yellow scales appear in small patches or can cover the entire scalp. Cradle cap is not due to poor hygiene. Babies who suffer from it probably just have greasier scalps.

Is it serious?
Cradle cap may appear unsightly, but it is quite harmless unless it is accompanied by red, scaly areas elsewhere on your baby's body, in which case your baby may have seborrhoeic **eczema**.

Possible symptoms
● Thick, yellowish scales over part or all of the scalp.

C

What should I do first?

1 Do not try to remove the scales with your fingers. If they won't brush out, they must be loosened first.

Smear baby oil on to the scales

2 Smear a little baby oil or Vaseline on to your baby's scalp and leave overnight. This makes the scales soft and loose and they will wash away easily when you shampoo the next day.

3 Do not use anti-dandruff shampoos without consulting your doctor.

Should I consult the doctor?

Consult your doctor if you are worried about the condition or if your baby has any red, scaly areas elsewhere.

What might the doctor do?

☐ Your doctor will prescribe a special shampoo to prevent the scales from forming and give you general advice on how to prevent cradle cap with brushing and other home treatments.

What can I do to help?

☐ You can prevent scales from building up by brushing through your baby's hair daily, even if there is very little of it, with a soft-bristled brush.
☐ Never rub the scalp very hard when washing your child's hair. Shampoos remove dirt within seconds, so you only need to bring the shampoo to a lather and then rinse it off thoroughly.
☐ If the cradle cap becomes quite hard and thick, you may have to continue the baby oil or Vaseline treatment over a ten-day period to loosen all the encrustations.

SEE ALSO:
Dandruff, *page 106*
Eczema, *page 123*

99

Croup

Croup is the name given to the sound made when air is breathed in through a constricted windpipe, past inflamed vocal cords. It usually occurs only in young children, who are susceptible because their air passages (*bronchi*) are narrow and become blocked with mucus when inflamed—most commonly because of a virus such as a **common cold**, or an infection such as **bronchitis**. In rare cases, croup can be caused by an inhaled foreign body. In older children the condition is less serious and is known as **laryngitis**.

The first attack of croup can come on quickly, usually at night, and it may last a couple of hours. Your child will have a croaking cough and laboured breathing.

Is it serious?
If your child has a severe attack of croup, he could develop breathing difficulties. This should be treated as an emergency.

Possible symptoms
- Croaking cough.
- Laboured breathing when the lower chest caves in at every inhalation.
- Wheezing.
- Face colour becoming grey or blue.

What should I do first?

1 Stay calm and try to calm your child so that he won't panic and make his breathing more difficult.

2 Your child's air passages will be soothed by moist air. If the air outside is cool and damp, take him to the window and get him to take a deep breath of air, or take him into the bathroom and turn on the hot taps to build up a steamy atmosphere.

3 Prop your child up in bed with pillows or hold him on your lap. It will be easier for him to breathe if he is sitting up.

Should I consult the doctor?

Consult your doctor immediately if your child's skin turns grey or blue and he has to fight for breath. Consult your doctor as soon as possible to tell him that your child has had an attack of croup.

What might the doctor do?

☐ In a serious attack your doctor will give your child oxygen.
☐ If necessary, your doctor will prescribe antibiotics to eradicate any underlying infection.
☐ You will be given advice on what to do should there be another attack.
☐ If the attack is caused by an inhaled foreign body, your doctor will remove the foreign body.

What can I do to help?

☐ In future attacks, stay with your child and follow your doctor's instructions.

SEE ALSO:
Bronchitis, *page 73*
Common cold, *page 90*
Laryngitis, *page 172*
Nose, foreign body in, *page 189*

Words in **bold** are A-Z entries

Crying

All babies cry but some cry much more often than others. Crying is a baby's means of communicating and you will soon come to recognize whether the crying is a symptom of an illness or not. By the age of about six weeks, your baby will be passing part of his waking hours by taking in his surroundings and making gurgling noises instead of just crying, feeding and sleeping. By six months, babies spend most of their waking time playing and communicating in all sorts of ways. A baby who cries rather than plays by the age of six months may be an anxious child, or cutting teeth, or one who is easily bored, or, in a minority of cases, one who has some physical illness. Most healthy babies stop crying as soon as they are fed, cuddled and made comfortable. If there are certain times of the day (especially in the evening) when nothing stops the crying, your baby could be suffering from **colic**, which is a common cause of crying in babies. A toddler will usually cry only for obvious reasons of illness or injury or as a show of temper.

C

Is it serious?
Crying is not normally serious. Persistent crying can, however, cause problems if you become angry, resentful and over-tired. A crying baby is a common cause of baby battering.

What should I do first?

1 Pick your baby up and cuddle him or give him a pacifier if he finds sucking calming.

Nurse your baby

2 Feed him or, if you have fed him recently, give him a spoonful of cooled, boiled water.

3 Change your baby's nappy and make sure he isn't too hot or too cold in what he's wearing.

Should I consult the doctor?

Consult your doctor as soon as possible if the crying seems to be following a different pattern from usual and there are symptoms of illness, such as **diarrhoea**, **fever** or **vomiting**. Consult your doctor as soon as possible if you are exhausted by your active baby and you think you might lash out in anger.

What might the doctor do?

☐ Your doctor will question you about the extent of your baby's crying. He will examine your baby for any symptoms of illness. If your baby is healthy, your doctor will probably reassure you that there is nothing to be anxious about.

Continued on next page ▶

Crying

C

◀ Continued from previous page

What can I do to help?

☐ You must think of ways to help yourself if you have a particularly demanding baby. Rest whenever you can and take turns with your partner if your baby is difficult at night and seems to need little sleep.

☐ Stay calm yourself; try not to resent your baby's need to be close to you.

Prop your baby in a bouncing chair so that he can see around him

☐ Keep your baby near to you when he is awake. Prop him up in a bouncing chair so that he can watch you at work. Carrying him round in a sling may also give him comfort and reassurance.

☐ Always go to your crying baby. Parental apathy and lack of response can inhibit a child's attachment to others in later life. There is no such thing as spoiling a baby.

SEE ALSO:
Colic, *page 88*
Diarrhoea, *page 112*
Fever, *page 134*
Sleeplessness, *page 217*
Teething, *page 232*
Vomiting, *page 256*

Words in **bold** are A-Z entries

Cuts and grazes

A cut is an injury which breaks the skin and underlying tissue, causing bleeding. A graze is an injury in which the skin's surface is not actually broken, but rubbed so that the blood vessels under the skin surface ooze slightly. Small cuts and grazes can be treated at home, and should be cleaned up and possibly dressed to prevent germs entering and causing infection. The best dressing for a cut or graze is a piece of sterile gauze held in place with adhesive tape so that the air can get to the wound. Skin closure tapes can be used to hold the edges of a cut together and prevent it from healing in a gaping shape.

Are they serious?

Few cuts and grazes are serious enough to need medical attention. However, if a cut is deep (from a nail, a rose or an animal) there is a risk of tetanus, or another infection, developing, and if it is very bloody there is the risk of shock (*see page 293*), so you must seek medical aid.

C

What should I do first?

If the wound is large and bleeding

Press pad on to wound

1 You must get medical help immediately. Take your child to the nearest casualty department, but before you go, press directly on to the wound with a clean pad, a handkerchief or your hand if you have nothing else.

2 Elevate the affected part to slow down the blood flow. Lay your child down.

3 Place a sterile dressing over the cut and tie it in place with a knot directly over the wound to keep pressure on it until you've got medical help.

If the wound is small or a graze

1 Hold the affected area under a cold tap or wash with soap and water or antiseptic lotion.

Hold edges together with skin closure tapes

2 Pat the skin dry. Hold the edges of a straight cut together with skin closure tapes to help the cut heal neatly. Apply a sterile dressing, held in place with adhesive tape, if the cut or graze needs it.

Continued on next page ▶

Cuts and grazes

◀ Continued from previous page

Should I consult the doctor?

Consult your doctor immediately or take your child to the nearest casualty department if the wound is large, if bleeding persists after 10 minutes of pressure, if the wound is very deep and bloody, if the wound is on the face, if the wound is gaping, if there is dirt or a foreign body in the wound that you can't get out, if the wound is deep but has only a small puncture hole in the skin or if your child was playing in an area where horses are kept and the wound has been contaminated by dirt or gravel. Consult your doctor as soon as possible if, after a day or two, you notice red streaks extending from the wound as this could be a sign of infection.

What might the doctor do?

☐ The doctor will clean the wound and stitch it, if necessary, under a local anaesthetic; any wound on the face will be stitched to minimize scarring.
☐ If the bleeding doesn't stop, a blood vessel may have been lacerated; this will be tied off by the doctor under an anaesthetic.

☐ If there is a deep wound or a wound contaminated with dirt, the doctor will ask you when your child last had a tetanus booster. If there is any doubt, your child will be given a tetanus injection.
☐ If there is any sign of infection, the doctor will cover the area with an antibiotic dressing and he may also prescribe antibiotics to be taken by mouth to eradicate the infection.

What can I do to help?

☐ Change the dressing daily. Your doctor may advise you to leave the dressing off at night as wounds heal more quickly if exposed to the air.
☐ When you change the dressing check for any redness extending from the wound. If you notice any, contact your doctor as soon as possible.
☐ A graze tends to cover a larger area, and it may need to be protected against rubbing. Use a dry gauze strip and hold it in place with surgical tape. Don't apply any adhesive dressing directly on to the wound as it will be very painful to remove.
☐ Put a handful of salt in your child's bath water to clean the skin and deter infection.

Words in **bold** are A-Z entries

Cystic fibrosis

Cystic fibrosis is a rare, congenital disease —that is, it is present at birth and inherited from both parents. If the mother and father are healthy but each carries one defective gene for cystic fibrosis, each child conceived has a 25 per cent chance of inheriting two defective genes and being born with cystic fibrosis. The disease causes several glands in the body to be defective, particularly the glands in the lining of the bronchial tubes. Instead of producing the normal thin mucus, the bronchial glands produce a thick, sticky phlegm, which results in blockages of the air passages, and this leads to lung infections. When small parts of the lungs collapse, **pneumonia** results. This is a common and recurrent infection in cystic fibrosis sufferers.

In the intestines of a child with cystic fibrosis, the pancreas fails to produce certain vital enzymes. These enzymes aid digestion, breaking down food so that it can be absorbed by the body more easily. Lack of these digestive enzymes means that food is poorly absorbed, which leads to diarrhoea and foul-smelling stools. Because food goes undigested, the body does not absorb many of the nutrients essential to good health and the child will be small, underweight and fail to thrive. The bouts of diarrhoea may alternate with constipation, which can actually block the intestine.

Possible symptoms

● Recurrent chest infections with a cough and some breathing difficulty.
● Diarrhoea, alternating with constipation.
● Greasy and foul-smelling bowel motions.
● Failure to thrive.
● Swollen abdomen and wasted limbs.

What can be done?

There is no cure for cystic fibrosis, but early detection of the condition lessens the chance of permanent damage to the lungs. Simple tests on the blood or stools of a newborn baby can be carried out but the definitive test for cystic fibrosis is a sweat test because there is an increased salt level in the sweat of sufferers. This test will be done on all brothers and sisters of a child with cystic fibrosis, or if a baby has recurrent bouts of pneumonia or fails to thrive, and will be carried out when the baby is old enough to sweat (around three months).

A child with cystic fibrosis has to have a special diet, with vitamin supplements and enzyme replacements, which can be taken by mouth. Fat in the diet is reduced. Physiotherapy and breathing exercises must be given daily to loosen and drain mucus from the lungs. The child's lungs will be helped by exposure to moist air, and a cold steam vaporizer is a good investment for a child's room. Respiratory infections are treated with antibiotics; sometimes a spray form is used for speedy inhalation.

FOR HELP AND ADVICE CONTACT:
Cystic Fibrosis Research Trust
5 Blyth Road
Bromley
Kent
01-464 7211

105

Dandruff

Dead cells are shed constantly from the surface of the skin. However, on the scalp they tend to become trapped and build up because of the hair. This build-up of cells is known as dandruff. It is not a disease, nor is it infectious or contagious; it is simply a variation of the normal. The amount of dandruff seen on the scalp varies from person to person according to how rapidly the skin cells are being shed and how greasy the scalp is. If the scalp is irritated, for example, by vigorous rubbing or by a medicated shampoo, more dead cells will be shed. If dandruff-like flakes appear on your child's eyelashes, this may be part of seborrhoeic **eczema** known as **blepharitis.**

Is it serious?

Dandruff is never serious; it can, however, be embarrassing, particularly as your child gets older. Although dandruff cannot be prevented if your child's scalp is greasy, it can be controlled.

Possible symptoms

● Flakes of white skin that are present on the scalp and can be easily wiped away with a finger.
● White flakes that appear on your child's shoulders after hair brushing.

What should I do first?

1 If you notice white flakes on your child's scalp, try to wipe them off with your fingers. If they move easily, this is dandruff. If not, don't pick at them; it could be an infestation of **lice.**

2 Wash your child's hair every other day using a baby shampoo.

3 Don't rub the scalp hard thinking that this will get rid of the dandruff. It will make it worse by stimulating the scalp.

Should I consult the doctor?

Consult your doctor as soon as possible if home treatment fails to clear up the white flakes.

What might the doctor do?

☐ Your doctor will reassure you, and advise you how best to cope with the dandruff.

What can I do to help?

☐ Don't use anti-dandruff shampoos more than once every two weeks. Avoid those containing selenium; this can irritate a child's scalp. Wash your child's hair with baby shampoo at other times.

> **SEE ALSO:**
> **Blepharitis,** *page 66*
> **Eczema,** *page 123*
> **Lice,** *page 174*

Words in **bold** are A-Z entries

Deafness

Deafness, either partial or total, is usually the result of a congenital defect—that is, present at birth—or of an illness during a baby's first six weeks. There is normally some residual hearing, so with early diagnosis, hearing aids will help to develop speech, as will the stimulation of touch and vision. A child may also suffer a hearing loss as the result of an ear infection such as **glue ear** or **otitis media,** or a build-up of wax in the external ear canal. The problem for parents is how to recognize whether their child is deaf or not. It is not easy to spot deafness in a newborn baby: all babies make gurgling noises up to the age of six months, and loud noises don't seem to disturb very young babies. However, after about four to six months, a deaf baby may become quiet, and won't chatter the way a normal baby does, because he hasn't been stimulated by his own or other people's voices.

D

Is it serious?
If a baby cannot hear properly, learning to talk can be a much more difficult task. Much of a child's language should have been learned before he starts to talk. Therefore, the longer a child is unable to hear, the greater will be the delay in communicating. Even partial deafness will interfere with speech development.

What should I do first?

Test your child's hearing by making a fairly loud noise when your child's head is turned away from you to see if he turns around. Make sure he doesn't see you. If he responds, make the sounds gradually fainter and note the level at which he ceases to hear.

Should I consult the doctor?

Consult your doctor as soon as possible if you suspect a hearing problem. Consult your doctor immediately if your child has had an ear infection and you detect some hearing loss.

What might the doctor do?

☐ Your doctor will perform routine hearing tests on your child and examine his ears. If a hearing difficulty is diagnosed, your doctor will refer your child to an ear, nose and throat specialist for audiometric tests to determine the extent of the deafness. In most cases, a hearing aid will be fitted. A baby can wear a hearing aid from six months. Your child will probably have aids fitted to both ears even if the hearing difficulty is only in one ear. You will be given advice on how to talk to your child.
☐ If the deafness is the result of repeated attacks of otitis media, surgery may be necessary to insert tubes to drain the fluid causing the deafness.

What can I do to help?

☐ Don't be concerned if your child remains silent for several months after hearing aids are fitted. It may take time for him to start to use what he's hearing by way of speaking the words -themselves.
☐ Communicate with your child as clearly as you can. Make sure everyone else talks to him clearly, too, but never shout.
☐ If your child is at school, ask if he can sit near the front of the class so that his school work won't suffer as a result of the disability.

SEE ALSO:
Glue ear, *page 144*
Otitis media, *page 196*
Wax in the ear, *page 258*

Dehydration

D

The body needs adequate supplies of water to carry the essential minerals through the system to maintain body chemistry and to get rid of waste from the body. If your child loses water by **vomiting**, **diarrhoea** or **fever**, and doesn't take in enough to replace the lost fluid, dehydration will result. Diarrhoea in babies can cause dehydration to develop rapidly as the intestines are not given enough time to absorb water. So, while a loose bowel motion is nothing to worry about, diarrhoea lasting six hours, especially if it is accompanied by vomiting, will definitely cause dehydration in a baby or child. Dehydration will be compounded if your baby or child has a fever and is losing fluid through sweating. The body chemistry will be upset, essential nutrients will be lost and the volume of blood circulating through the body will be dangerously lowered.

Is it serious?
Dehydration is extremely serious and should be treated as an emergency. If dehydration is advanced, this can lead to brain damage and even death.

Possible symptoms
- Dry mouth and lips.
- Lethargy.

Affected area

Sunken
fontanelle

- Sunken fontanelle in a child under 18 months.
- Concentrated urine (dark yellow colour) or dry nappies.

What should I do first?

Sponge child to reduce temperature

1 If your baby or child has diarrhoea or is vomiting, check his temperature to see if he has a fever. If he has, try to reduce it with tepid sponging.

2 If your bottlefed baby is not yet weaned, stop all milk feeds and give him only cooled, boiled water off a spoon or from a bottle or cup for six hours. Continue breastfeeding your baby. If the diarrhoea or vomiting hasn't stopped after six hours, consult your doctor immediately.

Continued on next page ▶

Words in **bold** are A-Z entries

Dehydration

◀ *Continued from previous page*

Give frequent drinks

3 Encourage your child to take small amounts of fluids frequently— every ten minutes or so. Don't give your child milk or undiluted fruit juices.

Glucose *20ml* **Salt** *2.5ml* **Water** *500ml*
(4 teaspoons) *(½ teaspoon)* *(1 pint)*

4 Add 20ml (4 teaspoons) of glucose and 2.5ml (½ teaspoon) of salt to every 500ml (1 pint) of water or what- ever drink your child prefers. As a rough guide, your child should drink at least 200ml (7fl oz) of liquid per kilogram (2.2lb) of his body weight in the first 24 hours of vomiting or diarrhoea. The glucose supplies energy, and the salt, though only in small quantities, is vital, as salt loss can add to the problems of dehydration.

5 Never give your child patent medicines for vomiting or diarrhoea unless prescribed by your doctor.

Should I consult the doctor?

Consult your doctor immediately if your baby or child has had diarrhoea for more than six hours, or is vomiting and cannot keep fluids down.

D

What might the doctor do?

☐ Your doctor will prescribe a powder to be added to your child's drinks. This will replace the essential minerals that have been lost. In severe cases, your child may be admitted to hospital and given essential fluids by intravenous drip.

☐ Your doctor may advise you to change your baby's formula milk feed to one that contains no sugars. Your baby may be allergic to the sugar in the milk (lactose).

What can I do to help?

☐ Check the colour of your child's urine. When it becomes clear and more regular, this is a good sign that his body fluid levels are getting back to normal.

☐ When the illness has passed, rein- troduce milk feeds gradually. Dilute your baby's normal formula milk feed with three times the usual amount of boiled water. Gradually reduce the water in the feed to the normal pro- portion over the next two or three days.

☐ If you are weaning your child on to solid foods, remember to keep his fluid intake up. Breast and formula milk have a high percentage of water and when they are replaced by solid foods, your child's fluid levels may be reduced without you realizing it.

SEE ALSO:
Diarrhoea, *page 112*
Dysentery, *page 118*
Fever, *page 134*
Food poisoning, *page 136*
Gastroenteritis, *page 139*
Vomiting, *page 256*

Diabetes mellitus

There are two forms of diabetes: one affects children and young adults, and one comes on in middle age. Both are due to a lack, or relative lack, of insulin in the body. Insulin is the hormone responsible for the normal metabolism of glucose in the body (we take in glucose in our diet mainly in the form of carbohydrates). Insulin is produced by the pancreas and it then promotes the absorption of glucose from the blood into the cells of the body and into the liver for storage. If the body is short of insulin, glucose collects in the blood and the body cells are deprived of their energy source. To make up for this deficiency, the body starts to break down fats and proteins to replace the lost energy. This means of energy production leads to weight loss and results in the production of poisonous waste substances, such as acetone and ketones.

Diabetes can start quite suddenly, for no known reason, though the disease may be inherited. Because the excess glucose spills over into the urine, the first symptom in a child is the frequent passing of large amounts of urine every hour; and because of the loss of body fluid, your child will be very thirsty. He may also start to wet the bed.

Possible symptoms

● Large amounts of urine passed every hour, possibly leading to bed-wetting.
● Increased thirst.
● Weight loss.

● Irritability and listlessness.
● Smell of pear drops on the breath, signifying presence of acetone.
● Reduced resistance to infection.

What can be done?

The diagnosis is confirmed by blood tests that show an inappropriately high blood level of glucose. Your child will be prescribed a regime of insulin injections—the digestive juices destroy insulin taken by mouth—and you and your child will be taught how to administer them. Many children over the age of five confidently give themselves injections, under parental supervision. Insulin injections must be given daily and often twice a day to keep blood glucose levels to normal limits.

Your child will also need a special diet to keep the glucose steady in the blood throughout the day. No meals should be missed.

The hospital will provide you with special equipment to use at home to test the urine for sugar every day. The result will help you to adjust the dose of insulin to keep glucose levels normal in your child. You may also be shown how to measure the blood glucose level by using a drop of blood from a finger. It is advisable for your child to wear a bracelet or medallion engraved with details of his condition in case problems occur when you are not with him. As diabetic children are extremely prone to infectious illnesses, consult your doctor as soon as your child gets any infection; infection can change your child's insulin requirements.

FOR HELP AND ADVICE CONTACT:
British Diabetic Association
10 Queen Anne Street
London W1M 0BD
01-323 1531

Diarrhoea

See also page 112

Consult your doctor if your child has loose, watery bowel motions for more than six hours, especially if he's under one year old. Consult your doctor immediately if the diarrhoea is accompanied by vomiting or fever.

Accompanying symptoms	Common causes
Your child has no symptoms except looser stools than normal, and seems perfectly well and contented.	He has possibly eaten too much of a food high in dietary fibre (such as prunes). Unless the stools are very watery or frequent, this is not true diarrhoea and you have no need to worry.
Your child has a sudden attack of diarrhoea and vomiting, with a slight fever.	He possibly has "gastric" 'flu, *page 139* or a bowel infection such as **Food poisoning**, *page 136.*
Your child has no symptoms other than the diarrhoea, but he is anxious about something, for example, school.	Stress can cause bouts of diarrhoea in older children. If this happens often, consult your doctor.
Your child has other symptoms, such as a cough, for example, for which your doctor has given him medicine.	Many medicines cause diarrhoea. Tell your doctor, but don't stop giving the medicine.
Your child has abdominal pain around his navel and to the lower right side of his groin.	**CONSULT YOUR DOCTOR IMMEDIATELY** Your child may have **Appendicitis**, *page 53.*
Your baby has severe abdominal cramps, is vomiting and his bowel motions are filled with blood and mucus, resembling redcurrant jelly.	**CONSULT YOUR DOCTOR IMMEDIATELY** Your baby may have a bowel blockage known as **Intussusception**, *page 169.*
Your child soils his underpants involuntarily, even though he is toilet-trained.	This is not true diarrhoea, but possibly a condition called **Encopresis**, *page 126.*
Your child fails to thrive and his stools are pale, bulky and foul-smelling and float when you try to flush them down the toilet.	He could have **Coeliac disease**, *page 85.*

Diarrhoea

Diarrhoea is the frequent passage of loose, watery stools. It is a sign of an irritation of the intestines in which the intestines contract more than normal, hurrying food along. Consequently there is not sufficient time for water from foodstuffs to be absorbed into the body and this can result in profound water loss or **dehydration**, especially in babies.

Babies on a milk diet pass liquid motions many times a day. This is perfectly normal. Once a baby begins to take solid foods, bowel motions become firmer and more regular. Loose, frequent stools can result when a baby or child eats too much of a certain food that is rich in dietary fibre, such as fruit, or they may be a symptom of an infection. Infection in the intestines is commonly caused by viruses or bacteria. Food may have been contaminated with bacteria (**food poisoning**) or an infection from contaminated stools may have been spread to the mouth by unwashed hands. The infection need not be in the intestines; diarrhoea can also be the symptom of a non-intestinal infection, such as **otitis media** or **influenza**, when the diarrhoea may be accompanied by a **fever.**

Ironically, stools similar to those of diarrhoea may be caused by **constipation**. If an older child soils himself, this may be because constipation has resulted in a blockage but the liquid stools manage to escape past it. This involuntary soiling is known as **encopresis**.

Is it serious?

Diarrhoea in a baby is always serious because of the dangers of dehydration. Diarrhoea accompanied by **vomiting** in a young child is also serious for the same reason, especially if it is accompanied by fever and sweating. Diarrhoea in which the stools are greasy and foul-smelling can be a symptom of a more serious long-term condition such as **coeliac disease** or **cystic fibrosis**, in which there is a failure by the body to absorb the nutrients in food.

What should I do first?

1 If your baby is under one year old and has had diarrhoea for six hours, consult your doctor immediately.

2 Don't give an older child any food or milk but give frequent drinks of diluted fruit juice or water with a pinch of salt and 5ml (one teaspoonful) of glucose added.

3 Check your child's temperature to see if he has a fever. Reduce any fever with tepid sponging (*see page 31*).

4 Check the chart on page 111 to find a possible cause of your child's diarrhoea.

Pay close attention to hygeine

5 Pay close attention to hygiene. The infection could spread throughout the family if your child doesn't wash his hands after going to the toilet or if you don't wash yours after changing his nappies, if he wears them.

Continued on next page ▶

Words in **bold** are A-Z entries

Diarrhoea

◀ *Continued from previous page*

Should I consult the doctor?

Consult your doctor immediately or take your baby to the nearest casualty department if he has diarrhoea for more than six hours. Consult your doctor immediately if your child has diarrhoea with fever and vomiting, or if he still has diarrhoea after 12 hours, or if the stools are greasy or contain mucus or blood.

What might the doctor do?

☐ After diagnosing the cause of the diarrhoea, your doctor will treat the illness accordingly.
☐ Your doctor may prescribe a powder to be added to all your child's drinks. This contains glucose and essential salts that will have been lost. Your doctor will recommend bed rest and a liquid diet until any fever has passed. As a rough guide, your child should drink at least 200ml (7 fl oz) of liquid per kilogram (2.2 lb) of his body weight in 24 hours while he has diarrhoea. For a bottlefed baby, your doctor will probably suggest that you replace milk feeds with glucose and salt solution and then slowly reintroduce the milk.

If your baby is breastfed, you will be advised to continue breastfeeding.
☐ If your baby is seriously ill, your doctor may admit him to hospital so that he can be given fluids intravenously.

What can I do to help?

Sterilize all feeding equipment

☐ Be meticulous about hygiene. Wash your hands before preparing food and after changing your baby's nappies. If your baby is under six months, sterilize all feeding equipment.
☐ Advise anyone with diarrhoea to stay away from your baby.
☐ When the diarrhoea has cleared up, introduce bland foods such as yogurt, bananas, rice and soups.

Diphtheria

Diphtheria is a serious bacterial infection that is very contagious. It produces symptoms like those of **tonsillitis**—a **sore throat**—accompanied by a **cough**, which sounds like **croup**. If diphtheria is not treated promptly, the infection may cause **pneumonia** to develop and heart failure due to paralysis of the cardiac muscle. Muscles of the limbs may weaken and become paralysed, too. A fine web of grey membrane forms over the tonsils and may make breathing difficult if the windpipe is affected. However, a child can be rendered immune from the infection in the first year of life with a series of injections, and this immunization programme has virtually eradicated the disease.

Is it serious?
Diphtheria is always serious as it is both life-threatening and contagious.

Possible symptoms

● Mild fever.
● Sore throat.
● Cough and hoarseness of voice.
● Headache.

Affected area

Grey patches

● Enlarged tonsils, covered by greyish patches.

What should I do first?

1 Diphtheria rarely occurs spontaneously; there are nearly always several cases in the community, so you should be on the alert if you hear of any outbreaks and your child has not been immunized.

2 Check to see if your child's tonsils are swollen and coated with greyish patches.

Should I consult the doctor?

Consult your doctor immediately or take your child to the nearest casualty department if you suspect diphtheria.

What might the doctor do?

☐ Your doctor will admit your child to hospital immediately. Your child will be given powerful antibiotic drugs and if there are breathing difficulties, a

tracheotomy will be performed to keep the airways open. This is a surgical procedure to insert a tube into the windpipe, by-passing the blockage in the throat.

What can I do to help?

☐ You will need to help medical staff to trace all known contacts of your child so that they can be checked for immunity.
☐ Make sure your child has a full course of immunization injections as the disease itself does not give immunity.

SEE ALSO:
Cough, *page 97*
Croup, *page 100*
Pneumonia, *page 200*
Sore throat, *page 220*
Tonsillitis, *page 241*

Words in **bold** are A-Z entries

Dizziness

Dizziness describes a feeling of unsteadiness and spinning about. When a child is out of breath, he may feel a bit dizzy because there is a relative lack of oxygen to his brain. Your child may also feel dizzy if he is suffering from **anaemia**. A bang on the head that results in loss of consciousness, or a **convulsion** may be preceded by dizziness. Under normal circumstances, dizziness should pass off within a few minutes.

Is it serious?
Momentary dizziness is not serious, but if dizzy spells fail to pass off within 12 hours, they may be caused by anaemia.

What should I do first?

Put your child's head between his knees

1 Sit your child down and put his head between his knees to increase the flow of blood and therefore oxygen to his brain. Tell him to take a few deep breaths in and out.

2 Keep him quiet and calm if that is what he wants.

3 Note how long he says the dizzy feeling lasts.

Should I consult the doctor?

Consult your doctor immediately if your child experiences dizzy spells over a 12-hour period but has no other symptoms. Consult your doctor as soon as possible if your child is always complaining of dizziness after strenuous activity; this may be a sign of anaemia.

What might the doctor do?

☐ After examining your child, your doctor will determine the cause of the dizziness. If the dizziness is a symptom of a more serious disorder, such as anaemia, your doctor will treat this accordingly.

SEE ALSO:
Anaemia, *page 52*
Convulsion, *page 95*
Head injury, *page 153*

Down's syndrome

D

Down's syndrome is the most common chromosomal abnormality. Children with Down's syndrome have 47 chromosomes instead of the normal 46 in each cell. The extra chromosome, chromosome 21, usually comes from the mother's egg. The incidence of Down's syndrome babies rises sharply with maternal age, but a form of screening in pregnancy known as amniocentesis can identify the condition in the fetus and a termination can be performed if the parents wish. An amniocentesis test, in which a sample of amniotic fluid is extracted and examined for abnormalities, is usually offered to all pregnant women of 37 or over.

Children with Down's syndrome share obvious physical characteristics. The bridge of the nose is wide and the eyes generally have an upward slant (hence the former term for this condition, mongolism). The hands are short and broad, there is a deep crease running across the middle of the palm, and there may be a large gap between the first and second toes. In addition, Down's children may suffer some degree of mental handicap, and approximately 50 per cent have a heart defect; a smaller number are born with a blockage in the intestine.

Possible symptoms

● Small upward-slanting eyes, nose with a wide bridge, short, broad hands with a deep crease across the palm, gap between first and second toes.

● Some degree of mental handicap.
● Even-tempered and affectionate nature.

What can be done?

Down's children are invariably outgoing, happy and affectionate, with a love of music and rhythmic games. The degree of mental handicap varies widely, and some children are within the normal intelligence range. Modern theories reject the idea that Down's children should all be educated in special institutions. The education of a Down's child must be determined by the mental handicap of the particular child. Excellent work in Israel has shown that with a sympathetic and stimulating environment, these children can develop alongside normal children and be accepted by them and by the community as a whole.

Many Down's children need help with dressing and feeding, while others can hold down jobs and make a contribution to society if they are given the chance and encouragement. It is important that parents of a Down's child help him to rise above the social stigma that used to be attached to Down's syndrome. As with all disabled children the emphasis should be on what a Down's child can do rather than what he cannot.

FOR HELP AND ADVICE CONTACT:
Down's Children's Association
4 Oxford Street
London W1N 9FL
01-580 0511

Words in **bold** are A-Z entries

Drowsiness

Drowsiness in a normally alert child can be a symptom of a **fever**, hypothermia (when the body temperature falls below normal), or **dehydration**. It can also occur before or after a **convulsion**, or as a result of medication, such as antihistamines.

Is it serious?
If a child is drowsy but contented, is feeding well and has a normal temperature, there is no cause for alarm, your child is probably just feeling a little sleepy. If, however, a child becomes drowsy while recovering from an infectious disease such as **measles** or **chickenpox**, and he complains of headache and neck pain, this could be **encephalitis**, **meningitis**, or **Reye's syndrome**, all of which are serious conditions and should be treated immediately.

What should I do first?

1 Check your child's temperature. If it is over 38°C (100.4°F) he has a fever; if it is under 35°C (95°F) he will be suffering from hypothermia.

2 If drowsiness is accompanied by vomiting and diarrhoea, keep up your child's fluid intake to prevent the risk of dehydration.

3 Check to see if your child has received a blow to his head.

4 Check if your child has a headache, or neckache.

5 Smell your child's breath and check the liquor cabinet—he may have drunk alcohol. Check the medicine cabinet for sleep-inducing drugs.

6 If your child has had a convulsion, leave him to rest after the fit has passed.

Should I consult the doctor?

Consult your doctor immediately if your child's temperature is over 38°C (100.4°F) or below 35°C (95°F) and he is difficult to rouse. Consult your doctor immediately if he has a headache or neckache, or if he has just had measles, chickenpox or mumps.

What might the doctor do?

☐ After examining your child, your doctor will determine the cause of the drowsiness, and will treat your child accordingly.

Dysentery

Dysentery is the inflammation of the lining of the large bowel and causes the symptoms of **diarrhoea** and **fever**. The bacterium (*Shigella bacillus*) is passed out with the faeces, and if the hands are not washed after going to the toilet, they become contaminated. The bacterium will then be passed on by contact. Dysentery is rare in countries where sanitary conditions are good.

Is it serious?

Dysentery is especially serious in children, because of the risk of **dehydration**.

Possible symptoms

- Griping abdominal pain.
- Loose, frequent motions, every half-hour or so, which may contain mucus, blood or pus.
- Fever.
- Nausea.
- Lethargy and weakness.
- Vomiting.

What should I do first?

1   If you are living or travelling in an area of poor sanitation and your child has frequent loose stools, check the stools for any blood, mucus or pus. If you notice any, consult a doctor immediately.

2   Check your child's temperature to see if he has a fever.

3   Give your child frequent drinks to keep his fluid levels up.

Should I consult the doctor?

Consult a doctor immediately if you notice mucus, blood or pus in your child's loose bowel motions. Consult a doctor as soon as possible if your child's bowel motions are still loose after 12 hours, or if his urine is infrequent and concentrated (dark yellow colour).

What might the doctor do?

☐ The doctor will treat your child for dehydration and send a sample of your child's faeces to a laboratory for investigation.

☐ If your child has a severe case of dysentery, he might be admitted to hospital and put on an intravenous drip to counteract the dehydration.

In many places, public health authorities must be notified of any cases of dysentery, and not only will your child's stools be tested but those of the whole family as well. The child will not be allowed to return to school until the stools are free of the bacterium.

What can I do to help?

Train your child to wash his hands after going to the toilet

☐ Insist on meticulous hygiene when your child goes to the toilet.

SEE ALSO:
Dehydration, *page 108*
Diarrhoea, *page 112*
Fever, *page 134*

Words in **bold** are A-Z entries

Dyslexia

Dyslexia is a specific learning disorder concerning reading and writing. Dyslexic children have problems interpreting visual symbols. Although their hearing and vision are normal and they have the manual dexterity to form letters, they may have difficulty in perceiving letters or words in their proper order, or they may confuse certain letters, such as b and d, and p and q. Dyslexic children may misread words which have a similar overall configuration, they may disregard punctuation and read monotonously, and quite often they produce incorrect spellings that nevertheless reflect the sound of words (for example, lite for light) or that transpose letters (lihgt for light).

Dyslexic children are of average or above average intelligence, though many of them appear clumsy. If the problem is not diagnosed and handled properly, the frustration with learning can lead to behavioural problems and unnecessary emotional strain.

D

Possible symptoms

● Written words that have the letters misplaced.
● Poor reading ability.

● Difficulty in visualizing words, even those just seen.

What can be done?

Dyslexia need not be educationally disabling. Provided the problem is detected early on, and the child is given the correct tuition from educational psychologists and teachers (this can be done within a normal school), he should be able to overcome reading problems and reach the standards required for examinations. Dyslexic children are helped if emphasis is given to their non-verbal skills and activities.

The artistic and creative side of their development should be stressed so that they never become insecure and develop behavioural problems to mask feelings of inadequacy.

Parents and teachers must persist if they believe a child has been wrongly assessed as being of low intelligence or as having some problem with sight or hearing. Dyslexic children need to be encouraged and have their confidence boosted.

> **FOR HELP AND ADVICE CONTACT:**
> **British Dyslexia Association**
> **Church Lane**
> **Peppard**
> **Henley-on-Thames RG9 5JN**
> *049 17699*

Ear, foreign body in

The most common foreign bodies to become stuck in a child's ear are small objects, like beads, pushed in by the child or by a playmate. Very rarely, a small insect may fly into the ear and be trapped there.

E

What should I do?

1 If the object is small and soft, try to remove it with a pair of tweezers. If you cannot grasp it without poking around in the ear, leave it and consult your doctor immediately.

Flush out the ear with water

2 If the foreign body is an insect, lay your child on his side with the affected ear uppermost and pour warm water into the ear. The insect should float out.

Is it serious?

Any foreign body in the ear that cannot easily be removed should be regarded as serious because it may cause an infection of the external ear canal, **otitis externa,** or damage the eardrum.

Should I consult the doctor?

Consult your doctor immediately if the object cannot be removed, or if your child complains of pain and tenderness in his ear.

What might the doctor do?

☐ After examining your child's external ear canal, your doctor will remove the object and will treat any damage to the skin, or any infection that may have been caused by the foreign body.

What can I do to help?

☐ Don't let a child under four play with small objects which he could put in his nose, or mouth, thus risking choking.

SEE ALSO:
Otitis externa, *page 194*

Words in **bold** are A-Z entries

Earache

There are a number of causes of earache. The most common cause is an infection of the middle ear called **otitis media.** This is especially true in children under six because the tube that runs from the throat to the ear—the Eustachian tube—is relatively short, and so infections of the nose and throat can be easily spread to the middle ear cavity. A baby may not be able to isolate the site of the pain, and will scratch and rub the side of his face if the pain is severe. A child may complain of earache if he is suffering from **toothache, tonsillitis** or **mumps;** when the glands in his neck are swollen; or if he has been out in a cold wind without protective headgear. Earache with intense pain will result from an infection of the outer ear (**otitis externa**) if, for example, a foreign body has been poked into the ear or if a **boil** has developed.

Is it serious?

Earache plus loss of hearing is serious. If the condition is not diagnosed and treated, it could cause permanent damage to the middle ear, resulting in a loss of hearing that will affect your child's speech development and learning ability.

Possible symptoms

● Pain in the area around the ear.
● A temperature of over 38°C (100.4°F).
● Discharge of pus from the ear.
● Deafness.
● Inflammation of the tonsils.
● Pain when the ear is touched.
● Swollen glands.
● Rubbing and pulling of the ear in a young child.

Cross-section of the ear

Middle ear cavity
Eustachian tube
Cochlea
Eardrum

E

What should I do?

1 Take your child's temperature to see if he has a fever.

2 Check whether there is any discharge from the ear.

3 Check whether your child's hearing is diminished. To do this, call his name quietly when his head is averted. See if he turns around.

4 Examine the back of your child's throat to see if the tonsils are abnormally enlarged or red (*see page 241*). This could indicate tonsillitis.

5 Check to see if there is any inflammation in the outer ear cavity; such inflammation could be caused by a boil. Do not put anything into the ear, not even a cotton-wool swab.

6 Never use eardrops, or put anything into your child's ear, unless your doctor advises it.

Should I consult the doctor?

Consult your doctor as soon as possible if your child complains of earache; most earache is caused by infection. Consult your doctor immediately if your child is in pain with a high fever, and especially if you notice a discharge from the ear. Consult your doctor immediately if your child is too young to tell you he's in pain but is crying, generally off colour and possibly pulling or rubbing one of his ears.

Continued on next page ▶

Earache

◀ *Continued from previous page*

What might the doctor do?

☐ Your doctor will examine your child to determine the cause of the earache. If it is caused by a bacterial infection, your doctor will probably prescribe antibiotics.

What should I do to help?

Use a hot-water bottle to ease the pain

☐ Place a hot-water bottle, covered by a towel, next to your child's ear to relieve pain, as long as the source of the earache is not a boil.
☐ Prevent water from entering the ear during bathing until the infection has cleared up.

SEE ALSO:
Boil, *page 68*
Ear, foreign body in, *page 120*
Mumps, *page 182*
Otitis externa, *page 194*
Otitis media, *page 196*
Tonsillitis, *page 241*
Toothache, *page 243*

Words in **bold** are A-Z entries

Eczema

Eczema is an allergic skin condition which produces an extremely itchy, dry, scaly, red rash on the face, neck and hands, and in the creases of the limbs.

The most common form of eczema in children is atopic eczema, which usually develops when a baby is about two to three months old, or at around four to five months, when solid foods are introduced. Certain foods, most commonly dairy products, eggs and wheat, and skin irritants such as pet fur, wool or washing powders, are among the main causes. An attack of eczema can also be triggered by stress or an emotional upset. It is common for eczema to be followed by other allergic complaints such as **hayfever** and penicillin sensitivity. It is also quite common for a child with eczema to suffer from **asthma**. Although most children grow out of eczema by the age of three, the associated allergic conditions may remain.

Another form of eczema, known as seborrhoeic eczema, occurs where the sebaceous glands are numerous. This is most commonly found on the scalps of young babies (**cradle cap**), on the eyelashes and eyelids (**blepharitis**), in the external ear canal (**otitis externa**) and in the greasy areas around the nostrils, ears and groin. This seborrhoeic eczema is not as itchy as atopic eczema and it responds well to treatment.

Is it serious?
Eczema is not serious, although it can be very irritating.

Possible symptoms

● Dry, red scaly skin which is extremely itchy. The rash usually starts off as minute pearly blisters beneath the skin's surface.
● Sleeplessness if the itchiness is very bad.

Affected areas

What should I do first?

1 If your child is scratching, inspect his neck and scalp, his face, his hands and the creases of his elbows, knees and groin for any rash.

2 Keep his fingernails short to minimize the possibility of breaking the skin. If the skin becomes broken, put mittens on him to prevent infection.

3 If you've just started weaning your breastfed child, return to breast-feeds only until you have seen your doctor. If you have been using formula milk, return to that.

4 Apply an oily calamine lotion to ease irritation and soothe the skin. Don't apply any astringent lotions.

Continued on next page ▶

Eczema

◀ *Continued from previous page*

Should I consult the doctor?

Consult your doctor as soon as possible if you suspect eczema.

What might the doctor do?

☐ Your doctor will question you on your family's medical history, particularly whether anyone has ever suffered from eczema-related conditions such as asthma or hayfever.

☐ Your doctor will ask you about any changes in your child's diet, whether you have recently changed washing powders, whether you have just brought a pet into the house, and whether your child wears natural or synthetic fibres next to his skin.

☐ Your doctor will probably advise you to avoid foods such as dairy products, eggs and wheat, which may have caused the reaction.

☐ If you have just started weaning your baby from the breast or bottle, your doctor may recommend that you avoid dairy products and continue breastfeeding or formula milk. If you don't want to do this, he may recommend that you wean your baby on to soya milk instead.

☐ Your doctor may prescribe an anti-inflammatory skin cream to reduce redness, scaliness and itchiness. In severe cases, very weak steroid creams may be prescribed. These should be used only sparingly on a child's skin.

☐ Your doctor may prescribe anti-histamine medication to help your child to sleep if the itching is causing sleepless nights.

☐ If your child has scratched the eczema and the skin has become infected, your doctor may prescribe antibiotics.

☐ Your doctor will advise you to add bath oil to your child's bath water and to stop using soap. Soap can be an irritant to the already sensitive skin; the oil will help to keep your child's skin supple and less dry.

What can I do to help?

☐ Use an emollient cream whenever your child washes. This will keep his skin soft, prevent it from drying out and damp down the itchiness.

☐ Underplay the condition in front of your child. Your anxiety can make the condition worse.

☐ Keep your child's fingernails short and put gloves or mittens on his hands at night so that scratching doesn't cause the skin to break and give rise to infection.

☐ Make sure all your child's clothes, and anything that comes next to his skin, are rinsed thoroughly to remove all traces of powders and conditioners.

☐ You may need to consider giving your family pet away if the reaction is found to be caused by pet fur.

☐ Dress your child with cotton next to his skin at all times.

☐ Don't eliminate any foods from your child's diet without your doctor's supervision.

☐ Remove as many irritants from your child's environment as possible. For example, feather and down pillows can be a source of irritation.

SEE ALSO:
Asthma, *page 58*
Blepharitis, *page 66*
Cradle cap, *page 99*
Hayfever, *page 151*
Itching, *page 170*
Nappy rash, *page 185*
Otitis externa, *page 194*
Sleeplessness, *page 217*

Words in **bold** are A-Z entries

Encephalitis

Encephalitis is an inflammation of the brain. The most common causes in children are viral infections like **chickenpox** or **mumps**. The major symptoms of encephalitis are fever, headache, pain when the neck is stretched and intolerance of bright light. Very rarely, encephalitis occurs as a severe reaction to the **whooping cough** vaccine. If your child is irritable, with a fever, and especially if he has a **convulsion**, this could be the first sign of sensitivity.

Is it serious?
Encephalitis is always serious and in babies it can be fatal.

Possible symptoms

- Fever.
- Severe headache.
- Pain when the neck is stretched.
- Intolerance of bright light.
- Loss of appetite and perhaps vomiting.
- Drowsiness.
- Listlessness.
- Confusion, and, in later stages, convulsion and coma.

What should I do first?

Bend your child's neck forward

If your child is recovering from an infectious disease and seems unwell, with a fever, ask him to bend his neck forward so that his chin touches his chest. See if this causes him pain.

Should I consult the doctor?

Consult your doctor immediately if you suspect encephalitis.

What might the doctor do?

☐ Your child will be admitted to hospital where diagnostic tests will be carried out to determine the severity of the disease. These will include a lumbar puncture in which spinal fluid is drawn off under anaesthetic for examination.
☐ The hospital staff will treat the accompanying symptoms of encephalitis and your child should be better in a couple of weeks.

What can I do to help?

☐ Once your child has been discharged from hospital, keep him comfortable and well fed.
☐ If there has been any weakness or stiffness of your child's muscles, you may have to do exercises with him to help him regain control over them. You will be advised how to do this by a hospital physiotherapist.

SEE ALSO:
Chickenpox, *page 82*
Cold sore, *page 87*
Convulsion, *page 95*
Drowsiness, *page 117*
Headache, *page 155*
Mumps, *page 182*
Whooping cough, *page 259*

Encopresis

If a child frequently soils his underpants after he has been toilet trained, this is known as encopresis. In a child of four or five, uncontrollable bowel motions should be regarded as a symptom of a problem rather than of slow development. The most common cause of encopresis is chronic **constipation**, when hard, dry stools accumulate in the bowel and loose, watery motions trickle out past them. You may even mistake this for **diarrhoea**. The problem often starts as the result of some emotional disturbance in the child's life, such as a new baby in the house. Occasionally, children persist in soiling their pants from infancy onwards. This soiling may be a reaction against over-fussy toilet training.

Is it serious?
Encopresis is not a serious problem.

Possible symptoms

- Involuntary bowel motions after the child has been toilet trained.
- Chronic constipation.

What should I do first?

1 Try to determine whether your child is constipated or not. Ask him when he last went to the toilet.

2 Check to see if your child is affected by any obvious causes of stress, such as a new baby, moving house or starting school.

Should I consult the doctor?

Consult your doctor as soon as possible if you think your child has chronic constipation. If you can find no reason for the involuntary soiling, your doctor may be the best person to uncover the tension that is affecting your child.

What might the doctor do?

☐ If your child is constipated, your doctor will prescribe a mild laxative, specially formulated for babies and children, which is safe to give your child for short periods.
☐ Your doctor will advise you on mea-

sures to avoid constipation in future.
☐ If there is some emotional reason for the encopresis, your doctor will assess the situation after discussion with you and your child. If further investigation is needed, your doctor may refer you and your child to a psychotherapist.

What can I do to help?

☐ Make sure your child has a diet rich in dietary fibre and liquids.
☐ Don't punish your child or show disgust if he soils his pants; this will make the condition worse.
☐ Watch for signs of poor school performance. Your child may become a target of scorn because of the odour if he soils himself at school. Provide him with spare underpants.

SEE ALSO:
Constipation, *page 93*
Diarrhoea, *page 112*

Epilepsy

Epilepsy is a disorder that causes periodic seizures, and these occur when the normal electrical impulses in the brain are disturbed. There are two main forms of epileptic seizure. The *grand mal* form involves recurring attacks of **convulsions**. These involve a loss of consciousness and a stiff phase lasting a minute or less, followed by a series of rhythmic jerks of the limbs, clenching of the teeth (when your child might bite his tongue), involuntary urination and frothing at the mouth. The child then usually lapses into sleep.

The *petit mal* form of epilepsy has no convulsions. There is only a second or two of unconsciousness—like day-dreaming —when the child's eyes glaze over; the child appears not to see or hear anything. This form of epilepsy is often not recognized and not diagnosed as epilepsy. Although the scale of the problem is different from the grand mal convulsions, frequent petit mal seizures can interfere with a child's life, particularly with school performance and certain physical activities, such as bike-riding. There is not usually any mental disability associated with either form of epilepsy, which tends to run in families.

About three to five per cent of children under the age of six have an occasional convulsion but nearly all of these are harmless febrile convulsions, when the electrical disturbance in the brain is caused by a high temperature preceding or during an infectious illness.

Is it serious?
Epilepsy is not a life-threatening disorder. All children grow out of the petit mal form of epilepsy by late adolescence. However, children who suffer from the grand mal form of epilepsy may need special consideration throughout their lives, even though the condition is controlled by drugs. They will need supervision during activities such as swimming and cycling.

Possible symptoms

Grand mal
- Loss of consciousness.
- Clenching of teeth.
- Stiffness, followed by rhythmic jerking of the limbs.
- Involuntary urination.
- Frothing at the mouth.

Petit mal
- Day-dream-like state lasting one or two seconds, from which the child cannot be roused.

E

What should I do first?

During a *grand mal* seizure

1 Protect your child from injury by moving any furniture away from him so that his jerking limbs don't hit any solid objects.

2 Loosen the clothing around his neck and chest.

3 Stay with your child until the seizure has finished.

4 Don't try to hold your child's teeth apart if they are clenched, or put anything in his mouth. Any injury to his tongue will occur at the beginning of the attack, therefore there is nothing you can do until the attack is over.

Turn on to side

5 As soon as your child stops moving violently, turn him gently on to his side so that he cannot choke on his tongue or saliva.

6 Watch what happens during your child's seizure—your account will help your doctor make a diagnosis.

Continued on next page ▶

Epilepsy

◀ *Continued from previous page*
During a *petit mal* seizure:

1 Guide your child to safety if he is in the street or near a stairway, for example.

2 Stay with your child until the seizure has passed.

Should I consult the doctor?

Consult your doctor as soon as the convulsion has passed, whether you think it is a grand mal seizure or a febrile convulsion. Consult your doctor as soon as possible if you think your child has petit mal seizures.

What might the doctor do?

☐ If your child has a convulsion, your doctor will examine him and question you about the attack in order to determine what form of seizure your child suffered from.

☐ If your child has recurrent convulsions, he will be referred to hospital for laboratory examinations. These may include blood tests for glucose and calcium, an EEG (electroencephalogram), and possibly a brain scan to find out if an abnormal area of the brain is causing the seizures. During the scan the child is stimulated, for example, with strobe lights, so that any abnormal behaviour in the brain can be picked up with the scanning equipment. Some of these tests are also used to diagnose petit mal seizures.

☐ The hospital paediatrician will prescribe anti-convulsant drugs to be taken daily to reduce the frequency of grand mal seizures. There are no drugs to cure the condition.

☐ Your child's condition will be reviewed periodically by the paediatrician. If there are no seizures for a year or two, the doctor may decide to phase out the drugs.

What can I do to help?

☐ It can be a shock to realize that your child has epilepsy. Both you and your child will need to get your confidence back. You can do this through your doctor who can advise you how to cope with the seizures.

☐ Make a note of the frequency of your child's petit mal seizures so that you can tell your doctor.

☐ Watch your child carefully and report any mental or personality differences which may be the result of the drugs. It is important that your child's medication is given in the proper amounts so as not to cause any undesirable side-effects.

☐ Treat your child as normally as possible. Tell his friends and teachers about the condition so that they will not be frightened and shocked if your child has a convulsion in their presence.

☐ Have a bracelet or medallion engraved with information about your child's epilepsy in case of an attack when you are not there and make sure your child wears it all the time.

☐ If your child is prescribed anti-convulsant drugs, do not stop them without medical advice. To do so could cause a severe, prolonged convulsion after a few days.

☐ Teach your child to recognize the signs of an on-coming attack. Some sufferers from epilepsy experience strange sensations, such as unpleasant smells, distorted vision or an odd feeling in the stomach, just before a convulsion. This is known as an "aura" and if your child is old enough to identify these sensations as warning signs, he may be able to avoid having an accident.

SEE ALSO:
Convulsion, *page 95*

Words in **bold** are A-Z entries

Eye, foreign body in

If a foreign body such as a speck of dust or grit enters your child's eye, the eye will water and your child will be loathe to open it. If you can see something moving loosely over the white part of the eye, you can try to remove it. If, however, the foreign body is embedded in the eyeball or is on the coloured part of the eye (the iris), don't touch it.

Is it serious?

Small specks of dust or grit are not serious as they are washed out naturally by the tears, but if your child's eyeball is scratched, if an object has pierced it or there is a cut on the eyeball or eyelid, this is serious and should be treated as an emergency.

Possible symptoms

- Watery eye.
- Reluctance to open eye.
- Pain and irritation.
- A visible embedded object.

What should I do first?

Look closely to see whether the foreign body is moving or is embedded in the eye. Encourage your child to blink; this may dislodge the foreign body, as may tears if your child has been crying because of the pain and irritation.

If the foreign body is embedded in the eye

Keep eye closed

1 Do not attempt any first aid. Keep your child's eye closed by putting a pad or clean handkerchief over the eyelid and taping it in place. Go straight to the nearest casualty department.

If the foreign body is not embedded in the eye

Remove object with a clean handkerchief

1 Ask your child to look upwards. Pull down eyelid to see if the object is there. If it is, remove it with the corner of a clean handkerchief or a cotton-wool swab.

Continued on next page ▶

Eye, foreign body in

◄ *Continued from previous page*

Fold eyelid back over matchstick or cotton-wool swab

2 To expose the area beneath the top lid, lay a matchstick or a cotton-wool swab along the middle of the top lid. Take hold of the eyelashes and pull them back over the matchstick or swab. Remove the object with a handkerchief or cotton-wool swab. If your child won't co-operate, you will need someone to help you. You may have to restrain your child bodily if he resists.

3 If these methods don't work, try to flush the foreign body out by pouring a glass of water, to which you have added a pinch of salt, across the open eye.

Should I consult the doctor?

Go immediately to the nearest casualty department if the eyeball is scratched or if a foreign body has pierced the eye. Consult your doctor immediately if you have failed to remove a floating foreign body from your child's eye within one hour. Consult your doctor as soon as possible if your child still complains of pain an hour or two after you have removed the object.

What might the doctor do?

☐ The hospital doctor will remove an embedded foreign body from your child's eye after putting drops of a local anaesthetic into the eye.

☐ If the eyeball is scratched, the doctor will prescribe antibiotic drops to guard against infection and may bandage the eye to keep it closed for about 24 hours.

☐ If you went to your doctor because your child's eye was still sore, your doctor will examine the eye and remove any foreign object that he finds.

What can I do to help?

☐ After the removal of a foreign body, the pain should subside in an hour or so. If it does not, consult your doctor as soon as possible.

SEE ALSO:
Eye, injury to, *page 131*

Words in **bold** are A-Z entries

Eye, injury to

Injuries to the eye should be treated promptly because they could have long-term consequences for your child's sight.If your child receives a blow to the eye, the eye socket will probably protect the eye itself, but the surrounding area will swell and **bruise** as the tiny blood vessels beneath the skin break.

If a chemical substance is accidentally splashed into the eye, this should be treated as an emergency. Soap in the eye may cause your child to make a lot of fuss but it will do no damage. If a toy or other sharp implement penetrates the eyeball or makes a **cut** near the eye, or on the eyelid, this should be treated as an emergency.

Is it serious?
A black eye looks bad but it is rarely serious. However, if a chemical substance or a sharp object injures your child's eye, this is serious and should be treated as an emergency.

What should I do first?

Put a cold compress on the eye

1 If your child receives a blow to his eye, place a cold compress over the eye for half an hour to limit the extent of the bruising.

Flush the eye with water

2 If your child's eye is injured by a chemical substance, try to flush the chemical out with water immediately, before consulting your doctor or going to the nearest casualty department. If you can, carry your child to a sink or basin and hold his head under the cold tap with the injured eye lowermost so that no chemical can run into the unaffected eye or down on to his face. Hold the eye open and let the water run in from the inner corner. Do this for 15 minutes. Alternatively, lay your child on the ground with his head turned to one side so that the injured eye is lowermost and pour cold water from a jug, bowl or bucket into the eye. Apply a pad or clean handkerchief, held in place with tape, to the eyelid to keep it closed.

3 If there are chemical particles sticking to the eyeball, don't attempt to remove them. Apply a pad or clean handkerchief, held in place with tape, to the eyelid to keep it closed, and take your child to the nearest casualty department.

Continued on next page ▶

Eye, injury to

◀ *Continued from previous page*

Cover the injured eye

4 If the injury is caused by a sharp implement, cover the injured eye with a pad or clean handkerchief, tape in place and go at once to the nearest casualty department.

5 If there is blood coming from the wound, hold a pad firmly against the cut to stem the blood flow, and take your child to the nearest casualty department.

Should I consult the doctor?

Consult your doctor immediately or go to the nearest casualty department after flushing the chemicals from your child's eye. Go to the nearest casualty department immediately if your child suffers any other injury to his eye other than a black eye or minor cut.

What might the doctor do?

☐ How the doctor in the casualty department will treat the eye depends on the cause of the injury. If the problem was caused by a chemical substance, take the bottle containing the chemical with you; otherwise note what caused the damage and tell the doctor at the hospital.

☐ If your child's eyelid was cut, the doctor will stitch the cut to reduce scarring.

SEE ALSO:
Bruise, *page 75*
Cuts and grazes, *page 103*
Eye, foreign body in, *page 129*

Words in **bold** are A-Z entries

Fever

See also page 134

A fever is a temperature of 37.7°C (100°F) or over. Consult your doctor if your baby's temperature remains high despite tepid sponging (*see page 31*). Consult your doctor immediately if your child's temperature is as high as 40°C (104°F).

F

Accompanying symptoms	Common causes
Your child has a cough and a runny nose.	He possibly has a **Common cold**, *page 90.*
Your child has a cough, sore throat and aches and pains.	He possibly has **Influenza**, *page 166.*
Your child has a sore throat and difficulty in swallowing.	He may have **Tonsillitis**, *page 241.* If his voice is hoarse, he may have **Laryngitis**, *page 172.* If his neck glands are swollen, he may have **Glandular fever**, *page 142.*
Your child has a rash of itchy, red spots starting on the trunk.	He may have **Chickenpox**, *page 82.*
Your child passes urine frequently and if he is old enough complains of a burning sensation.	He may have a **Urinary tract infection**, *page 250.*
Your child had a runny nose and sore eyes and now has a brownish-red rash.	He possibly has **Measles**, *page 176.*
The sides of your child's face and the area under his chin are swollen.	He possibly has **Mumps**, *page 182.*
Your child has earache, or if he is too young to tell you, he cries and tugs at his ear.	He possibly has a middle ear infection, **Otitis media**, *page 196.*
Your child has diarrhoea.	He could have "gastric" 'flu, *page 139* or **Food poisoning**, *page 136.*
Your baby or child is breathing rapidly and with great difficulty.	**CONSULT YOUR DOCTOR IMMEDIATELY** Your child may have **Bronchitis**, *page 73,* **Bronchiolitis**, *page 72,* **Pneumonia**, *page 200* or **Croup**, *page 100.*
Your child cannot bend his neck without pain, and turns away from bright light.	**CONSULT YOUR DOCTOR IMMEDIATELY** Your child may have **Meningitis**, *page 177.*

Fever

The range of normal body temperature is 36°-37°C (96.8°-98.6°F). Anything over 37°C (100°F) is a fever, although the height a temperature reaches is not necessarily an accurate reflection of the seriousness of the sickness. A fever is not in itself an illness, but rather a symptom of one (*see page 133*). Apart from any illness, your child's temperature will reflect the time of day and activity level: after a very strenuous game of football, for example, the temperature could temporarily be over 38°C (100.4°F).

Is it serious?

A temperature of over 37.7°C (100°F) is always serious in a baby under six months old. If the temperature remains high, there is also a slight risk of a convulsion occurring.

What should I do first?

1 If you suspect that your child has a fever, take his temperature, then check it again in 20 minutes to see if it has varied. Note down each reading.

2 Put your child to bed and remove most of his clothing, even if the room is cool. A child with a fever need only be covered by a light sheet.

Sponge child to reduce temperature

3 Lower a temperature of over 40°C (104°F) by sponging your child all over with tepid water (*see page 31*). But take the temperature every five minutes and stop tepid sponging when the temperature drops to 38°C (100.4°F). Never use cold water for this as it causes the blood vessels to constrict, preventing heat loss and therefore driving the temperature up.

4 Give paracetamol elixir *only* if other methods of reducing the fever (see above) have failed. Never give aspirin to a child with the symptoms of **chickenpox** or **influenza** as this has been linked to the development of **Reye's syndrome**.

Give frequent drinks

5 Encourage your child to drink as much liquid as possible by offering small amounts of fluid at regular intervals.

Should I consult the doctor?

Consult your doctor immediately if your child is under six months old. Consult your doctor immediately if your child has a **convulsion**, if he has had a convulsion in the past, or if febrile convulsions run in the family. Consult your doctor as soon as possible if the fever lasts for more than 24 hours, or if you are worried about any of the accompanying symptoms.

Continued on next page ▶

Fever

◀ Continued from previous page

What might the doctor do?

☐ The course of treatment will depend on the underlying cause of the fever. If the cause is bacterial infection, antibiotics will probably be prescribed. If the cause is an ailment like chickenpox, or a **common cold**, then most likely no medication will be given, just advice on how to make your child comfortable.

What can I do to help?

☐ Change the sheets on your child's bed frequently and cover him with a sheet only.
☐ Place a cold compress or a wet facecloth on your child's forehead.
☐ Don't wake your child to take his temperature. Sleep is more important.

F

SEE ALSO:
Chickenpox, *page 82*
Common cold, *page 90*
Convulsion, *page 95*
Influenza, *page 166*
Measles, *page 176*
Reye's syndrome, *page 206*

Food poisoning

Food poisoning is a form of **gastroenteritis** caused by eating food that is contaminated with poisons, usually bacteria. Within 3 to 24 hours, depending on the poison, the symptoms of abdominal cramps, **fever**, **vomiting**, and **diarrhoea** occur with unpleasant ferocity. If the food was contaminated with bacteria, they release their own poisons, known as toxins, which have a direct effect on the lining of the bowel, causing inflammation There are many types of bacterium that cause food poisoning, but the most common are *salmonella, shigella, staphylococcii,* and *E. coli,* which is the bacterium most commonly responsible for food poisoning among babies, usually in bottlefed babies. Of the non-bacterial types of food poisoning, symptoms can arise from eating chemicals, insecticides, or certain plants.

Is it serious?
In a baby, this condition is serious because the symptoms can rapidly lead to **dehydration**.

Possible symptoms
- Abdominal cramps.
- Fever.
- Vomiting.
- Frequent, loose stools that may contain blood, pus, or mucus.
- Muscular weakness and chills.
- Loss of appetite.

What should I do first?

1 If your child is vomiting and has diarrhoea, check his temperature to see if he has a fever.

2 Check your child's stools for mucus or blood.

3 Put your child to bed and stop all foods, but keep up his fluid levels by offering frequent small drinks of water with a pinch of salt and 5ml (one teaspoonful) of glucose added to every drink.

4 Try to determine what your child could have eaten to cause the symptoms.

Should I consult the doctor?

Consult your doctor immediately or take your baby to the nearest casualty department if vomiting and diarrhoea continue for more than six hours and you cannot bring them under control with a fluids only diet. Consult your doctor immediately if your child's condition has not improved within 24 hours or if you suspect that your child has drunk an insecticide or eaten a poisonous plant. If your doctor is delayed in such cases, take your child to the nearest casualty department, taking the suspected poison with you.

Continued on next page ▶

Words in **bold** are A-Z entries

Food poisoning

◀ *Continued from previous page*

What might the doctor do?

☐ In the majority of cases there is no special treatment for food poisoning except to replace the fluid and salts that have been lost through diarrhoea and vomiting. Your doctor will probably prescribe a powder containing glucose and essential salts to be added to all your child's drinks and to replace all milk feeds in a bottlefed baby.

☐ If your baby or child is in danger of dehydration, your doctor will admit him to hospital to be given fluids intravenously. If the vomiting is very severe, your doctor may give your child an injection of an anti-emetic drug to stop the vomiting.

What can I do to help?

☐ Place a bucket next to your child's bed for him to be sick into, so that he doesn't have to run to the toilet.

Cool your child's forehead

☐ Keep him cool and refreshed with an icepack or a damp facecloth if he has a fever.

☐ Help your child to rinse his mouth out with water after he has been sick.

☐ Be meticulous about hygiene. Food poisoning is infectious so make sure your child washes his hands after every visit to the toilet. Wash your own hands after changing nappies.

☐ To prevent food poisoning, refrigerate all cooked food, and if you reheat it, do so thoroughly. Salmonella thrives in warmed food but is killed by high temperatures.

☐ If your child refuses to drink enough fluids, or doesn't like the taste of the special powder, give him cubes of melon to suck.

☐ Defrost foods well before cooking, particularly poultry and pork, and make sure they are thoroughly cooked.

☐ Reintroduce foods that are easily digested, such as soups, yogurt, jellies and non-fatty foods, as soon as your child asks for something to eat. The effects of the illness usually pass within a week.

☐ Follow your doctor's instructions for reintroducing milk feeds for a bottlefed baby.

☐ Check back over what your child has eaten in the previous 24 hours. Throw out any cooked meats, fish, dairy products or pastries that you suspect may have caused the illness.

SEE ALSO:
Dehydration, *page 108*
Diarrhoea, *page 112*
Fever, *page 134*
Gastroenteritis, *page 139*
Vomiting, *page 256*

Frostbite

Frostbite occurs after exposure to extreme cold when the blood flow to the exposed area stops and the affected area of skin becomes frozen. Typically the skin first becomes red, then shiny and then a dull, greyish colour. Occasionally blisters may form. The fingers, toes, nose and ears are most often affected.

Is it serious?
Frostbite is serious and should be treated as an emergency but there is a first-aid routine (see below) that you should carry out immediately. If treated quickly, frostbite has no lasting effect but severe cases can lead to gangrene and amputation of the affected part.

Possible symptoms
- Hard, red, cold skin, usually on the hands, toes, nose or ears, which becomes shiny then a dull, grey colour.
- Tiny blisters on the affected area.
- Numbness in the affected area.

What should I do first?

1 Get your child out of the cold immediately. If you can, get someone else to call for medical help. If you are on your own, don't stop to call a doctor until you have followed the first-aid procedure.

2 Do not apply direct heat or rub the affected part. If the fingers or toes are frostbitten, immerse them in warm water and keep adding warm water so that the temperature remains constantly warm. If you have no access to warm water, keep the affected part warm by putting your child's hands or feet under your armpits, or holding his face against your body.

3 Wrap your child in blankets and give him hot drinks. Feed the drinks to him yourself if his hands are affected. Don't let your child walk on a frostbitten foot.

4 When the affected part becomes pink, stop warming, wrap in gauze or cotton wool or any soft, warm fabric that you have to hand and go at once to the nearest casualty department.

5 While you are travelling to the hospital, keep the affected part level with your child's chest to encourage blood flow. For example, raise his feet or put his hands across his chest.

Should I consult the doctor?
Take your child to the nearest casualty department as soon as you have restored pinkness to the affected skin.

What might the doctor do?
☐ The doctor will check that circulation has returned to the frostbitten area. Drugs to improve blood circulation may be necessary if the blood flow has not returned to normal.

What can I do to help?
☐ Always wrap your child up warmly in cold weather.

Gastroenteritis

Gastroenteritis is inflammation of the stomach and intestines. The symptoms include **vomiting**, nausea, **diarrhoea**, abdominal cramps and loss of appetite. The most common cause of gastro-enteritis in children is the *rotavirus*, which can be inhaled and tends to spread easily through a community. It may also be caused by direct infection of the intestines with bacteria, usually from contaminated food, when it is known as **food poisoning**, or by a parasite, when the condition is sometimes known as **dysentery**. Gastroenteritis may also be a symptom of another infection, such as **influenza**, when the infecting bacteria may spread to the bowel through the bloodstream. When vomiting and diarrhoea accompany 'flu symptoms, this is often referred to as "gastric 'flu".

Gastroenteritis in babies is most common in bottlefed babies and is usually the result of poor sterilization of feeding equipment.

Is it serious?
Gastroenteritis is very serious in children, especially babies, because the symptoms of vomiting and diarrhoea can rapidly lead to **dehydration**.

Possible symptoms
- Vomiting.
- Nausea.
- Diarrhoea.
- Abdominal cramps.
- Loss of appetite.
- Raised temperature.

G

What should I do first?
1 Stop all foods and milk and give your child only water in small amounts every 15 minutes.

2 Put your child to bed with a bowl by the bed in case he vomits.

Maintain good hygiene

3 Make sure he washes his hands after going to the toilet to prevent the spread of the infection.

Continued on next page ▶

Gastroenteritis

◄ Continued from previous page

Should I consult the doctor?

Consult your doctor immediately if your child has diarrhoea and vomiting for more than six hours and you cannot bring them under control with a fluids only diet.

What might the doctor do?

□ Your doctor will probably prescribe a powder to be added to all your child's drinks. This contains the glucose and essential minerals that have been lost through vomiting and diarrhoea. To avoid dehydration, your child should be given 200 ml (7½ fl oz) of water for every kilogram (2.2 lb) of his body weight in the first 24 hours of diarrhoea and vomiting.

□ Your doctor will recommend bed-rest and a liquid diet until the vomiting and diarrhoea have subsided.

□ For a bottlefed baby, your doctor may recommend that you replace all milk feeds with the glucose solution and he will then provide you with a regime for reintroducing the formula feeds.

□ If your baby is seriously ill, your doctor may admit him to hospital so that he can be given fluid intravenously to counteract dehydration.

What can I do to help?

□ If your child is admitted to hospital, try to stay with him. Most hospital authorities now encourage parents to do this.

□ Be meticulous about hygiene. Sterilize all feeding equipment if your baby is bottlefed. Wash your hands before preparing any food for your child and after changing nappies.

□ Avoid giving your child acidic drinks such as orange and grapefruit juice. They may irritate the stomach further.

□ Reintroduce foods slowly when your child seems interested, starting with bland, easily digested foods such as jellies, yogurt, soups and non-fatty foods.

Glucose 20ml   Salt 2.5ml   **Water** 500ml
(4 teaspoons)   (½ teaspoons)   (1 pint)

□ If your child refuses to drink enough fluids, or doesn't like the taste of the special powder, give him cubes of melon or watermelon to suck, or make your own glucose drink with 20 ml (4 teaspoonful) of glucose and 2.5 ml (½ teaspoonful) salt to every 500 ml (1 pint) of boiled, cooled water.

SEE ALSO:
Appetite, loss of, *page 55*
Dehydration, *page 108*
Diarrhoea, *page 112*
Dysentery, *page 118*
Food poisoning, *page 136*
Influenza, *page 166*
Vomiting, *page 256*

Words in **bold** are A-Z entries

German measles

German measles, or rubella, is a mild, infectious disease that is caused by a virus. It is contagious and has an incubation period of 14 to 21 days. The rash usually starts behind the ears before spreading to the forehead and the rest of the body. It looks more like a large patch of redness than a series of spots. The rash lasts about two to three days and is rarely accompanied by serious symptoms, just a mild fever and enlarged glands at the back of the neck. The main danger with German measles is not to your infected child but to any pregnant woman who may contract the disease from your child. Rubella can cause birth defects such as blindness and deafness.

Is it serious?
This is not a serious childhood illness. However, you should keep your child in isolation for five days after the rash appears. Like other childhood infectious diseases, rubella carries a slight risk of **encephalitis**.

Possible symptoms
● Slightly raised temperature.
● Tiny pink or red spots, starting behind the ears and spreading to the forehead, then the rest of the body.

Site of swollen glands

● Enlarged, swollen glands at the back of the neck.

What should I do first?

1 Make sure that anyone who might be pregnant and has been in contact with your child is informed of your child's infection.

2 Keep your child away from school and from public places.

3 If your child's temperature rises above 38°C (100.4°F), give him paracetamol elixir.

4 If your child is feeling unwell, put him to bed.

Should I consult the doctor?

Consult your doctor by telephone to confirm that your child has German measles. Consult your doctor immediately if your child complains of a stiff neck or a headache.

What might the doctor do?

☐ There is no treatment for German measles, but your doctor will advise you to alert any women you know who might be pregnant, if you haven't already done so.

What can I do to help?

☐ If you have daughters, make sure they are vaccinated against the disease.

SEE ALSO:
Encephalitis, *page 125*
Rash, *page 204*

141

Glandular fever

Glandular fever, or infectious mono-nucleosis, is a viral infection, and starts in much the same way as **influenza**, with a runny nose, **sore throat**, aches, pains, and tiredness, or, in a small number of cases, with a rash like that in **German measles**. It is a fairly common disease affecting mostly teenagers and young adults; children can also contract it, but they tend to be less severely affected by the disease. In common with other viral infections, there is no known cure for glandular fever; it has to run its course— generally at least a month. As part of the body's reaction to the infection, the glands become swollen and the spleen may become enlarged. This does not in itself give rise to unpleasant symptoms, and the spleen, which is part of the lymphatic gland system, returns to normal once the infection is gone.

Is it serious?
Although debilitating, glandular fever is not usually serious, but as so many of its symptoms are similar to those of other illnesses, you should consult your doctor for a diagnosis.

Possible symptoms
- Runny nose.
- Sore throat.
- Aches and pains.

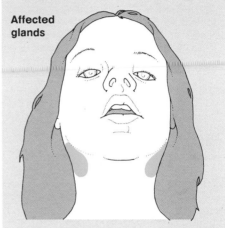

Affected glands

- Swollen glands, most commonly in the neck, accompanied by a fever.
- Depression and lethargy.
- Rash which starts behind the ears, spreading to the forehead.

What should I do first?

1 While many of the early symptoms of glandular fever are similar to those of other ailments, be alerted if the neck glands are swollen and there is a **fever**. Check your child's temperature regularly if his glands are swollen. If it remains high, give him a dose of paracetamol elixir.

2 Keep your child isolated until you have a definite diagnosis. The virus is infectious and is passed on by intimate contact, such as kissing.

Should I consult the doctor?

Consult your doctor immediately if you suspect that your child is not just suffering from influenza or a **common cold**.

What might the doctor do?

☐ Your doctor will take a blood sample for analysis. Glandular fever can be diagnosed with certainty only by finding the virus in the blood. You will be advised to keep your child indoors and to make sure he has plenty of rest; no further treatment is required.

What can I do to help?

☐ Your child will not be able to return to school for at least a month. Don't send him back without your doctor's advice. Arrange for school work to be sent home for him once he feels up to it.

Continued on next page ▶

Words in **bold** are A-Z entries

Glandular fever

◀ *Continued from previous page*
☐ If your child wants to stay in bed, let him. If he doesn't, keep him indoors at least until the fever subsides.

Give frequent drinks

☐ If your child has a temperature, offer him plenty of fluids to prevent dehydration.
☐ Glandular fever is debilitating and it may be six months before your child is completely fit and his old self again.
☐ Keep him entertained and cheerful. The length of time the disease takes to run its course can lead to boredom and depression. So, although your child needs plenty of rest, keep him busy in quiet ways with books, puzzles, and television.
☐ The virus may reappear during the two years after the first attack, so watch for a recurrence of the symptoms and consult your doctor if you are at all worried.

G

SEE ALSO:
Common cold, *page 90*
Fever, *page 134*
German measles, *page 141*
Influenza, *page 166*
Sore throat, *page 220*

Glue ear

Glue ear is the non-medical term for a condition that results when the Eustachian tube and middle ear fill with fluid as a result of infection. The Eustachian tube, which runs from the throat to the ear, produces large quantities of fluid as a response to chronic infections such as **sinusitis**, enlarged adenoids, **tonsillitis**, or, most commonly, **otitis media**. If the tube in either ear is blocked by inflammation, the fluid cannot drain and becomes glue-like, impeding the efficient vibration of sound, causing loss of hearing.

Is it serious?
Although painless, glue ear should be treated seriously because it can lead to **deafness** and eventually permanent loss of hearing in the affected ear. If undetected, it can cause problems with speech development and learning.

Possible symptoms
● A feeling of fullness in the ear.
● Partial loss of hearing or deafness in one or both ears.

What should I do first?

Call your child from behind

If your child seems inattentive and has recently had some upper respiratory tract infection, such as otitis media or a **common cold**, do a hearing test. Call quietly when the head is averted and see if there is a response. Even if your child can hear you, the hearing may be impaired in such a way that the child cannot tell where you are calling from.

Should I consult the doctor?
Consult your doctor as soon as possible if you suspect your child's hearing has deteriorated in any way.

What might the doctor do?
☐ Your doctor will examine your child's ears with a special instrument (an otoscope), and treat the glue ear according to the severity of the blockage.
☐ In mild cases, your doctor will prescribe antibiotics to clear up the infection, and he may also prescribe vasoconstrictor drugs, which promote drainage by reducing swelling in the Eustachian tubes.

Continued on next page ▶

Words in **bold** are A-Z entries

Glue ear

◀ *Continued from previous page*

Grommet

Eustachian tube

Middle ear cavity

Position of the grommet

☐ In severe and recurrent cases, your child will probably be referred to an ear, nose and throat specialist and may be admitted to hospital to have the fluid drained off under a general anaesthetic. At the same time, the specialist may insert grommets in the affected ear. These are tiny plastic tubes that allow mucus to drain away, thus preventing further build-up of the sticky secretions. The grommets either fall out after several months when the ears are healthy again or can be removed by the specialist at a regular check-up. If glue ear is a result of repeated infections or enlarged adenoids, the underlying problem will also be treated to prevent recurrences.

What can I do to help?

☐ If your child has had grommets inserted, he must always wear a bathing cap when swimming. Some ear, nose and throat specialists advise against swimming altogether when grommets are in place.
☐ Keep the ear as dry as possible at all times.

SEE ALSO:
Common cold, *page 90*
Deafness, *page 107*
Otitis media, *page 196*
Sinusitis, *page 215*
Tonsillitis, *page 241*

G

Growing pain

A growing pain is a dull, vague ache in a limb; it doesn't last long and the child can usually be distracted from it. One in six children of school age suffers from some kind of growing pain. Such pains can occur when your child is going through a growth spurt; the muscles and bones grow at slightly different rates, leading to an aching soreness that is worse in the evening. They can also occur after strenuous activity. It is important to distinguish a growing pain from joint pain. A growing pain is felt between the joints of a limb; joint pain is specific to the joint area. In a child, a joint pain can also be a symptom of **rheumatic fever** or **arthritis**.

Is it serious?

A growing pain is not serious, but any pain in the joint may be, particularly if it is accompanied by a fever. This could be septic arthritis.

Possible symptoms

● Aches and pains in the arms or legs, most often in the legs.
● Disturbed sleep if the pain is severe.
● Painful muscles after strenuous activity.

What should I do first?

1 Check your child's joints for swelling and tenderness by pressing on and around them. If there is neither, check the muscles in the same way.

2 See if your child limps when he walks.

3 Ask your child when the pain started and how long it lasts.

Should I consult the doctor?

Consult your doctor as soon as possible if the pain is sited over a joint and is accompanied by a fever, or if it lasts longer than 24 hours.

What might the doctor do?

☐ After excluding other possible causes of the pain, your doctor will reassure you and your child that there is no cause for concern.

What can I do to help?

☐ Show sympathetic interest in the pain—this may be sufficient to relax your child.
☐ Give your child a warm bath or a hot-water bottle: these can be soothing if your child is having difficulty sleeping.
☐ Gently massage the affected muscles to relax any tension.

SEE ALSO:
Arthritis, *page 56*
Limp, *page 175*
Rheumatic fever, *page 207*

Words in **bold** are A-Z entries

Growth hormone deficiency

The growth hormone, as it name implies, ensures that development of physical stature proceeds normally. In a very small percentage of children, the pituitary gland in the brain, which produces the growth hormone, fails to produce enough and this leads to stunted growth. Very occasionally the deficiency is caused by a tumour in the pituitary gland. Deficiency of growth hormone is often picked up at regular childhood check-ups when your child's weight and height are plotted on a graph to check that he is within the range of the average for his age. If your child is small for his age, a variety of laboratory tests can be performed to give a full clinical evaluation. Generally the tests involve a stay in hospital so that a full profile of the hormonal activity in your child's body can bo compiled by a specialist in hormones—an endocrinologist. A series of blood samples is used to assess the rise of growth hormone in the body in response to a stimulus, such as exercise or a test drug. In a normal child, this kind of stimulus would cause the pituitary gland to produce and release the growth hormone.

Possible symptoms
● Exceptionally short stature.
● Slow rate of growth.

What can be done?
The treatment for growth hormone deficiency is sophisticated, and replacement therapy is easily controlled, giving good results. The hormone may be given by intramuscular injections two or three times a week. The maximum growth response occurs during the first year of the treatment: the rate at which your child grows may be twice that expected for his chronological age as he makes up for lost time. The treatment usually continues until your child reaches adolescence. In the rare cases where the deficiency is caused by a pituitary tumour, the tumour will be removed surgically or with radiotherapy.

Gum boil

A gum boil, or dental abscess, is a pus-filled cavity that develops at the root of a decayed tooth. In a primary tooth, a gum boil can damage the underlying permanent tooth if it is left untreated. Gum boils are nearly always very painful as they are in such a confined area and the pain does not always respond to painkillers.

Is it serious?
A gum boil should be treated seriously as it causes great discomfort and can result in a lost tooth.

Possible symptoms

● Red, inflamed lump on one side of the tooth in the gum.
● Throbbing pain.
● Tenderness and swelling on the affected side of the face.
● Swollen neck glands.
● Pain below the ear on the affected side of the face.

What should I do first?

1 Examine the gum around the tooth and if you notice a red lump, gently feel it with your fingertip. It will be soft and spongy because of the underlying collection of pus.

2 Give your child doses of paracetamol elixir to try to relieve the pain. Do not use local anaesthetics such as oil of cloves. These can damage the gum margin, leading to more dental problems.

3 Rinse your child's mouth with a weak salt-water solution to speed the bursting of the boil and to wash away any pus that has seeped out.

A hot-water bottle will help to soothe the pain

4 Apply a covered hot-water bottle to your child's cheek to soothe the pain.

Should I consult the doctor?

Consult your dentist immediately or take your child to the nearest casualty department.

What might the doctor do?

☐ The dentist or doctor will drain the pus by either opening the gum or removing the tooth if there is no possibility of saving it. Both will be done under an anaesthetic.
☐ Your dentist or doctor will prescribe a course of antibiotics to eradicate the infection. Your child may also be prescribed a mouth wash to be used three or four times a day until the wound has healed.

What can I do to help?

☐ Maintain regular tooth brushing to minimize tooth decay.
☐ Take your child to the dentist regularly from the age of three.
☐ Cut down on sweets and sugary foods in your child's diet.

SEE ALSO:
Earache, *page 121*
Toothache, *page 244*

Haemophilia

Haemophilia is an inherited disease of the blood, caused by a faulty gene. It is carried by some females, in whom the disease does not show. A carrier female may pass it to her daughter, who then becomes a carrier herself, or to her son, who will be a haemophiliac.

Haemophiliacs lack a substance called *antihaemophilic globulin (AHG)* which is essential for the blood to clot. A haemophiliac therefore bleeds profusely from even small wounds, and the blood flow does not stop. In a normal person, a trivial knock produces a little bleeding into the tissues, which results in a bruise; in a haemophiliac, it produces deep bruising, swelling and quite severe pain for several days.

Possible symptoms

● Profuse and prolonged bleeding from any open wound.
● Heavy bruising, pain and swelling after even a light knock.
● Stiff joints or muscles due to internal bleeding.

What can be done?

Most haemophiliac families are aware that the disorder exists. Boys in such families should be tested after birth to see if haemophilia is present. Women in such families are advised to consult their doctor and a genetic counsellor before conceiving, to assess the risks involved. During pregnancy, amniocentesis—a process in which amniotic fluid is drawn off from around the fetus through a needle—can determine the sex of the baby. If it is a boy, and the mother is a carrier of the haemophiliac gene, a termination will be offered.

In unsuspected cases, the symptoms tend to show themselves when the baby boy is several months old and is becoming more active, learning to crawl and walk.

The main treatment for haemophilia is replacement of the missing AHG by intravenous injection, as soon as possible after bruising, swelling or injury, or before dental and surgical procedures. In the case of injury, this injection may have to be repeated daily until the bleeding or swelling has ceased. Many older boys can insert the needle themselves, with the help of the parent or telephone supervision by a doctor.

You should be swift to apply the correct first-aid techniques if your child is injured. Bleeding must be staunched at once with firm pressure and the affected part raised to reduce blood flow. Keep your child very still while waiting for medical assistance.

A haemophiliac should wear a disc that states he has the disease, his blood group, and what to do in an emergency.

The doctor or nurse may also pass on advice on how to protect your son against injury. For example, your child should sleep on a low bed, be careful on slippery floors, and avoid playing with hazardous toys that may lead to physical injury.

FOR HELP AND ADVICE CONTACT:
The Haemophilia Society
16 Trinity Street
London SE1
01-407 1010

Hair loss

Children rarely lose their hair. However, in newborn babies, the first fluffy hair is often lost just after birth and the second growth may be slow, so your baby will appear to be bald for several months. Babies also lose hair through friction. Simply by the pressure of their heads on the cot sheet, they may have large bald patches on the back of their heads. This is because newborn baby hair is not very firmly embedded in the skin and only a small amount of friction is needed to rub it loose.

By far the most common cause of hair loss in older children is the fungal infection of the scalp known as **ringworm**. This produces circular patches of pink or grey, scaly baldness in the scalp and it is extremely itchy. Another cause of temporary baldness in children is a condition known as *alopecia areata*. Round, bald patches appear suddenly and within a few months fine white hairs break through into the bald area, followed by normal hair. Some children can actually inflict hair loss on themselves with a nervous **tic** or mannerism, compulsively pulling, twisting and breaking their hair. This condition, which is called *trichotillomania*, is often worse when your child is concentrating on something.

Is it serious?

Hair loss is not normally serious, though your child may feel self-conscious until the hair grows back again.

What should I do first?

1 Check any patches of baldness on your child's scalp. If the skin is pink or grey, and scaly, this indicates ringworm. If not, your child could be suffering from alopecia areata.

2 Notice if your child has the nervous tic of pulling and tugging at his hair while concentrating.

Should I consult the doctor?

Consult your doctor as soon as possible if you suspect ringworm. This is infectious but can be easily cleared up with medication. Consult your doctor as soon as possible if you are unsure about the cause of the patches of baldness on your child's head, or if you are worried about the tic.

What might the doctor do?

☐ Your doctor will treat the underlying cause. If your child has ringworm, your doctor will prescribe an antifungal ointment for the skin, and tablets for the scalp.

☐ If alopecia areata is the cause, your doctor will advise you that there is no treatment and that the condition is only temporary.

What can I do to help?

☐ If your child has ringworm, keep him away from school until the scaly patches have healed.

☐ Let your child wear a hat if he feels self-conscious about the bald patches.

☐ Check for regrowth regularly and encourage your child not to be disheartened.

☐ Try not to make a fuss about the baldness; treat it as a normal condition. Inform your child's teacher so that your child does not suffer too much teasing.

☐ If your child fiddles with his hair, try not to let him see that it annoys you. Discourage him gently and make sure he doesn't get over-tired or anxious as this can make such tics worse.

SEE ALSO:
Ringworm, *page 208*
Tic, *page 240*

Words in **bold** are A-Z entries

Hayfever

Hayfever is similar to **asthma** except that the allergic reaction occurs in the mucous membranes of the nose and eyelids, not the chest. The condition is also known as allergic rhinitis and causes sneezing, a runny nose and itchy, watery eyes. It occurs in spring and summer and is usually due to a reaction to pollen from flowers, grasses and trees. Most hayfever sufferers are sensitive to more than one pollen and, short of isolation in an air-conditioned room, it is difficult for them to avoid the symptoms. Children who suffer from hayfever can become mouth-breathers because the nose is so blocked. Hayfever tends not to occur before the age of five, but it can start or stop at any time, and it tends to run in families. Some children who are allergic to animals and house dust as well as pollens suffer all year round from hayfever; this condition is called perennial allergic rhinitis.

Is it serious?
Hayfever is periodically troublesome, but it has no serious consequences.

Possible symptoms
- Sneezing.
- Runny nose with clear discharge.
- Itchy, watery, red-rimmed eyes.

H

What should I do first?

1 If your child is sneezing a lot, check his temperature to make sure he isn't ill with an infection such as **influenza** or a **common cold**.

2 Discourage your child from rubbing his eyes; this will make them worse. Bathe his eyes with cool water to ease the irritation.

Should I consult the doctor?

Consult your doctor as soon as possible if you think your child may be suffering from a more serious infection, or if the hayfever is making your child miserable.

What might the doctor do?

A nasal spray may ease the symptoms

☐ Your doctor will probably prescribe decongestant nasal drops or antihistamine spray, elixir or tablets to relieve the symptoms.

Continued on next page ▶

Hayfever

◀ Continued from previous page
□ If your child's condition is severe, your doctor may arrange for your child to have a series of skin tests to track down the allergen that is causing the symptoms of hayfever. Once one or more allergens have been determined, a special vaccine can be made for your child and a course of desensitizing injections given over a period of weeks to protect him. These don't always work, however, and have to be given during the winter.

What can I do to help?

□ Watch the pollen count each day and if it is high, discourage your child from playing near freshly-mown grassland, for example.
□ Avoid feathers in your child's bedding and fluff in his clothing.
□ Keep your house as dust-free as possible. Even if your child isn't allergic to dust, a dusty atmosphere makes hayfever worse.

Moist towel

Paper handkerchiefs   Eye drops   Nasal spray

□ Prepare an emergency pack for outings. It should contain paper handkerchiefs, eye drops to reduce the eye irritation, a moist towel to soothe your child's eyes, and whatever medication has been prescribed.

SEE ALSO:
Asthma, *page 58*
Common cold, *page 90*
Influenza, *page 166*

Words in **bold** are A-Z entries

Head injury

Children hit their heads frequently and in the majority of cases the child has stopped crying and is playing normally within 10-15 minutes of the accident. With some harder knocks to the head, there is **headache** and local swelling; if the skin is broken, the blood flow may be alarming from even a small cut.

When there is no outward sign of injury, a mild headache is probably all your child will complain about. If, however, he lapses into unconsciousness, complains of **dizziness**, or appears stunned and vomits, this may be concussion, when the brain is shaken inside the skull. The symptoms of concussion may not appear for several hours.

Is it serious?
A head injury resulting in unconsciousness, dizziness or **vomiting** should always be treated as serious. If your child has any bleeding or straw-coloured discharge from his nose or ear after a blow to his head, treat this as an emergency because it indicates a skull fracture. If there is a fracture and an open wound, or any bleeding into the brain, the chances of brain damage are higher.

Possible symptoms
- Headache.
- Stunned and dazed state.
- Drowsiness.
- Period of unconsciousness.
- Irritability.
- Vomiting.
- Discharge of blood or straw-coloured fluid from the nose and ears.

What should I do first?

1 If your child has fallen on his head or suffered a blow to his head, check for any of the symptoms of concussion or a fracture of the skull, whether or not there is an open wound. Treat any symptoms other than just a mild headache as an emergency and take your child to the nearest casualty department.

2 If your child complains of a headache but seems otherwise alert, let him lie down for an hour in a dark room, but keep a watch on him to check that he doesn't lose consciousness.

Press down on wound

3 If the wound is bleeding, press a clean pad or handkerchief on to it for about 10 minutes, or until the

Continued on next page ▶

Head injury

◀ *Continued from previous page*

bleeding has stopped. It it is a small wound, clean the area with soap and water, place a clean pad over it and secure with a bandage to keep pressure on the wound. If the wound is jagged or long, take your child to the nearest casualty department for stitching.

4 If there is discharge coming from ears or nose, do not try to stop the flow—put a pad against the ear or nose to absorb it. Take your child to the nearest casualty department.

Should I consult the doctor?

Consult your doctor immediately or take your child to the nearest casualty department if he loses consciousness, even for a short time, if he complains of a severe headache and dizziness, if he vomits or if there is any discharge from his nose or ears. Take your child to the nearest casualty department if there is a cut that needs stitching. Consult your doctor immediately if you are at all worried about your child's behaviour even hours after a head injury, particularly if he is pale, unnaturally quiet and has lost interest in food. Be sure to tell the doctor what sort of fall or incident caused the injury.

What might the doctor do?

☐ If there is any likelihood of a skull fracture, your child will be given a skull X-ray.

☐ If there is a cut, the doctor will stitch it under local anaesthetic.

☐ If there are no signs of a fracture but your child is dizzy and has a headache, the doctor will admit him to hospital for overnight observation.

SEE ALSO:
Cuts and grazes, *page 103*
Dizziness, *page 115*
Headache, *page 155*
Vomiting, *page 256*

Words in **bold** are A-Z entries

Headache

About one in five children suffers from recurrent headaches, although a serious physical cause is hardly ever found. Most commonly children complain of pain in their heads after sitting in a hot, stuffy room, if they are worried or anxious about something, if they have a **fever**, or they have **sinusitis** or **toothache**, for example. Some children complain frequently of headache and tummy ache. Such pain is known as abdominal **migraine**.

Is it serious?
Headaches are rarely serious but if a single headache is accompanied by a temperature, neck stiffness, confusion or an intolerance of bright light, this may be a symptom of a more serious illness, such as **encephalitis** or **meningitis**, and you should seek medical advice. Similarly, if your child has had a recent injury to his head, you should get immediate medical attention.

What should I do first?

1 Ask your child if he has pain anywhere else. Run your hands over the area around his cheeks, jaw and ears to see if sinusitis, a **gum boil,** toothache or **earache** are the problem.

2 Check your child's temperature to see if he has a fever. Headache and fever could be among the first symptoms of an infectious illness such as **measles** or **influenza**.

3 Check to see if your child has any injury to his head.

4 If the headaches are frequent, find out if your child is worried about anything, such as his school work.

5 If your child complains of nausea or vomits, this could be a migraine headache.

6 If your child has no other symptoms to concern you, give him something to drink and a single dose of paracetamol elixir to relieve the pain, and put him to bed in a darkened room for half an hour.

Should I consult the doctor?

Consult your doctor immediately if the headache is accompanied by a temperature of 38°C (100.4°F) with vomiting, neck stiffness and intolerance of bright light, or if your child has had a recent head injury. Consult your doctor as soon as possible if the headaches are persistent.

What might the doctor do?

☐ Your doctor will examine your child to try to determine the cause of the headache. The examination may include taking your child's blood pressure and looking at the retina in the eye. Further tests will be carried out only if your doctor finds something wrong apart from the headaches.

☐ If the headache is a symptom of a more serious condition, such as meningitis, your doctor will treat the condition accordingly.

What can I do to help?

☐ If your child complains of headaches at the end of the school day, give him a drink and a nutritious snack and encourage him to go out and play in the fresh air.

H

SEE ALSO:
Earache, *page 121*
Encephalitis, *page 125*
Fever, *page 134*
Gum boil, *page 148*
Head, injury to, *page 153*
Influenza, *page 166*
Measles, *page 176*
Meningitis, *page 177*
Migraine, *page 178*
Sinusitis, *page 215*
Toothache, *page 243*

Heat exhaustion

Heat exhaustion results when too much body fluid is lost through sweating, and occurs when the body becomes over-heated, either by excessive exposure to sunshine, excessive humidity or through over-exertion. Although a strenuous game can raise the tempera-ture to over 38°C (100.4°F), the rise is usually temporary and the temperature returns to normal quite rapidly. However, if it doesn't, your child will develop the symptoms of heat exhaustion and will become pale and clammy and may complain of **dizziness**, nausea and **headache**.

Is it serious?
Heat exhaustion isn't serious as long as you recognize the problem and cool your child down, thus preventing **heatstroke.**

Possible symptoms
- Temperature over 38°C (100.4°F).
- Pale and clammy skin.
- Dizziness.
- Nausea.
- Headache.
- Rapid pulse rate.
- Muscle cramps.

What should I do first?

1 Lay your child down in a cool place with his feet raised a little. Remove most of his clothing.

2 Use tepid sponging (*see page 31*) to cool the skin down quickly.

3 Keep the air in the room as cool as you can.

4 Give your child plenty of fluids and add 5ml (one teaspoonful) of salt to every litre (1¾ pints) of liquid.

5 Take his temperature every half hour to make sure that it is coming down.

Should I consult the doctor?

You should not need to consult your doctor if your child is suffering only from heat exhaustion, and is cool and feels better within one hour. Consult your doctor immediately or take your child to the nearest casualty depart-ment if, after an hour, your child is still extremely hot but his skin is dry. He could be suffering from heatstroke. Consult your doctor immediately if

your child's temperature fails to come down after an hour; he may be suffering from some other illness.

What might the doctor do?

☐ If your child is suffering from heat-stroke or an infection, your doctor will deal with this accordingly.

☐ Your doctor may advise you to keep your child inside during the heat of the day or until he is acclimatized.

What can I do to help?

☐ Discourage your child from playing active games in strong sunshine.

☐ Keep a watch on your child if he has a tendency to become exhausted in hot weather.

SEE ALSO:
Dizziness, *page 115*
Headache, *page 155*
Heatstroke, *page 158*

Heat rash

Heat rash is a faint red **rash** in the areas of the body where the sweat glands are most numerous—on the face, neck, shoulders and in the skin creases, such as the elbows, groin and behind the knees. It is quite common in babies because their sweat glands are still primitive and not efficient at regulating body temperature. Heat rash is not due to exposure to sunlight but arises when the body becomes overheated and the skin responds with excessive production of sweat.

Is it serious?
Heat rash is never serious.

Possible symptoms

Areas affected

● Faint, red rash over the face, neck, shoulders and in the creases, such as the elbows, groin and knees.
● Flushed and hot appearance.

What should I do first?

1 Check your baby's clothing. He may be wearing too many clothes for the air temperature.

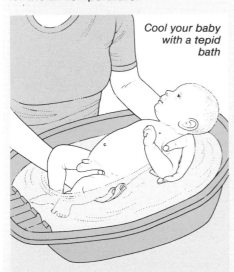

Cool your baby with a tepid bath

2 Undress your baby and bath him in tepid water. Pat him dry to remove most of the moisture. Allow the rest to evaporate—this will cool his skin down.

Should I consult the doctor?

There is no need to consult the doctor for a heat rash. Consult your doctor as soon as possible if the rash does not disappear 12 hours after the baby has cooled down.

What might the doctor do?

☐ Your doctor will examine your baby to exclude any other reason for the rash, and will probably advise you to dress your baby in natural fibres, which do not trap the sweat.

What can I do to help?

☐ Check that the temperature in your baby's room is not too high. Keep the air flowing by opening a window slightly.
☐ Don't overdress your child in hot weather.
☐ Don't put wool or manmade fibres directly against your baby's skin. Dress him in a cotton vest first.

> **SEE ALSO:**
> **Rash,** *page 204*

Heatstroke

Heatstroke, or sunstroke, is due to exposure to extreme heat, which causes the body's temperature-regulating mechanism to break down. The sweat glands fail to work and the body cannot cool itself in the normal way by producing sweat. Your child's skin will remain dry instead of sweaty, and he may become drowsy with a rapid pulse. He may then become confused and lapse into unconsciousness. If your child is not first acclimatized to the sun and heat, **heat exhaustion** and heatstroke can easily result.

Is it serious?

Heatstroke is very serious and may even be fatal. It should be treated as an emergency, although there are first-aid procedures you should follow while you are waiting for help.

Possible symptoms

● Temperature as high as 40°C (104°F).
● Hot skin which remains dry, not sweaty.
● Drowsiness.
● Rapid pulse.
● Confusion followed by unconsciousness.

What should I do first?

1 Undress your child completely and lay him down in a cool room.

2 Check his pulse (*see page 26*), and take his temperature to see if he has a fever. If his temperature is as high as 40°C (104°F), consult your doctor immediately, or take your child to the nearest casualty department.

3 If your child's temperature isn't this high, try to bring it down slowly. Play a fan over him and sponge his whole body with tepid water, (*see page 31*).

4 Place an icepack on your child's forehead and give your child plenty of cool drinks.

5 Take your child's temperature regularly to make sure it is dropping.

Should I consult the doctor?

Consult your doctor immediately or take your child to the nearest casualty department if his temperature is as high as 40°C (104°F).

What might the doctor do?

☐ The doctor will continue to cool your child's body. There are special drugs that can be given in emergencies to bring the body temperature down.

What can I do to help?

☐ Apply a sunblock cream to your child's skin before he is exposed to the sun. Get him to wear a hat.
☐ Watch your child when he plays in very hot or sunny conditions. An older child will probably rest in the shade, but a young child is often incapable of exercising this much caution, so you must be careful to monitor the time he spends in full sunlight if he has not been acclimatized.

> **SEE ALSO:**
> **Heat exhaustion,** *page 156*

Words in **bold** are A-Z entries

Hepatitis

Hepatitis is an infection which causes inflammation of the liver. The most common form of the illness in children is acute hepatitis A, caused by the type A virus, and It is highly contagious. The virus is found in the stools of a sufferer, and, if the hands are not washed after going to the toilet, the infection can easily be passed on to others by contaminated food and drink. The virus is also found in the blood and saliva. The first symptom is loss of appetite. **Influenza**-like symptoms then develop, followed by **jaundice**, with its associated symptoms of yellowing of the skin and whites of the eyes, dark brown urine, and abnormally pale stools.

Is it serious?

Hepatitis itself is rarely a very serious illness in children, who usually make a recovery. However, because it is contagious and can spread quickly through a household or school, it should be treated promptly.

Possible symptoms

● Loss of appetite.
● Influenza-like symptoms of headache, fever, aching joints.
● Jaundice (yellow skin), dark brown urine and pale stools.

What should I do first?

1 If your child loses interest in food and has 'flu-like symptoms, keep a check on his skin, urine and stools for any changes in colour.

2 If your child won't eat, give him frequent drinks of diluted fruit juice or water with a pinch of salt and 5 ml (one teaspoonful) of glucose added, to prevent dehydration and to keep up his energy level.

3 If you suspect hepatitis, keep your child home from school.

Be meticulous about hygiene

4 Be meticulous about your child's hygiene—make sure he washes his hands after going to the toilet. Keep his towel and facecloth, and his eating and drinking utensils, separate from those of the rest of the family.

Continued on next page ▶

Hepatitis

◀ *Continued from previous page*

Should I consult the doctor?

Consult your doctor immediately if you suspect your child has hepatitis, especially if jaundice develops.

What might the doctor do?

☐ Your doctor will take a blood sample to test for hepatitis.
☐ Your doctor will recommend bed-rest and isolation measures for at least two weeks, until the 'flu symptoms have passed. After another two weeks your child will probably feel well enough to return to school.
☐ Although there is no specific treatment for hepatitis other than bed-rest, some doctors advise a high-calorie, low-fat diet to reduce the strain on the liver. Others, however, don't consider this worthwhile.
☐ Your doctor may suggest that the rest of the family have a gamma globulin injection to minimize the risk of their contracting the infection.

What can I do to help?

☐ Observe the isolation measures for at least two weeks, or until your doctor says otherwise. Nurse your child in his own room, restrict physical contact with others, keep his eating utensils, toys and other objects separate from those of the rest of household.
☐ Maintain high standards of hygiene. Wash out the toilet bowl with disinfectant after your child has used it, wash his eating things separately from those of the family, and continue to keep his facecloth and towel separate, too.
☐ Despite these measures, try not to make your child feel left out. Put a television in his room, allow him books and tapes, and aim to keep him cheerful but quiet. Check with your doctor before you reduce isolation measures and before you send your child back to school.
☐ Post-hepatitis symptoms like lethargy, difficulty in concentrating and moodiness may persist for up to six months, so be patient and understanding with your child.

SEE ALSO:
Appetite, loss of, *page 55*
Influenza, *page 166*
Jaundice, *page 171*
Rash, *page 204*

Words in **bold** are A-Z entries

Hernia

A hernia results when a small defect in the muscular wall of the abdomen allows soft tissue to protrude through. This appears as a slight bulge in the skin and can be seen even more clearly if your child coughs or strains. The most common hernia in children is the *umbilical hernia.* This appears near the navel and results from a weakness that occurs in the abdominal wall at birth. An *inguinal hernia* appears lower down in the groin and is most common in boys, the defect occurring after the testicles have descended into the scrotum. Umbilical hernias rarely need any treatment; they heal spontaneously. Inguinal hernias may also heal themselves but if a small part of the bowel becomes trapped in the hernia it will have to be corrected by minor surgery.

Is it serious?
A hernia is not usually serious unless the bowel is trapped.

Possible symptoms

Areas affected

Umbilical hernia

Inguinal hernia

- Painless bulge in the skin's surface near to the navel or in the groin; the bulge increases in size when the child coughs, sneezes or cries.
- Vomiting with sharp abdominal pain if the bowel has become trapped.

What should I do first?
Try to push the hernia gently inwards. Most hernias respond to gentle pressure by sliding back inside the muscular wall.

Should I consult the doctor?
Consult your doctor immediately if you notice a bulge in your baby's abdomen before he is six months old. Consult your doctor immediately if a hernia becomes hard, the bulge won't go back with the application of gentle pressure and there is accompanying abdominal pain and vomiting.

What might the doctor do?
☐ If the hernia is hard or won't go back, your doctor will refer you to a paediatric specialist as the hernia will probably have to be repaired surgically. The operation for a hernia repair is simple. If your child is under six months old and has an inguinal hernia, your doctor may recommend surgical repair to avoid any trapping of the bowel.

What can I do to help?
☐ As long as the umbilical hernia is there, check periodically, say at bathtime, to make sure that it is not enlarging, that it is not hard and that it goes back when gently pushed.
☐ Discuss future action with your doctor and decide jointly whether or not you are going to let the hernia heal spontaneously or whether it should be operated on.
☐ Take your child for a check-up at regular intervals, as decided with your doctor.

H

Hives

Hives, urticaria, or nettle rash, is a skin condition. The **rash** that results is easy to recognize: the skin erupts into white lumps on a red base. These are known as weals. The weals can be as small as pimples or centimetres across. Hives can be caused by skin contact with an allergen, such as primulas, or it can result from eating certain foods, most commonly strawberries and shellfish, or from taking certain drugs, particularly penicillin and aspirin. Hives is most common after a nettle sting. Each crop of weals is extremely itchy and lasts up to an hour. It then disappears, to be replaced by more weals elsewhere on your child's face or body.

Is it serious?

Hives is not serious, but if it appears on the face, especially in or around the mouth, and is accompanied by swelling, get medical assistance immediately. This allergic reaction is known as *angioneurotic oedema,* and if the swelling spreads to the tongue or the throat, it can cause severe breathing problems.

Possible symptoms

Classic appearance of rash

- White lumps on a red base.
- Extremely itchy rash.
- Weals which disappear within an hour or so to be replaced elsewhere by other weals.
- Swelling on the face.

What should I do first?

1 Apply calamine lotion to the weals to soothe the skin.

2 Give your child a warm bath to relieve itching.

Should I consult the doctor?

Consult your doctor immediately if hives on your child's face causes swelling, particularly in and around the mouth. Consult your doctor as soon as possible if the weals have not gone after several days, or if your child is miserable with the itchiness.

What might the doctor do?

☐ Your doctor may prescribe antihistamine tablets or medicine to relieve the itchiness of your child's skin.

☐ Your doctor may give your child an injection of adrenalin if the swelling is causing breathing problems.

What can I do to help?

☐ If your child has frequent attacks, make a note of any new foods he might have eaten. Provided it is not an essential food for a growing child, you can exclude the suspected allergen for a week or two, then reintroduce it and watch for a reaction.

SEE ALSO:
Itching, *page 170*
Rash, *page 204*

Words in **bold** are A-Z entries

Hydrocephalus

The term "hydrocephalus" means water on the brain, and this condition results when there is an excessive build-up of the fluid that surrounds the brain. This fluid, known as cerebrospinal fluid or CSF, carries nutrients to the brain and acts as a protective, fluid buffer. If the circulation of CSF is blocked for some reason, or if the fluid is produced in too great a quantity, the build-up of fluid increases pressure inside the brain. The brain tissue becomes thinner and the bones of the skull stretch to accommodate the excess fluid. The pressure on the brain can cause brain damage and, if untreated, more than 50 per cent of hydrocephalic infants die.

The symptoms of hydrocephalus depend on the age at which it develops in the child. If it is present at birth, the head is abnormally large because the skull bones have been pushed apart by the fluid; the baby in such cases will prob ably also suffer from spina bifida. In milder forms of hydrocephalus, the head may be normal at birth but grow at an excessive rate in the following months. Hydrocephalus can also develop later in childhood as the result of a tumour, or an infection such as meningitis, when there may be no appreciable enlargement of the head, although the pressure of the fluid on the brain may cause the symptoms of headache and vomiting.

Possible symptoms

- Abnormal head size at birth, or rapid growth of it in following months.
- Veins standing out on scalp.
- Swollen fontanelle.
- Headache.
- Vomiting.

What can be done?

If the condition is present at birth, this will normally be noticed by the doctor at delivery, or at regular check-ups when your baby's head is measured to check the head size. A careful initial evaluation by a paediatrician is necessary to deter- mine the exact cause of the build-up of fluid. In mild cases, drugs may be used to prevent excess production of CSF. Otherwise, provided the hydrocephalus is not too advanced, the condition will be relieved surgi- cally. Under anaesthetic, a fine tube with a one-way valve is inserted into a hole in the skull. The other end is inserted into a major blood vessel, thus draining the fluid from the brain directly into the bloodstream. After these treatments the baby's head gradually returns to normal; about 40 per cent of hydrocephalic infants

then go on to develop near normal intelligence. (If at some stage after the operation your child becomes irritable and is vomiting, a blockage of the tube will be suspected. The tube will be replaced or the blockage removed.)

FOR HELP AND ADVICE CONTACT:
Association for Spina Bifida and
Hydrocephalus
Tavistock House North
Tavistock Square
London WC1B 9HI
01-388 1382

Hyperactivity

The word "hyperactive" has come to be used as a label for children with minor behavioural problems, such as disruptive behaviour, poor attention span, **sleeplessness** and excitability. In fact, most hyperactive children are simply extremely active and normal.

Although research in the United States has found that certain food colourings and flavourings contribute to patterns of hyperactive behaviour in children, proper handling and tolerance by parents can solve most of the problems of individual behaviour in a child.

Is it serious?
There are few degrees of hyperactivity in children that are abnormal or serious.

Possible symptoms

- Disruptive behaviour.
- Restlessness.
- Short attention span.
- Sleeplessness.
- Foolhardiness and unpredictability.

What should I do first?

1 Try to determine whether your child is bored or restless for some reason. Intelligent children need a lot of stimulation.

2 Don't exaggerate the problem. Most parents would agree that their pre-school child is hyperactive some of the time.

Should I consult the doctor?

Consult your doctor for advice if you find your child difficult to live with or if his behaviour is interfering with schooling.

What might the doctor do?

☐ It is difficult to find two doctors who agree on the origin, features, or even the fact of hyperactivity. If minor behavioural problems are combined with any form of learning disability, such as **dyslexia**, the confusion is compounded. Your doctor may refer your child to a child psychotherapist for assessment in case there is any learning disability. This is more likely

to be spotted when your child begins school. Your doctor will not prescribe any drugs unless a definite diagnosis is made.

What can I do to help?

☐ The essential approach for parents with hyperactive children is proper handling. You should both adopt the same approach so that your child cannot manipulate either of you.
☐ Learn to live with your child by treating him as an exciting, unpredictable, but nevertheless normal child. While your child is young, this will be exceedingly difficult, but by the time he goes to school, he should have learned, with your help, to concentrate.
☐ You will need to be more vigilant if your child is foolhardy, and more inventive at providing games, so that he won't become bored.

> **SEE ALSO:**
> **Dyslexia,** *page 119*
> **Sleeplessness,** *page 217*

Words in **bold** are A-Z entries

Impetigo

Impetigo is a bacterial skin infection that is most often seen around the lips, nose and ears. It is caused by a common skin organism (*staphylococcus*), which is carried in the nose and on the skin. The rash starts as small **blisters**, which break and crust over to become yellow-brown scabs that look rather like brown sugar. The condition is most often seen in school-age children and is contagious.

Is it serious?
Impetigo rarely has serious effects, but because it is highly contagious, it should be treated immediately.

Possible symptoms

Common sites

● Tiny blisters around the nose and mouth or ears, which ooze and harden to form crusty, yellow-brown scabs.

What should I do first?

1 If the rash on your child's face starts to weep, stop him from touching it. Wash away any crusts with warm water and pat dry with a paper towel. Keep your child's facecloth and towel separate from those of the rest of the family to avoid spreading the infection.

2 Keep your child away from school until you have visited the doctor.

Should I consult the doctor?

Consult your doctor as soon as possible if you suspect impetigo.

What might the doctor do?

☐ Your doctor will prescribe an anti-biotic cream which should clear up the impetigo within five days.
☐ Your doctor might also prescribe a course of antibiotics to be taken by mouth to eradicate the infection from your child's body, or a nasal cream to prevent the infection being spread from there.

What can I do to help?

☐ Before applying the ointment, wash away any yellow crusts with warm water and pat dry with a paper towel.
☐ Be meticulous about hygiene. Wash your hands before and after administering the treatment, and encourage your child to keep his hands away from his face. Keep his fingernails short to reduce the risk of spreading the infection to other parts of the body.
☐ Be very strict with your child if he sucks his thumb, bites his nails or picks his nose. This can spread the infection.
☐ When the infection has cleared, keep the area moist with emollient cream.

SEE ALSO:
Blister, *page 67*

Influenza

Influenza ('flu), like the **common cold**, is caused by a virus and has similar symptoms such as a runny nose, **sore throat**, **cough** and **fever**, as well as shivering and aches and pains all over the body. Because it is a viral infection there is no cure for 'flu and it lasts, on average, three to four days. Unless there is a secondary infection, treatment of the symptoms is all that is necessary in most cases.

Is it serious?

Even if influenza is accompanied by a high temperature, it is rare for serious complications to occur. However, as with any viral infection, natural resistance is reduced, and a secondary infection, such as **pneumonia**, **bronchitis**, **otitis media** or **sinusitis**, may result. Influenza is always serious in a child who has lungs weakened by **asthma**, or a condition such as **diabetes mellitus**.

Possible symptoms

- Runny nose.
- Sore throat.
- Cough.
- Temperature above 38°C (100.4°F).
- Shivering.
- Aches and pains.
- Diarrhoea, vomiting or nausea.
- Weakness and lethargy.

Areas affected

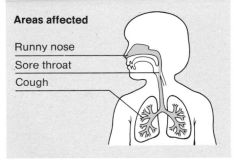

Runny nose

Sore throat

Cough

What should I do first?

1 Check your child's temperature every three or four hours and if it doesn't come down within 36 hours, consult your doctor.

2 Give your child paracetamol elixir to reduce the fever and the aches and pains, and put him to bed.

Give frequent drinks

3 Don't force your child to eat; make sure he gets plenty to drink, but don't give him milk if he has diarrhoea. Small quantities of diluted fruit juice or water taken often are the best way of replacing fluids lost through sweating and fever.

4 If a rash appears just after the onset of 'flu symptoms, your child may have **measles** and not influenza.

Should I consult the doctor?

Consult your doctor immediately if your child's temperature fails to come down within 36 hours. Consult your doctor immediately if you notice a deterioration in your child's condition after 48 hours. Be on the look-out for a worsening cough, which suggests that the infection has gone to your child's chest; earache, which may suggest otitis media, or yellow, pussy discharge from the nose, which may indicate sinusitis. Consult your doctor as soon as possible if you suspect measles.

Continued on next page ▶

Words in **bold** are A-Z entries

Influenza

◀ Continued from previous page

What might the doctor do?

☐ Your doctor will confirm whether or not there is a secondary infection. If there is, he will prescribe an antibiotic medicine to eradicate the infection. If not, your doctor will advise you to continue with paracetamol elixir and bed rest. If your child has a persistent cough, your doctor may prescribe an appropriate cough mixture.

What can I do to help?

☐ Your child should rest in a constant, warm temperature. If he is bored, make him up a bed in the kitchen or the living room so he can be near you during the day.
☐ As soon as he wants to be active, let him, but if his temperature rises again make him rest.

☐ Don't leave dirty paper handkerchiefs lying around. Encourage your child to throw them away as soon as they are used. If he uses linen handkerchiefs, wash them in boiling water to prevent the spread of the virus through the household.
☐ You might consider protecting your child each winter with an injection of influenza vaccine. This has been shown to protect some children. However, every year a different strain of the virus appears and immunity, whether from a vaccine or contracting the virus, is only short-lived.
☐ If, after your child should have recovered, his temperature rises and he vomits, consult your doctor immediately. A rare, but serious, childhood illness, **Reye's syndrome**, could be the cause of his deterioration.

Ingrowing toenail

When a toenail fails to grow straight out from the nailbed, but instead curves over into the sides of the toe, it is referred to as an ingrowing toenail. This occurs most often to the nail of the big toe, and causes pain and discomfort. An ingrowing toenail is more likely to occur if the toe is broad and plump, if the toenail is cut down at the sides instead of straight across, if the toenail is small, or if tight shoes and socks push the nail into the skin. If untreated, the nail will penetrate the skin, possibly becoming infected, causing painful inflammation and a pussy discharge around the edges of the nail.

Is it serious?
An ingrowing toenail is painful but it is not serious.

What should I do first?

1 Examine the skin around the nail to see if the nail has penetrated the skin.

Cut a V shape

2 Cut a tiny V shape in the top edge of the nail to relieve pressure on the sides of the nail.

3 Apply an antiseptic cream to the sides of the nail to prevent infection.

4 If there is any sign of redness or pus, stop your child walking about and get him to lie down with his foot propped up. Apply a sterile dressing to the toe.

Should I consult the doctor?

Consult your doctor as soon as possible if the nail has penetrated the skin, if you notice any redness or pus around your child's toenail, or if ingrowing toenails are a recurrent problem.

What might the doctor do?

☐ Your doctor may prescribe antibiotic tablets to clear up the infection, and an antiseptic cream to apply to the affected toe. Your doctor may also prescribe an astringent lotion to toughen up the skin around the toenail.
☐ If the problem is recurrent, your doctor may refer your child to an orthopaedic surgeon to see whether the ingrowing edge of the toenail should be removed. This is a minor operation.

What can I do to help?

Incorrect   Correct

☐ Cut your child's toenails straight across and not too short. Cut them regularly; don't let them get too long.
☐ Make sure your child's shoes and socks are not too tight and allow him enough space to wriggle his toes.
☐ If your child's toenail becomes infected, don't put socks on him; cut the toe out of an old shoe or let him wear sandals while the infection is clearing up.

Words in **bold** are A-Z entries

Intussusception

Intussusception is a condition that occurs when part of the small intestine telescopes inside the intestine ahead of it, rather like a finger in a glove being turned inside out. The twisted intestine swells and this causes a blockage. In an effort to overcome this blockage, the affected intestine goes into spasm. There is no known cause for intussusception and it can happen at any age; however, it most often affects baby boys under 12 months of age who have previously been in excellent health. The baby may suddenly cry out as the muscular spasms begin and may vomit and be pale and feverish. In between spasms, he may appear quite normal and pass normal bowel motions for the first few hours. However, as the attacks continue, the bowel motions characteristically look like redcurrant jelly because they contain mostly blood and mucus.

Is it serious?
Though rare, intussusception is a serious condition. If left untreated, it can be fatal.

Possible symptoms

● Severe abdominal pain, possibly accompanied by screaming.
● Vomiting.
● Paleness.
● Slight fever.
● Bowel motions, containing blood and mucus, that resemble redcurrant jelly.

Affected area

Large intestine

Telescoped intestine

Blockage

Small intestine

What should I do first?

1 If your baby has a number of spasmodic attacks when he screams and pulls his legs up to his stomach in pain, yet he appears quite well in between attacks, consult your doctor immediately.

2 Check your baby's bowel motions for any blood and mucus.

3 In between attacks, take your baby's temperature to see if he has a fever.

Should I consult the doctor?

Consult your doctor immediately if your baby has a number of attacks of abdominal cramps, or if you notice any blood or mucus in your baby's bowel motions.

What might the doctor do?

□ Your doctor will refer your baby to hospital for a barium enema to confirm the diagnosis of intussusception. This is a painless investigation in which fluid is pumped into the intestines through your baby's rectum; the condition of the intestines can then be seen on X-ray. The barium enema sometimes causes the condition to right itself; if it does not, your baby will have an operation to push the intestine back into its normal position.

SEE ALSO:
Colic, *page 88*
Vomiting, *page 256*

Itching

Itching is nearly always a symptom of some underlying skin problem (**eczema**, **ringworm**), the result of an infestation (**scabies**, fleas or **worms**), sensitivity to some foodstuff or drug, skin contact with an irritant (**hives**), or the result of an infectious disease (**chickenpox**). Some-times nervous tension and worry can cause itching, and scratching can make the itchiness even worse.

Is it serious?
Itching is rarely serious but it should not be ignored.

What should I do first?

1 Try to determine the cause of the itching. The site may give you a clue. For example, itching around the anus and genitals could indicate worms or **thrush**, itchiness in the hair, ringworm, on the feet, **athlete's foot**, or between the fingers, scabies.

2 Check any pets your child comes into contact with for fleas.

3 Check to see if your child has eaten any new foods recently.

4 Note whether your child is taking any new medicines.

5 Try soothing the itching with calamine lotion or give your child a cool bath with a handful of bicarbonate of soda dissolved in the water.

Should I consult the doctor?

Consult your doctor as soon as possible if you can find no apparent reason for the itching or if your child is having difficulty sleeping because of constant itchiness.

What might the doctor do?

☐ Your doctor will examine your child and determine the cause of the itching. If itching is a symptom of another condition, he will treat this accordingly. He may prescribe antihistamine tablets, elixir or cream to curb the itching.
☐ If your child is having difficulty sleeping, your doctor may prescribe a mild sedative.

What can I do to help?

☐ Dress your child in cotton underwear so that fabrics such as wool and nylon, which irritate, do not touch his skin.
☐ If you have recently changed your washing powder or fabric conditioner, change back to the old brand and see if the irritation subsides. Rinse clothes well.
☐ Use a mild soap and shampoo for your child.

Keep your child's nails short

☐ To stop your child scratching, put mittens on him whenever possible, and keep his nails short to prevent infection should he break the skin by scratching too hard.

SEE ALSO:
Athlete's foot, *page 60*
Chickenpox, *page 82*
Chilblains, *page 83*
Eczema, *page 123*
Hives, *page 162*
Ringworm, *page 208*
Scabies, *page 210*
Thrush, *page 238*
Worms, *page 261*

Words in **bold** are A-Z entries

Jaundice

Jaundice is a symptom of an underlying disease, and it causes a yellow coloration of the skin and the whites of the eyes.

The condition is due to the presence of yellow bile pigment, *bilirubin,* in the blood. Bile pigment is made during the normal breakdown of old red blood cells, but when certain illnesses are present, the bile pigment accumulates in the blood, tinging the skin yellow. Possible causes include **hepatitis** (liver infection), a blockage or malformation of the bile duct, and certain types of **anaemia**. The yellowish skin coloration is often accompanied by dark brown urine. This is because bile pigment overflows from the blood into the urine. There may also be pale stools because the pigment is no longer present in the intestinal contents to darken their colour.

Jaundice also occurs in one-third of babies during the week after birth, when it is called "physiological jaundice". In nearly all such cases there is no underlying disease. The condition is merely due to the baby's liver and digestive system adapting to life outside the womb.

Possible symptoms

- Yellowish coloration of the skin and the whites of the eyes.
- Dark-brown urine.
- Pale-coloured stools.
- Nausea and loss of appetite.

Is it serious?
Jaundice should be treated seriously because it is usually a symptom of an underlying complaint.

What should I do first?

1 Look to see if your child's urine is a darker colour and check if his stools are abnormally pale.

2 If your child feels sick and will not eat, give him frequent drinks to prevent dehydration.

3 Be meticulous about hygiene until you have consulted your doctor; your child may have hepatitis, which is contagious.

Should I consult the doctor?

Consult your doctor immediately if you suspect your child is jaundiced. Consult your doctor immediately if your baby seems yellow or unusually suntanned. A baby who is jaundiced must be checked by a doctor since excess bilirubin can damage internal organs; he must also be checked for any underlying disease.

What might the doctor do?

☐ The underlying disease will be identified and treated as necessary. If it is hepatitis, your child may need to be isolated.

☐ Your child will need regular check-ups at the hospital clinic for some weeks or months after the problem has cleared up, to ensure that there are no after-effects.

What can I do to help?

☐ Ensure that your child keeps to any special diets and treatments.

☐ Be sympathetic. Your child may have difficulty understanding why he has to eat special food, and he may feel tired and depressed for some weeks.

SEE ALSO:
Anaemia, *page 52*
Appetite, loss of, *page 55*
Hepatitis, *page 159*

J

Laryngitis

Laryngitis is an inflammation of the larynx, or voice box. Many minor viruses, and occasionally bacteria, can enter the body through the throat and quickly infect the larynx. The most obvious symptoms of laryngitis are hoarseness and a dry **cough**, and sometimes **fever**.

Is it serious?

Laryngitis is rarely serious and lasts less than seven days, even if it is part of a more serious infection, such as **tonsillitis** or **bronchitis**. However, in young children a swollen larynx can obstruct the passage of air causing breathing difficulties and **croup**, which is a serious complication. If laryngitis develops into croup, you should seek urgent medical treatment.

Possible symptoms

- Hoarseness or loss of voice.
- Dry cough.
- Slight fever.
- Sore throat.
- Croup, a barking type of cough.

Cross-section of the throat

| Larynx | Epiglottis

What should I do first?

1 If the hoarseness is not accompanied by any other symptoms of a respiratory tract infection such as bronchitis, keep a check on your child's temperature. If it rises above 38°C (100.4°F), there may be another infection present.

2 Listen closely for the barking cough of croup.

3 Keep the air in your child's room moist if possible. Open a window to allow air to circulate. This is usually an effective atmosphere for suppressing a dry cough.

Should I consult the doctor?

Consult your doctor immediately if you think your child has croup. Consult your doctor as soon as possible if your child has a fever or you think he has contracted another infection.

What might the doctor do?

☐ If there is a bacterial infection such as bronchitis or tonsillitis, your doctor will prescribe antibiotics.

What can I do to help?

☐ Discourage your child from talking out loud. You could make a game of it and have the whole family talking in whispers.

☐ Give your child plenty of warm drinks to soothe his throat. Try hot lemon and honey or heat any fruit juice drink by diluting it with hot water.

SEE ALSO:
Bronchitis, *page 73*
Cough, *page 97*
Croup, *page 100*
Fever, *page 134*
Tonsillitis, *page 241*

Words in **bold** are A-Z entries

Leukaemia

Leukaemia is a rare form of cancer caused by the rapid overgrowth of millions of primitive white blood cells. The cancerous white blood cells prevent the normal growth of red blood cells, leading to anaemia; they cause a lack of mature white blood cells, which reduces immunity to infection; and they prevent the growth of platelets, which help in the blood-clotting mechanism of the body. Quite often the first indication of leukaemia is the anaemic condition of the child and his failure to recover quickly from an infectious illness.

Possible symptoms

- Anaemia—paleness, tiredness and shortness of breath.
- Susceptibility to infection.
- Pain in the limbs; if in the legs, perhaps seen as a limp.
- Purpura—a purplish-red rash which doesn't disappear with pressure.
- Tendency to bruise easily.
- Recurrent nosebleeds.

What can be done?

At one time the outlook for children with leukaemia was not good, but over the last ten years therapy has improved the chances of a complete cure for 50 per cent of those children suffering from the commonest type of childhood leukaemia.

All children with the disease will be treated by a paediatrician who is experienced in childhood leukaemic diseases. Several drugs are given at the same time, some by mouth and some by injection. In the commonest type of childhood leukaemia, radio-therapy and special drugs may be used to kill the cancer cells in the brain. A blood transfusion may be given at the beginning of the treatment. If the number of white blood cells falls to a very low level, your child will be isolated against infection, and all visitors will need to wear masks and gowns. After several weeks, your child should be allowed to return home to lead as normal a life as possible. Regular check-ups will be necessary to keep track of the condition.

The important role for you as parents is to support your child through the long and arduous treatment by keeping up his morale with the prospect of an eventual cure. Children with leukaemia must not be exposed to the common childhood infectious diseases, such as chickenpox, unless they are already immune, so you will need to screen your child's playmates carefully.

L

FOR HELP AND ADVICE CONTACT:
Leukaemia Society
PO Box 82
Exeter
Devon EX2 5DP
0392 218514

Lice

The head louse is a tiny insect which infests the hair on the human head. The adult louse lays its eggs (nits) at the root of the hair, to which they become firmly attached. This distinguishes them from dandruff, which can be flaked off easily with a fingernail. The eggs hatch after two weeks and the lice bite the scalp to get blood. Your child's head will be itchy where the lice bite, particularly after strenuous exercise when he is hot. Your child can become infested by contact with another infested child or adult.

Are they serious?
Lice and nits are irritating, but they can be easily eradicated and are therefore not serious.

Possible symptoms

● Itchy scalp, particularly when the head is hot.

Nit

Hair root

Adult louse

● Tiny, pearly-white eggs covering the roots of the hair.

What should I do first?

1 If your child scratches, inspect the roots of the hair for nits.

2 If you find them, keep your child away from school or nursery until you have administered the treatment, and inform the headteacher of the outbreak so he can inform the health authorities.

3 Ask your chemist to recommend a shampoo for removing nits. Rub the shampoo, which will contain malathion, into your child's wet hair, leave it for five minutes and then rinse it off in clean water. (Alternatively, ask the chemist for a malathion-containing lotion—this is left on the hair overnight.) Whichever treatment you buy, follow the manufacturer's instructions carefully.

4 Examine the heads of the rest of the family to check for any nits. Treat the other members of your family with the appropriate shampoo or lotion because contact with someone who has lice for less than one second is sufficient to transfer the lice.

5 After treatment remove any dead eggs with a fine metal comb.

Should I consult the doctor?

Consult your doctor as soon as possible if the treatment doesn't work—you may not have administered the treatment properly—or if you aren't sure your child has head lice.

What might the doctor do?

□ Your doctor will question you about any self-help treatment you have used. He may prescribe another shampoo.
□ Your doctor will probably report the outbreak of nits to the health authorities too; lice infestation is considered a public health hazard.

What can I do to help?

□ Repeat the treatment seven days later in case any eggs remain.
□ Clean any headgear, brushes or combs that have been used by your child with the anti-louse shampoo.

> **SEE ALSO:**
> **Itching,** *page 170*

Words in **bold** are A-Z entries

Limp

Your child is limping if he is not taking the full weight of his body on one leg as he walks. The cause, on investigation, may be obvious, such as a **cut**, a **blister** or a **splinter** on the sole of the foot or the heel, a protruding toenail, an **ingrowing toenail**, tight shoes, wrinkling of the inner sole in his shoes or a pebble in a shoe. A persistent limp which has no such obvious cause may be a symptom of some other, more serious, problem.

Is it serious?

Limping for no apparent reason should always be treated seriously in a child. An unexplained limp is a symptom of the rare form of blood cancer, **leukaemia**. If the limp is accompanied by swelling or tenderness of the joints, it may be caused by **rheumatic fever**, **arthritis** or **osteomyelitis**. These could have long-term complications and should therefore be treated seriously.

What should I do first?

1 Look for obvious injuries and examine any areas that your child claims are painful.

Check for swelling and tenderness

2 Check to see if the joints are swollen and inflamed.

3 If you suspect your child may have a **broken bone**, don't hesitate to get medical attention. The injury may not always be obvious.

Should I consult the doctor?

Consult your doctor immediately for a thorough investigation of the limp if you can't find a reason for it, or if you suspect a broken bone. Consult your doctor immediately if any of your child's joints is swollen or tender.

What might the doctor do?

☐ Your doctor will examine your child's leg thoroughly and may refer your child to a paediatric orthopaedic surgeon to find the cause of the problem.
☐ If a bone in your child's leg is broken, your doctor will refer your child to the nearest casualty department for an X-ray and to have the leg put into plaster.

What can I do to help?

☐ Never give up if your child has a limp. Continue taking your child to your doctor for investigation and be persistent until the cause is found.

L

SEE ALSO:
Arthritis, *page 56*
Blister, *page 67*
Broken bone, *page 70*
Cuts and grazes, *page 103*
Ingrowing toenail, *page 168*
Leukaemia, *page 173*
Osteomyelitis, *page 193*
Rheumatic fever, *page 207*
Splinter, *page 222*

Measles

Measles is a common infectious childhood disease caused by a virus. It is very contagious and has an incubation period of between eight and 14 days. The first indication of measles is usually symptoms similar to those of a **common cold**, with a **fever** that gets increasingly higher, and small, white spots inside the mouth, on the lining of the cheeks (Koplik's spots). Your child's eyes may also be red and sore. The initial symptoms are followed about three days later by small, brownish-red spots behind the ears that merge together to form a rash over the face and torso.

Is it serious?
Measles is an unpleasant childhood disease but it is not usually serious. However, in rare cases your child may develop complications, such as **otitis media**, **pneumonia** or **encephalitis**.

Possible symptoms

- Runny nose and dry cough.
- Headache.
- Fever, rising as high as 40°C (104°F).
- Small, white spots inside the mouth.
- Red, sore eyes, intolerant of bright light.
- Brownish-red rash of small spots starting behind the ears and spreading to the torso.

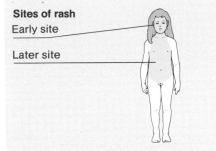

Sites of rash
Early site

Later site

What should I do first?

1 Check your child's temperature. If he has a fever, try to bring it down with tepid sponging (*see page 31*).

2 If his eyes are sore, bathe them with cool water.

3 Make sure he has plenty of fluids by offering small amounts regularly.

Should I consult the doctor?

Consult your doctor as soon as possible to confirm the diagnosis. Consult your doctor immediately if your child gets worse after seemingly recovering from measles, or if he complains of **earache**.

What might the doctor do?

☐ Your doctor will advise you to keep your child in bed for as long as his temperature remains high. He will examine your child's ears to check that there is no ear infection. If there is, he will prescribe antibiotics.

☐ Your doctor may prescribe eye drops for your child's eyes if they are sore.

What can I do to help?

☐ Don't send your child back to school until the rash has faded.

☐ Have any other children inoculated against measles. Immunization is advised at about 13 months of age.

SEE ALSO:
Common cold, *page 90*
Earache, *page 121*
Encephalitis, *page 125*
Fever, *page 134*
Otitis media, *page 196*
Pneumonia, *page 200*

Words in **bold** are A-Z entries

Meningitis

Meningitis is an inflammation of the membranes (*meninges*) that cover the brain and spinal cord, and most frequently results from an infection, either viral or bacterial. Viral meningitis occurs most commonly after **mumps**, but is not a very serious illness. Bacterial meningitis, however, is serious but can be treated successfully with antibiotics if it is diagnosed early enough. The symptoms of meningitis are fever, stiff neck, lethargy, headache, drowsiness and intolerance of bright light; in rare cases, there may also be a purple-red rash. Meningitis can be difficult to diagnose in babies and children, whose inability to communicate what they are feeling may lead to a delay in diagnosis. Under the age of two, the fontanelle will bulge slightly.

Is it serious?
Bacterial meningitis is a very serious disease and, if it is left untreated, it can prove fatal.

Possible symptoms

- Fever, as high as 39°C (102.2°F).
- Stiff neck.
- Lethargy.
- Headache.
- Inability to tolerate bright light.
- Bulging fontanelle.
- Drowsiness and confusion.
- Vomiting.
- Purple-red rash over most of the body.

Cross-section of the meninges

Skull | *Dura* | *Arachnoid*

Pia | *Cerebro-spinal fluid*

M

What should I do first?

1 If you suspect meningitis, or your child has just had mumps, bend your child's head forward so that his chin touches his chest to see if there is any stiffness or pain in his neck.

2 If your child is under two years old, see if he screws his eyes up in bright light. Feel the fontanelle to see if it bulges outwards.

Should I consult the doctor?

Consult your doctor immediately if you suspect meningitis.

What might the doctor do?

☐ Your doctor will refer your child to hospital for a lumbar puncture. This involves taking a sample of spinal fluid from your child for testing and

is done under local anaesthetic.
☐ If your child is suffering from bacterial meningitis, he will be given high doses of antibiotics intravenously. Viral meningitis clears up on its own but your child will be given painkilling drugs to relieve the symptoms.

What can I do to help?

☐ Contact your child's school as meningitis can be contagious.

SEE ALSO:
Drowsiness, *page 117*
Encephalitis, *page 125*
Fever, *page 134*
Headache, *page 155*
Mumps, *page 182*
Vomiting, *page 256*

Migraine

Migraine is a severe, recurrent **headache** (usually felt on only one side of the head) that is accompanied by **vomiting** and, in children, by abdominal pain. For this reason, it is often referred to as abdominal migraine. Migraine tends to run in families and starts in late childhood or in early adolescence. Headaches in younger children are not usually migraine headaches. It is not known what sets off a migraine headache but tension and certain foods, notably cheese and chocolate, are possible causes.

Quite often a migraine headache is preceded by an "aura", a series of strange sensations such as flashing lights, peculiár smells and numbness on the affected side of the head. Most children can pinpoint these sensations clearly.

Is it serious?
Migraine is not serious but it is debilitating.

Possible symptoms

- Severe headache on one side.
- Vomiting.
- Nausea.
- Abdominal pain.
- Paleness.
- Withdrawn, quiet behaviour.
- Aura, involving strange visual and physical sensations, preceding the attack.

What should I do first?

1 Put your child to bed in a cool, darkened room if he complains of headache and nausea. If the headache persists, it is best to give him some paracetamol elixir.

2 Put a bucket next to your child's bed for him to be sick into.

3 If your child complains of abdominal pain check for **appendicitis**, (*see page 53*).

Should I consult the doctor?

Consult your doctor immediately if your child is suffering severe abdominal pain, to exclude the possibility of appendicitis. Consult your doctor as soon as possible if your child suffers from recurrent migraine headaches.

What might the doctor do?

☐ Your doctor will ask your child to describe the headache. Your doctor may prescribe painkilling drugs for an acute attack. If your child's headaches are frequent, your child may be given drugs to take immediately an attack begins, or, in severe cases, to be taken regularly to prevent attacks.

What can I do to help?

☐ If the headaches are frequent, keep a diary of your child's diet to try to pinpoint a possible trigger food. Avoid any suspect foods for a couple of weeks to see if there is any reduction in headaches.

> SEE ALSO:
> **Appendicitis**, *page 53*
> **Headache**, *page 155*
> **Vomiting**, *page 256*

Words in **bold** are A-Z entries

Milia

Milia is a rash of tiny white- or yellow-headed spots that may appear on the nose and cheeks of a newborn baby within the first three weeks of life. The spots appear because the baby's sweat glands are not well enough developed to function properly. They remain until the sweat glands mature, usually within the first three months. The spots are not itchy and give rise to no unpleasant symptoms in the baby.

Is it serious?
Milia is never serious and resolves itself naturally without treatment.

Possible symptoms

● Tiny white or yellow spots, usually over the nose and cheeks.

What should I do first?

1 Do not squeeze the spots. Though they may appear to have heads of pus, they are not infected and the skin of a baby is too fragile to take any pressure or squeezing.

2 Don't put any creams or lotions on the spots.

Should I consult the doctor?

There should be no need to consult your doctor unless you are concerned about the cause of the rash.

What might the doctor do?

☐ Your doctor will reassure you and almost certainly not interfere with the milia.

What can I do to help?

☐ Ignore the milia. The spots will disappear in time.
☐ Try not to be vain about your baby even if you feel the spots make him appear ugly. Milia is very common in newborn babies, so try to relax and wait until they disappear.

Mouth ulcers

Children suffer from a variety of mouth ulcers, all of them painful, though most are relatively harmless. *Aphthous ulcers* are usually small and creamy-white and appear on the tongue, the gums or the lining of the mouth. They may be so painful that your child will be reluctant to eat. These ulcers are sometimes associated with stress and may come in crops during a particularly anxious time such as starting school. A *traumatic ulcer* is larger and usually starts as a sore patch on the inside of the cheeks, possibly after injury by biting or by the rubbing of a rough tooth. It enlarges to form a painful yellow crater. It heals very slowly and, regardless of treatment, takes 10-14 days to clear completely. White, painful blisters on the roof of the mouth, on the gums and inside the cheeks can be the result of a primary infection with the **cold sore** virus. White, curd-like blisters could indicate a **thrush** infection.

Are they serious?
Mouth ulcers are rarely serious, but because they are painful they can interfere with your child's eating.

Possible symptoms

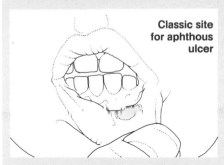

Classic site for aphthous ulcer

● Small, creamy-white, painful, raised areas anywhere on the tongue, gums or lining of the mouth.
● Large red area with a yellow centre, particularly inside the cheeks.
● White blister-like spots inside the mouth, sometimes accompanied by a fever.
● Loss of appetite because eating is painful.

What should I do first?

1 If your child complains of a sore mouth or tongue, check to see if there are any areas of soreness.

2 If the ulcer is large and is inside the cheek, check for a jagged tooth that might be rubbing the cheek lining and causing the injury.

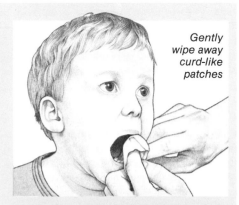

Gently wipe away curd-like patches

3 If the ulcers resemble white curds, try to wipe them off with a handkerchief. If this leaves red, raw patches, the ulcers could be caused by thrush.
Continued on next page ▶

Words in **bold** are A-Z entries

Mouth ulcers

◀ Continued from previous page

4 Smear an antiseptic jelly or glycerine over the ulcers with your fingertip, or give your child some paracetamol elixir

5 If your bottlefed baby has a traumatic ulcer on the roof of his mouth, check the teat. It may be too hard for your baby's tender mouth.

Should I consult the doctor?

Consult your doctor as soon as possible if the ulcers are very painful, or your home treatment (above) doesn't help. Consult your doctor as soon as possible if the mouth ulcers are recurrent. If the ulceration is caused by a jagged tooth, take your child to the dentist to have the tooth smoothed off.

What might the doctor do?

Apply cream regularly

☐ Your doctor will probably prescribe an anti-inflammatory cream for aphthous ulcers. The cream is not dissolved by saliva and therefore clings to the ulcers and speeds healing.
☐ If your child suffers from recurrent mouth ulcers, your doctor will refer him to hospital for blood tests to see if there is an underlying cause, other than stress.

What can I do to help?

☐ Liquidize foods to minimize chewing when the ulcers are most painful. Let your child feed through a straw if he wants.
☐ Don't give your child any salty or acidic foods. These will cause pain. Ice lollies and smooth, bland foods are best.
☐ Discourage your child from biting his lips or cheeks. This can lead to injury of the mouth and lip lining and eventually to ulceration.

M

SEE ALSO:
Cold sore, *page 89*
Thrush, *page 238*

Mumps

Mumps is a common infectious childhood disease, mostly affecting children over the age of two. It is caused by a virus and has an incubation period of 17 to 28 days. Your child will seem generally unwell for a day or two before the major symptoms appear. The salivary glands in front of and beneath the ears and chin swell up and there may be **fever**. The swelling will change the shape of your child's face; it can appear first on one side of the face, then the other, or on both sides at once. The swelling causes pain when swallowing and your child will complain of a dry mouth because the salivary glands have stopped producing saliva. A less common symptom is swelling of the testes or ovaries, causing local pain in boys and abdominal pain and tenderness in girls.

Is it serious?

Mumps is a mild disease. However, if after 10 days your child has a severe headache and a stiff neck, this could be **encephalitis** or **meningitis**, which are serious complications.

Possible symptoms

Affected areas

- Swelling of the glands on either or both sides of the face just below the ears and beneath the chin.
- Pain when swallowing.
- Dry mouth.
- Fever.
- Headache.
- Swollen, painful testes in boys, lower abdominal pain in girls.

What should I do first?

Sponge child to reduce temperature

1 Check your child's temperature to see if he has a fever. If he has, try to bring it down with tepid sponging (*see page 31*).

2 Liquidize your child's food and feed him through a straw if he is having difficulty eating.

3 Give him plenty to drink and encourage him to rinse out his mouth to alleviate the dryness.

4 Put your child to bed with a hot-water bottle wrapped in a towel to hold against the affected side.

Should I consult the doctor?

Consult your doctor as soon as possible to confirm the diagnosis of mumps, or if your son's testes are very painful or your daughter is suffering abdominal pain. Consult your doctor immediately if after 10 days your child's condition has worsened and he has a headache and a stiff neck.

Continued on next page ▶

Words in **bold** are A-Z entries

Mumps

◄ *Continued from previous page*

What might the doctor do?

☐ There is no specific treatment for mumps. Your doctor will advise you to keep your child away from school until five days after the swelling has gone down.

☐ If the testes are swollen, your doctor will advise complete bed rest until the swelling has subsided and he will probably prescribe paracetamol elixir to be taken for the pain of your son's swollen testes or if your daughter has abdominal pain from swollen ovaries.

What can I do to help?

Egg enriched milkshake

Yogurt

☐ Be inventive with liquid foods, such as egg-enriched milk shakes, soups and yogurt, which slip down easily.

M

> **SEE ALSO:**
> **Encephalitis,** *page 125*
> **Fever,** *page 134*
> **Meningitis,** *page 177*

Muscular dystrophy

Muscular dystrophy is the term given to a group of disorders which are usually inherited and result in a gradual wasting and weakening of the muscle fibres. The commonest form of the disease in children is Duchenne muscular dystrophy, which affects only boys. The boy will be slow at developing muscular power. He will be late for his age to sit, walk and run, but only about 25 per cent of boys suffering from this form of muscular dystrophy have any mental handicap. The disorder is usually diagnosed by the time the child is three years old.

As mobility deteriorates your child will walk with a waddling gait and an arched back because of the weakness of the pelvic muscles; he will have difficulty climbing stairs; his calf muscles, though weakened, will appear overdeveloped; and the muscles in the upper arm will also be abnormally large. Walking becomes impossible by the age of about 12. Because there is no known treatment, 75 per cent of sufferers die by the age of 20.

Because the cardiac muscles of muscular dystrophy sufferers also weaken, this increases the risk of serious or persistent chest infections, which can result in sudden death.

Possible symptoms

- Late development in ability to sit, walk and run.
- Waddling gait.
- Difficulty getting upright.
- Difficulty climbing stairs.
- Overdeveloped muscles, particularly noticeable in the calves.
- Deformation of the spine.

M

What can be done?

There is no effective treatment for muscular dystrophy. Sufferers may need to attend a school for the physically handicapped as they will usually be confined to a wheelchair by the age of 12. Until this time, the child should be kept active and walking as long as possible, without strenuous exercise, though, as this hastens the muscle deterioration. The use of lightweight splints and calipers can prolong walking. Too much bed-rest is not advisable as this speeds up muscular disintegration. Physiotherapy treatment is available to limit the physical disability.

As Duchenne muscular dystrophy is carried by women, you should seek genetic counselling before deciding to have a baby if there is any family history of muscular dystrophy. If a pattern of inheritance can be found, there is a 50 per cent chance of a male child being affected and the same chance of a female child being a carrier. Early in pregnancy, amniocentesis, where a sample of amniotic fluid is extracted and examined for defective cells, will determine the child's sex. The pregnant woman can then decide whether to terminate her pregnancy if the fetus is a male child and therefore at a 50 per cent risk of being affected. In the near future, more precise tests for muscular dystrophy will be available early in pregnancy.

FOR HELP AND ADVICE CONTACT:
**Muscular Dystrophy Group
of Great Britain
Nattrass House
35 Macaulay Road
London SW4 0QP**
01-720 8055

Words in **bold** are A-Z entries

Nappy rash

Nappy rash is a skin condition that affects the area normally covered by a baby's nappy, and can occur whether the nappies used are fabric or disposable. The skin may be slightly red, or broken and inflamed with pussy spots.

There are several causes of nappy rash, but it is most commonly caused by urine and stools being left in contact with the skin for too long. The bacteria in the baby's stools break down the urine and release ammonia, a strong irritant. (These bacteria grow best in an alkaline environment, and because the stools of bottlefed babies are alkaline—unlike those of breastfed babies, which are acid—bottlefed babies are much more likely to suffer from ammoniacal nappy rash.) In such cases the rash starts around the genitals, and, if left untreated, the skin becomes tight and shiny and pustules may develop. There is always a strong smell of ammonia from the nappy.

Nappy rash can also be caused by inadequate drying after bathing your baby. In such cases the nappy rash is usually confined to the skin creases at the top of the thighs. If the rash covers most of the

Possible symptoms

● Redness over nappy area.
● Redness which starts around the genitals and is accompanied by a strong smell of ammonia.
● Tight, papery skin with inflamed spots that have pussy centres.
● Redness which starts around the anus and moves over the buttocks and on to the thighs.

nappy area, and you use fabric nappies, nappy rash may be due to an allergic reaction to chemicals in the washing powder used to wash them, or to fabric conditioner. This reaction is an early sign of a form of **eczema**, known as atopic eczema.

A rash that starts around the anus and moves over the buttocks and on to the thighs may not be nappy rash at all but a **thrush** infection.

Is it serious?
Nappy rash is not serious and can be easily prevented and treated at home.

What should I do first?

Apply barrier cream

1 As soon as you notice any redness on your baby's bottom, wash his bottom with warm water and dry thoroughly. Apply liberal quantities of barrier cream, such as zinc oxide ointment, to prevent the urine from irritating his skin.

2 Change nappies and wash your baby's bottom frequently (at least every two to three hours and as soon as he's had a bowel motion). Leave your baby with no nappies on whenever possible.

3 Use one-way disposable nappy liners next to your baby's skin as these are designed to let urine pass through to the nappy while remaining dry next to the baby's bottom.

4 Don't use talcum powder around your baby's genitals. It cakes when wet and irritates the skin.

Continued on next page ▶

Nappy rash

◀ Continued from previous page

Wipe
away
any
white
patches

5 Check inside your baby's mouth. If you notice white patches, try to wipe them off with a clean handkerchief. If they leave raw, red patches, your baby has oral thrush and this may have caused the nappy rash.

Should I consult the doctor?

Consult your doctor as soon as possible if the measures above fail to clear the nappy rash within two or three days, or if you think your baby has thrush.

What might the doctor do?

☐ Your doctor will determine the cause of the nappy rash and will make sure you've been using the most suitable home treatment. He may suggest alternatives.
☐ If the nappy rash has become infected, your doctor may prescribe an antibiotic ointment.
☐ If your baby has the first signs of eczema, your doctor will question you about any washing powders or fabric conditioners you use to wash your baby's nappies and may advise you to change to another brand if your present brand contains a biological component. He may prescribe a cortisone ointment to be used sparingly.
☐ If the nappy rash is caused by thrush, your doctor will prescribe and anti-fungal cream.

What can I do to help?

☐ Continue to change your baby's nappies frequently, and always after a bowel motion.
☐ Try to use plastic pants as rarely as possible. They stop air from circulating around your baby's bottom.
☐ Wash your baby's fabric nappies thoroughly. Sterilize in nappy sterilizing solution, wash in very hot water and rinse them thoroughly to get rid of all traces of detergent and ammonia.
☐ If the condition is recurrent, change the type of nappies you use from one brand of disposables to another, or to cloth (or vice versa).

N

SEE ALSO:
Eczema, *page 123*
Thrush, *page 238*

Words in **bold** are A-Z entries

Nephritis

Nephritis is a disease that affects the kidneys, and it develops after a streptococcal infection such as **tonsillitis**. To combat this infection the body produces antibodies, but due to a defect in the body's immune system these antibodies may go on working after the infection has passed and begin to harm the kidneys, which become inflamed and cease to function normally. The condition comes on suddenly in children and produces symptoms of reddish-brown urine and mild swelling of the face and ankles.

Is it serious?
If nephritis goes untreated it can develop into a more serious disorder known as nephrotic syndrome.

Possible symptoms
- Reddish-brown urine.
- Slight swelling of the face, ankles and abdomen (oedema).
- Headache.
- High blood pressure.

What should I do first?

1 If your child has recently had a sore throat and you notice that he has reddish-brown urine, check to see if he has eaten any beetroot. This can cause red colouring of the urine.

2 If you notice that your child's face is puffy and swollen, check his ankles and abdomen for swelling.

Should I consult the doctor?

Consult your doctor immediately if you notice reddish-brown urine (and it is not related to something your child may have eaten) or if your child has any unusual swelling of the face, ankles or abdomen.

What might the doctor do?

☐ Your doctor will test your child's urine, take his blood pressure and take a sample of his blood for analysis.
☐ Your child will probably be admitted to hospital for bed rest, and a special diet will be suggested to reduce salt, fluid and protein levels.

☐ If a streptococcal infection is still present, your child will be prescribed antibiotics. His blood pressure will be closely monitored too.
☐ Once your child's urine has returned to normal, he will be allowed home. There is usually a complete recovery in one to two weeks.
☐ If there is a chronic condition, your child will have regular check-ups.

What can I do to help?

Take your child to see your doctor whenever he has a severe sore throat or has any other streptococcal infection such as **impetigo.**

N

SEE ALSO:
Impetigo, *page 165*
Rheumatic fever, *page 207*
Sore throat, *page 220*
Tonsillitis, *page 241*

Nightmares

Everyone dreams, and most children have occasional unpleasant dreams or nightmares. Your child may wake screaming in a panic or sobbing uncontrollably. He will seem to be in a state half-way between consciousness and sleep, with his eyes open, though he will not be in touch with reality and he may not even recognize you or understand what you are saying to him.

Nightmares can occur for a number of reasons. If your child has a high temperature or is uncomfortable because of illness, he may wake hot and frightened in the night. If he has gone to bed over-tired, he may wake crying within an hour or two of going to sleep. He may have seen a frightening television programme just before going to bed; he may be scared of the dark, or dislike being alone in his bedroom. In normal children, if nightmares occur with any frequency, the underlying cause is usually anxiety about school or home life, for example, the arrival of a new baby.

Are they serious?
Nightmares are not serious and don't require medical attention unless they occur very frequently.

What should I do first?

Go to your child immediately; don't let him get too hysterical. Turn on the light, hold him close to you and speak quietly to soothe him. Don't raise your voice and scold him; this may make him hysterical. Don't ask him why he woke frightened, or what his dream was about. Stay with your child until he drifts back to sleep.

Should I consult the doctor?

Consult your doctor for advice if the nightmares are frequent (every night, for example) and your child is losing sleep because of them.

What might the doctor do?

☐ Your doctor will probably do nothing but reassure you that your child will grow out of the habit.
☐ If your child is losing sleep, your doctor may prescribe a mild sedative to help him sleep.

What can I do to help?

☐ If he is old enough to explain, ask him what he thinks might have caused the nightmare but wait till the following day to do so.
☐ Try to reduce your child's anxiety by reassuring him. If you can guess the cause of his tension, such as the arrival of a new baby, do your best to allay his fears.

Nose, foreign body in

If there is a foreign body in your child's nose, it is most likely to have been pushed in by your child or a playmate. The problem may not be noticed by you or your child at first, but after two or three days there will be a **nosebleed**, or a blood-stained, foul-smelling discharge from the affected nostril.

Is it serious?

If the foreign body can be easily removed from the nose, it is not serious and should have no after-effects. The situation becomes serious, however, if your child inhales the object into his lungs. This may partially block the air passages causing breathing difficulties, **croup** or **choking.**

Possible symptoms

● Nosebleeds.
● Smelly, blood-stained discharge from the nostril.
● Red, swollen, tender area over the nose.
● Peculiar odour on your child's breath, sometimes said to smell like ripe cheese.

What should I do first?

Blow the affected nostril

1 If your child is old enough to understand, ask him to hold a finger against the good nostril (or do this for him) and blow the affected one. This may dislodge the foreign body. Don't ask a young child to do this—he might sniff the object back into his air passages.

2 Alternatively, lay your child on his back on a flat surface and shine a light on his face. If the object can be seen near the entrance to the nose, and if it is soft, remove it with tweezers. If it moves further up the nostril leave it alone. If your child has breathing problems, treat this as an emergency.

Should I consult the doctor?

Consult your doctor immediately or take your child to the nearest casualty department if you cannot easily remove a foreign body from your child's nose.

What might the doctor do?

☐ Your doctor will remove the foreign body with a pair of forceps. If your child is very young, or refuses to stay still, he may have to be taken to hospital and have the foreign body removed under general anaesthetic.

What can I do to help?

☐ Try not to allow a child under the age of three to play with toys or objects small enough to swallow or put up his nose.

> **SEE ALSO:**
> **Croup,** *page 100*
> **Nosebleed,** *page 190*

N

Nosebleed

A nosebleed occurs when a small area of blood vessels on the inner surface of the nose ruptures. This can be caused by hard nose blowing or sneezing when your child has a **common cold** or **hayfever**, by a knock on the nose, by picking the nose, or by a foreign body in the nose; in this last case the blood will be accompanied by a foul-smelling dis-charge. The blood loss from a nosebleed can look dramatic, but is usually very little.

Is it serious?
A nosebleed is hardly ever serious. However, if your child has frequent nosebleeds which don't stop easily, or if his nose bleeds after a blow to the head, medical advice should be sought.

What should I do first?

Pinch the nostrils

Don't try to staunch the blood by pushing anything into the nostrils. Sit your child down with his head forward over a basin or sink. Apply firm pressure to both nostrils, gripping his nose between your thumb and forefinger just where the bone ends. Squeeze for 10 minutes or until the bleeding stops. Don't let your child put his head back during a nosebleed. This allows blood to drip down the back of the nose into the stomach and can cause irritation and vomiting.

Should I consult the doctor?

Consult your doctor immediately if the nosebleed fails to stop after 30 minutes and your child is dizzy and pale. Consult your doctor as soon as possible if you think there may be a foreign body in your child's nose, or if the nosebleeds are frequent.

What might the doctor do?

☐ If your child has suffered a blow to the head, your doctor will probably arrange for an X-ray to discount the possibility of a fractured skull.
☐ If the nosebleed has failed to stop, your doctor will pack your child's nose with gauze to stem the blood flow. This will be done under a local anaesthetic. The gauze can be removed after a couple of hours.
☐ If your child has a foreign object stuck in his nose, your doctor will remove it, under local anaesthetic if necessary.
☐ If the nosebleeds are frequent, your doctor may refer you to an ear, nose and throat specialist for assessment. If the recurrent nosebleeds are caused by a fragile blood vessel the specialist may cauterize it. This involves burning off the end of the vessel, and is done under a general anaesthetic.

What can I do to help?

☐ Don't let your child blow his nose for at least three hours after a nose-bleed. The bleeding might start again.

SEE ALSO:
Common cold, *page 90*
Hayfever, *page 151*
Nose, foreign body in, *page 189*

Words in **bold** are A-Z entries

Obesity

A child is termed obese, or overweight, if he is 20 per cent heavier than the average for his height and age (*see page 304*). A child is not obese if he merely has a protruding tummy or round, chubby-cheeked face, both of which are quite common in children under the age of five. The best test for obesity is to look at the upper arms and thighs of your child: if there are rolls of fat, your child probably has a weight problem.

Obesity in babies and children is rarely due to any kind of family trait or hormonal disease. It is nearly always due to bad feeding habits, chiefly overfeeding by parents. It's for this reason that parents of a fat child rarely see that there's a weight problem.

Is it serious?

Obesity in children is serious. There will be an emotional strain on the child when he is teased by his playmates. More importantly, fat children tend to grow into fat adults who run higher than normal risks of heart disease, high blood pressure and joint disorders.

Possible symptoms

Overweight baby   *Normal-weight baby*

● Twenty per cent or more above average weight for height and age.
● Rolls of fat around the thighs, upper arms, breasts and chin.
● Breathlessness on exertion.

What should I do first?

1 Weigh your child and check the charts on page 304 to see if he is heavier than normal for his age.

2 Examine your child for rolls of fat around his upper arms and thighs, and see whether there are over-developed breasts.

3 Look at his diet. Do you give him high-calorie foods such as syrup drinks, lots of white flour and sugar products?

4 Compare your child with his playmates—is he as physically active?

Should I consult the doctor?

Consult your doctor as soon as possible if you think your child has a weight problem. If you are overweight your-self, you may be confusing your child's natural plumpness with the more serious problem of obesity. Your doctor can advise you.

What might the doctor do?

□ Your doctor will examine your child. In the rare cases in which obesity is due to a glandular disorder your doctor will refer your child to an endocrin-ologist (a specialist in hormonal disorders) for investigation.
□ If no disease is suspected, your doctor will give you advice on diet and advise you to encourage your child to use up more energy.

Continued on next page ▶

Obesity

◀ *Continued from previous page*

What can I do to help?

☐ Consider whether obesity is a family problem. If you plan changes in your child's diet, you should adopt these yourself to set an example. Find out about how to eat healthily.

Fresh fruit and vegetables

Wholemeal bread

☐ Don't put your child on a special diet to lose weight. Instead, change his diet to include more unrefined, fibre-rich foods such as wholemeal flour, brown rice, fresh fruit and vegetables. Cut out refined flours and sugar in cooking, and avoid cakes, biscuits, sweets and sugary drinks.
☐ Try not to fry food; grill or steam instead. Cut the fat off the meat before cooking.
☐ Always make up feeds using the correct amount of formula.
☐ Don't give your baby snacks of rusks or biscuits, both of which are full of sugar; give him dried wholemeal toast or pieces of celery or apple instead.
☐ Dilute fresh fruit juice with water, and avoid carbonated and squash drinks.
☐ Encourage your child to be active. Don't confine a toddler to a playpen or pushchair; let him use up his energy by crawling or walking. Play lively games with him.

Words in **bold** are A-Z entries

Osteomyelitis

Osteomyelitis is an extremely rare bacterial infection of the bone. Although it can affect any bone in the body, those of the arms and legs are the most commonly affected. The infection may arise because of an injury to the bone itself, or it may be carried in the blood from an infected cut elsewhere in the body. Pus forms in the bone and the area becomes tender and painful. Within a day or two the skin over the bone swells, and, if left untreated, a pus-filled abscess will form on the skin's surface.

Is it serious?
Osteomyelitis is always serious and can result in bone deformity or stiffness.

Possible symptoms

- Extreme pain and tenderness over an affected bone, usually in the arms or legs.
- Red, swollen area after a day or two, which may develop into a pus-filled abscess.
- Reluctance to use or move the affected part.
- Limping if the infection is in a leg.
- High temperature.
- Loss of appetite.

What should I do first?

1 If your child suddenly complains of pain in a limb, try to find out whether he has knocked himself or suffered an injury to the affected part.

Examine the limbs for tenderness

2 Try to determine how painful the area is by pressing it gently and noting your child's reaction.

3 Take your child's temperature to see if he has a fever.

4 Put your child to bed to rest the affected part.

Should I consult the doctor?

Consult your doctor immediately if your child has a fever and is in great pain for no apparent reason.

What might the doctor do?

☐ Your doctor will probably admit your child to hospital for blood tests and X-rays to make a definite diagnosis. If osteomyelitis is confirmed, your child will be given antibiotics.
☐ If an abscess has formed, the pus-infected bone and skin will be cleaned out surgically under an anaesthetic. The cavity left behind may take some time to heal completely but new bone usually forms within six months.

What can I do to help?

☐ If possible, try to stay with your child in hospital. When he is discharged, help him to exercise the affected limb according to instructions given by the hospital physiotherapist.

O

SEE ALSO:
Limp, *page 175*

Otitis externa

Otitis externa is an infection of the external ear canal—the passage which leads from the ear flap (pinna) to the eardrum. The infection may be caused by a foreign body in the ear, by a **boil** in the canal, or as the result of damage to the skin from over-vigorous cleaning or scratching. The infection is more common in children who swim a great deal. The symptoms of the infection are **earache**, inflammation, swelling, itchiness, dry, scaly skin or a discharge.

Is it serious?
As the external ear canal does not contain the ear's delicate hearing mechanisms, the infection is relatively minor. However, otitis externa should always be treated because the infection could spread to the bones of the skull, and possibly the brain. Any discharge from the ear should be treated seriously as this could be a symptom of the serious middle ear infection, **otitis media**.

Possible symptoms
- Earache.
- Redness and tenderness of the ear flap and external ear canal.
- Pus-filled boil in the canal.

Area affected

- Discharge from the ear.
- Itchy, dry, scaly ear.

What should I do first?

1 Look at the ear and into the external ear canal to check for any signs of infection or foreign objects. Remove the foreign object if you can do so easily.

2 Do not push or poke anything into your child's ear, and discourage him from touching or scratching it if it's sore.

3 Ask your child to open his mouth as wide as possible to see if this causes pain.

4 Pull back gently on the ear flap to see if this causes pain.

5 Clean away any discharge with warm water and soap.

6 Give your child a dose of paracetamol elixir to relieve pain, and place a cotton-wool pad over the ear to absorb any discharge.

Should I consult the doctor?

Consult your doctor as soon as possible if you notice any discharge from your child's ear or if you suspect infection of the external ear canal.

What might the doctor do?

☐ Your doctor will examine your child's ear with an otoscope and may then clean out the ear with a probe. He will probably prescribe antibiotic ear drops or tablets to clear up the infection.

☐ If there is still a foreign body in your child's ear, your doctor will remove it or refer your child to hospital for its removal.

☐ If the pain is the result of a boil, your doctor may lance it and drain the pus away; this will relieve the pain almost immediately.

Continued on next page ▶

Words in **bold** are A-Z entries

Otitis externa

◀ *Continued from previous page*

What can I do to help?

☐ Give your child junior paracetamol tablets or elixir on the advice of your doctor if the condition is still painful.

☐ Prevent water from entering the ear during bathing until the infection has cleared. Don't let your child go swimming.

Only wash the pinna

☐ Don't interfere with your child's external ear canal. Wash around the pinna but never poke cotton-wool swabs into the area to clear wax, for example. Wax is not abnormal. It is a natural lubricant, keeping infection at bay. Any cotton wool or twisted piece of facecloth will only push the wax further into the canal or damage the lining, increasing the chances of infection.
☐ Never use patent eardrops unless your doctor advises them.

O

SEE ALSO:
Boil, *page 68*
Earache, *page 121*
Ear, foreign body in, *page 129*
Otitis media, *page 196*

Otitis media

Otitis media is infection of the middle ear. The infection causes fluid to build up in the middle ear, producing **earache** and sometimes **deafness**. It is common in young children because the tube connecting the throat with the ear, the Eustachian tube, is relatively short, and because children spend a lot of time lying down. This means that any bacteria or viruses that invade the nose or throat have only to make a short journey to reach the middle ear. The infection may also result when enlarged adenoids block the entrance to the Eustachian tube. If the tube is blocked, mucus will not be able to drain away and may become sticky and glue-like, producing a condition known as **glue ear**.

Is it serious?

Otitis media is both painful and serious. If left untreated it can result in permanent loss of hearing.

Possible symptoms

- Severe pain in the ear; in a baby, the pulling or rubbing of an ear accompanied by crying.
- Temperature of over 39°C (102.2°F).
- Vomiting.
- Partial deafness.
- Pussy discharge from the ear.

Cross-section of the ear

Middle ear cavity

Eustachian tube

What should I do first?

1 Take your child's temperature to see if he has a fever.

2 Keep your child comfortable and cool. If the pain in the ear is severe, a well-wrapped hot-water bottle placed against it may relieve the pain.

3 Give your child junior paracetamol tablets or elixir to relieve the earache.

4 Check for any discharge from the ear.

Should I consult the doctor?

Consult your doctor immediately if you suspect a middle ear infection. Consult your doctor as soon as possible if you suspect any hearing loss.

What might the doctor do?

☐ Your doctor will examine your child's ear with an otoscope and will probably prescribe antibiotics to clear up the infection. If there is any build-up of fluid in the Eustachian tube, your doctor may also prescribe a drug to reduce swelling so that the fluid can drain away naturally down the throat.

☐ If the attacks are recurrent, your doctor will refer your child to an ear nose and throat (ENT) specialist for assessment.

What can I do to help?

☐ Check your child's hearing regularly (*see page 107*).

> **SEE ALSO:**
> **Deafness,** *page 107*
> **Earache,** *page 121*
> **Glue ear,** *page 144*

Words in **bold** are A-Z entries

Paronychia

A paronychia is an infection of the fold of the skin at the side of a fingernail or toenail. The bacteria which cause the infection are able to enter the skin if it is soggy because of prolonged immersion in water, or if the nail or adjacent skin is constantly picked at or bitten. While pus is building up in the nail fold the area will be painful.

Is it serious?
A paronychia is not serious and can be easily treated. Sometimes a fungus such as *Candida albicans*, which causes **thrush**, can complicate a paronychia and give rise to a chronic condition that has a greater risk of deformity and requires prolonged treatment.

Possible symptoms

Area affected

● Redness and swelling around the nail fold.
● Pus under or next to the nail.
● Throbbing pain.

What should I do first?

1 If your child complains of a throbbing pain around a nail and you can see that pus has collected under the skin, don't try to let the pus out yourself—you may damage the nail bed.

2 Apply a warm compress or a pad of cotton wool soaked in warm water to bring the pus to a head. It should then burst or drain away naturally.

3 Protect the finger or toe from knocks with a thick pad of cotton wool and a plaster.

Should I consult the doctor?

Consult your doctor as soon as possible if the pus does not drain within a few hours of coming to a head, or if the pain is severe.

What might the doctor do?

☐ If pus has collected, your doctor will probably lance it and let the pus drain away. This is usually done under a local anaesthetic. Sometimes, if the condition is severe, a small piece of nail has to be removed under anaesthetic to allow the pus to drain. This relieves the pain immediately.
☐ If there is an acute infection, your doctor will prescribe antibiotics to be taken by mouth, or in cream form to be spread on the nail, to eradicate the bacterial infection.
☐ If the paronychia fails to improve, your doctor may refer you to a dermatologist to see whether or not there is a fungal infection. If so, your child may be prescribed antifungal cream or tablets.

What can I do to help?

☐ Keep your child's nails short and file any rough pieces that your child may bite to make smooth.
☐ Discourage your child from biting or picking at his nails or at the skin around the edge of the nail.

SEE ALSO:
Thrush, *page 238*

P

Penis caught in zip

This situation may arise if your son is hurrying after going to the toilet or is not paying attention to what he's doing when he gets dressed, and catches both skin and fabric in the teeth of the zip.

Is it serious?

There should be no serious complications, but the pain your child will be suffering means that you should treat this as an emergency.

What should I do first?

1 Don't touch the penis or the zip unless you're sure that you can separate the two quickly and easily.

2 If your child will let you, place a cold compress or blocks of ice tied in a clean cloth over the zip and penis. This should numb the area and relieve the pain while you get help.

Should I consult the doctor?

Consult your doctor immediately or take your child to the nearest casualty department.

What might the doctor do?

Your doctor will inject a local anaesthetic into your child's penis. Because this can be painful, try to distract your son's attention while it is being done. When the penis is thoroughly numb, your doctor will undo the zip.

What can I do to help?

☐ Apply a thin smear of antiseptic cream to the damaged penis three or four times a day to soothe the area and prevent infection. Let your child do it if he wants to.

☐ Leave the skin open to the air as much as possible to promote healing and prevent rubbing.

☐ Give your child a bowl of warm water to pour over his penis as he urinates to stop the stinging. He will probably complain that it is painful to pass urine for about 48 hours.

☐ Keep your child quiet and calm so that he doesn't accidentally knock himself. There will be bruising and swelling for about four or five days.

☐ Give your child paracetamol elixir if he's in pain.

Words in **bold** are A-Z entries

Phimosis

Phimosis is the name given to an abnormal tightness of the foreskin which prevents it from being drawn back over the tip (*glans*) of the penis. Phimosis can result in infections such as **balanitis** because the penis cannot be properly cleansed; it may also cause problems with urination and pain with erections. If the foreskin fails to loosen naturally, circumcision is usually recommended.

Is it serious?

Abnormal tightness of the foreskin after the age of five should be treated seriously because of the pain and discomfort it may cause, and because of the increased risk of infection.

Possible symptoms

● Foreskin cannot be drawn back over the tip of the penis.
● Urine does not come out in a steady stream; It either dribbles out slowly or the foreskin balloons with the pressure of the urine, which sprays out in all directions.

What should I do first?

Never attempt to force the foreskin back, especially if your child is under five years old.

Should I consult the doctor?

Consult your doctor as soon as possible if you are concerned about the condition or if the foreskin has not loosened naturally by the time your child is five or six years old. Consult your doctor as soon as possible if either you or your child have forced the foreskin back and it will not slide forwards again.

What might the doctor do?

☐ Your doctor may refer you to a surgeon for permanent correction of the condition by circumcision. Your child will be admitted to hospital, and the foreskin will be removed under a general anaesthetic. Your child will be discharged from hospital within 24 hours.
☐ Your doctor will return the foreskin to its normal position if it has been pulled back and won't return.

What can I do to help?

☐ Try not to worry about the condition if your son is under five years old; it may correct itself in time.
☐ Make sure your child bathes frequently. A warm bath is the best way to keep an uncircumcised penis clean and to prevent infection. Retraction of the foreskin to clean the penis should not be necessary.
☐ If your child has just been circumcised, give him baths with a handful of salt in them twice a day for a couple of days to promote healing.
☐ Let him go about with no pants on—anything rubbing on a recently circumcised penis will make it sore.
☐ Give your newly circumcised child a bowl of warm water to pour over his penis when he urinates. There will be some pain urinating for about 48 hours after the circumcision operation.

P

SEE ALSO:
Balanitis, *page 62*

Pneumonia

Pneumonia is the term used to describe inflammation of the lungs. It may be caused by viral or bacterial infection, or by a foreign body which has been inhaled into the lungs. In young children, pneumonia is nearly always due to an upper respiratory infection such as a **common cold** or **influenza** spreading to the lungs. It can also be caused by **bronchitis** (when it is known as bronchopneumonia). Certain underlying conditions predispose to bronchopneumonia: these include **asthma**, **cystic fibrosis**, **whooping cough** and **measles**.

Older children may contract a type of pneumonia known as lobar pneumonia, where one or more of the lobes of the lungs may be infected by the *pneumococcus bacterium*. This form of pneumonia can start without warning, even when there is no other infection present.

The common symptom of all types of pneumonia is difficulty in breathing; with bronchopneumonia there will also be a noticeable deterioration of an existing illness and a high temperature.

Is it serious?
Pneumonia is always serious.

Possible symptoms

● Difficulty in breathing: the nostrils flare, the chest wall sinks with every breath, and efforts to breathe produce grunting sounds.
● Dry cough.
● Fever, up to 39°C (102.2°F).
● Vomiting and diarrhoea.
● Pain in the chest, made worse by deep breathing.

What should I do first?

1 If your child has an upper respiratory infection or an infectious illness and his condition worsens instead of getting better, look out for a dry cough and breathing difficulty.

2 Take your child's temperature to see if he has a fever. If he has, try to bring his temperature down with tepid sponging (*see page 31*).

Give frequent drinks

3 Give your child plenty of fluids to prevent him becoming dehydrated.

Continued on next page ▶

Words in **bold** are A-Z entries

Pneumonia

◀ Continued from previous page

Should I consult the doctor?

Consult your doctor immediately if your child's condition worsens and breathing becomes difficult. Any breathing problems in a child warrant immediate medical attention.

What might the doctor do?

☐ Your doctor will examine your child and he may prescribe antibiotics. If your doctor is in any doubt about the presence of pneumonia, your child may be sent to hospital so that he can be supervised and given a chest X-ray and oxygen if necessary.
☐ Your doctor will advise you about nursing procedures if your child is to be treated at home.

What can I do to help?

Prop your child up to ease breathing

☐ Prop your child up in bed; this may help his breathing.
☐ Keep the room moderately warm and well ventilated, but not hot and stuffy.
☐ Give your child plenty of fluids. When he feels like eating, give him foods that are easy to digest such as yogurt, fruits and soups.
☐ If he is feverish and too lethargic to go to the bathroom for a wash, give him a sponge-down to refresh him.

SEE ALSO:
Asthma, *page 58*
Bronchitis, *page 73*
Common cold, *page 90*
Cystic fibrosis, *page 105*
Influenza, *page 166*
Measles, *page 176*
Whooping cough, *page 259*

Poliomyelitis

Poliomyelitis (Polio) is a viral infection of the spinal cord and nerves. Polio has the same symptoms as many other viral infections, with a **fever**, **sore throat**, **headache** and stiff neck. In many cases, the disease does not progress to paralysis and there is a complete recovery without polio even being suspected. If it does progress, however, there is, most commonly, paralysis of the lower limbs, making walking difficult or even impossible. The disease is carried in the stools of an infected person and can quickly reach epidemic proportions. It is now entirely preventable with an immunization course of three doses of a vaccine taken by mouth.

Is it serious?
Polio is always serious. If it is not diagnosed and progresses, permanent paralysis will occur.

Possible symptoms
- High temperature, rising to 39°C (102.2°F).
- Sore throat.
- Headache.
- Pain and stiffness in the neck.
- Vomiting.
- Weakness.
- Paralysis of muscles, usually in the lower limbs, or in the chest causing breathlessness.

What should I do first?
If you know of any cases of polio in your community, be on the alert if you notice that your child has the symptoms of **influenza** with a stiff and painful neck and a fever.

Should I consult the doctor?

Consult your doctor immediately if your child has 'flu-like symptoms and then has difficulty in moving his limbs or becomes breathless—even if he has been immunized against polio.

What might the doctor do?

☐ Your doctor will admit your child to hospital for assessment if polio is suspected. Absolute quiet and bed-rest are the only treatment for polio, since antibiotics have no effect on viral illness. Your child may be returned home if you can manage the special nursing he will require.

☐ If your child is nursed at home, your doctor and physiotherapist will advise you about the diet and exercise regime your child should follow.

What can I do to help?

☐ Immunize your baby against polio within the first year of life. (The polio vaccine is given with the "triple vaccine", DTP, on the standard immunization schedule.) Even though polio is no longer the menace it once was, there is no reason for complacency. Risks from the vaccine are virtually unknown.

> SEE ALSO:
> **Fever,** *page 134*
> **Headache,** *page 155*
> **Influenza,** *page 166*
> **Sore throat,** *page 220*

Words in **bold** are A-Z entries

Pyloric stenosis

Pyloric stenosis is a congenital condition—that is, it is present at birth. The ring of muscle (*pylorus*), which links the stomach to the duodenum, thickens and narrows, preventing the contents of the stomach from passing through it to the intestine. The cause of this is not known, but when the baby is about one month old the symptoms begin. Food builds up in the stomach, which contracts powerfully in an attempt to force the food through the thickened pylorus. Because this is impossible, milk is vomited up violently after a feed. This is known as projectile **vomiting**, and the unpleasant-smelling milk curds and mucus can be thrown a metre or two (up to two yards) away. Projectile vomiting should not be confused with possetting, in which a baby naturally regurgitates milk after a feed.

Is it serious?
Pyloric stenosis is serious. The vomiting eventually leads to **dehydration** and a failure to thrive.

Possible symptoms

● Projectile vomiting after a feed, beginning at around four weeks of age.
● Failure to thrive.
● Weakness and listlessness.
● Lack of bowel movements.

Cross-section of the pylorus

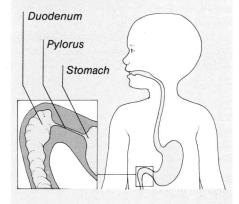

Duodenum

Pylorus

Stomach

What should I do first?

1 If your baby vomits violently after three consecutive feeds, consult your doctor immediately.

2 While you are waiting for medical attention, feed your baby frequent but small amounts of milk to keep up his fluid levels.

Should I consult the doctor?

Consult your doctor immediately if your baby vomits violently after every feed.

What might the doctor do?

□ If pyloric stenosis is suspected, your doctor will refer your baby to hospital. A paediatrician will examine your baby's abdomen during a feed to see if the enlarged pylorus can be felt.

□ A simple surgical operation to widen the thickened pylorus will be performed, giving a complete cure.

What can I do to help?

□ Stay with your baby in hospital. After the operation you will be advised to feed your baby gradually increasing amounts of milk. Forty-eight hours after the operation, his feeding routine should be back to normal.

SEE ALSO:
Dehydration, *page 108*
Vomiting, *page 256*

Rash

A skin rash can be a symptom of infection, either in the skin or elsewhere. It can also be an allergic reaction to something on the skin, or part of the body's reaction to an irritating chemical or to physical damage.

Many childhood infectious diseases have a rash as one of their main symptoms, among them **chickenpox**, **German measles** and **measles**. Localized rashes may be the result of a skin infestation by **scabies** mites, or **ringworm** fungus. A child who is allergic to a drug may break out in a rash when he takes the drug. Nettles and certain other plants cause a rash when touched.

The skin condition known as purpura looks like a rash but is the result of a blood disorder. If there is a problem with the blood's clotting mechanism, tiny areas of bleeding tend to occur in the skin, looking like small spidery "spots". These marks do not itch, nor are there other skin changes. Purpuric marks can be distinguished from other rashes by pressing the side of a drinking glass gently on them; if the marks are still visible, this indicates purpura. A purpuric rash may be brought on by infection or sensitivity to certain drugs.

Is it serious?

Skin rashes themselves are hardly ever serious, though they may be irritating. However, you should never ignore a rash since it may indicate a serious underlying illness. Purpuric rash, in particular, may be a symptom of a serious disorder such as **leukaemia**, **hepatitis** or **meningitis** as well as sensitivity to a drug.

What should I do first?

1 Note where the rash is on your child, and whether it has spread from one part of his body to another. He could have one of the common infections like chickenpox, measles or German measles.

2 Take his temperature to see if he has a fever.

3 Check whether your child has eaten something new (like shellfish or strawberries) or whether he has started a course of medicine (for example, penicillin).

4 Check whether your child has any symptoms of infestation, especially if his skin is very itchy between the fingers. This could indicate scabies.

Test for purpura

5 Press a drinking glass against your child's skin to see if the rash remains visible; the rash could be purpuric.

6 If the rash is itchy, use calamine lotion to relieve the irritation.

Should I consult the doctor?

Consult your doctor as soon as possible for an accurate diagnosis of your child's rash. Consult your doctor immediately if the rash is purpuric and your child has a fever: these two symptoms together could indicate meningitis.

Continued on next page ▶

Words in **bold** are A-Z entries

Rash

◄ *Continued from previous page*

What might the doctor do?

☐ Your doctor will examine your child to determine the cause of the rash, which will then be treated accordingly.
☐ If the rash is purpuric, your doctor will arrange for a blood test to determine the cause.

What can I do to help?

☐ If the rash is itchy, baths with a handful of bicarbonate of soda added to the water will ease the irritation.
☐ Keep your child's skin cool to reduce irritation.

Keep nails short

☐ Discourage your child from scratching the rash. Keep his hands clean and his nails short to prevent damage to the skin if he does scratch it.

R

SEE ALSO:
Chickenpox, *page 82*
German measles, *page 141*
Hepatitis, *page 159*
Leukaemia, *page 173*
Measles, *page 176*
Meningitis, *page 177*
Ringworm, *page 208*
Scabies, *page 210*

Reye's syndrome

Reye's syndrome is a childhood illness in which the child suddenly becomes ill with **vomiting** and **fever**. The body's reaction to the illness causes the brain to become inflamed, so your child may also become delirious and even lapse into unconsciousness and then a coma. Reye's syndrome usually occurs a few days after a child has had **chickenpox** or **influenza**, and it is particularly associated with these illnesses when aspirin was used to relieve symptoms or to reduce temperature. The cause of Reye's syndrome is only now becoming clear: a virus or some other poisonous agent damages cells in various parts of the body. However, only certain children

Possible symptoms
- Uncontrollable vomiting.
- Fever.
- Delirium.
- Drowsiness or unconsciouness.

seem susceptible. It is thought that susceptibility may be related to the body's inability to deal with certain chemical substances, especially fats.

Is it serious?
Reye's syndrome is very serious and can result in death if it is not identified quickly. It is, however, rare.

What should I do first?

1 If your child is recovering from chickenpox or influenza and he starts to vomit, take his temperature to see if he has a fever.

2 If he does have a fever, consult your doctor immediately. While waiting for medical help, *do not* give him any form of aspirin. Try tepid sponging (*see page 31*) to lower his temperature.

3 Consult your doctor immediately if your child has been vomiting and subsequently becomes drowsy or difficult to rowse.

Should I consult the doctor?

Consult your doctor immediately, or call an ambulance if there is any delay, if your child has a fever or has become drowsy and difficult to rouse.

What might the doctor do?

☐ If your doctor suspects Reye's syndrome, he will admit your child to hospital immediately. Usually a physical examination is all that is necessary to confirm the diagnosis, but if there is

any doubt, the doctor will remove a tiny piece of liver under local anaesthetic, using a hollow needle (a procedure called liver biopsy). This sample will then be analyzed for abnormal fat distribution, which is characteristic of the illness.
☐ Your child will be treated in an intensive care unit and given intravenous glucose. Various measures will be taken to control swelling of the brain.

What can I do to help?

☐ Stay with your child in hospital if possible.
☐ Be prepared for a long convalescence. Ask about any special precautions that should be taken to avoid a recurrence of the syndrome.

SEE ALSO:
Chickenpox, *page 82*
Fever, *page 134*
Influenza, *page 166*
Vomiting, *page 256*

R

Words in **bold** are A-Z entries

Rheumatic fever

Rheumatic fever is a rare disease characterized by inflammation of the joints and the heart. It is caused by an allergic response to streptococcal bacteria which exist in the throat, where they cause such infections as **tonsillitis**.

Rheumatic fever usually begins within a week or two of a throat or ear infection (for example, **otitis media**) and produces symptoms of general ill health, with fever and aching joints. In some cases there may be a circular, blotchy red rash on the trunk and limbs. Rheumatic fever is now less common because streptococcal infections are usually treated with antibiotics at an early stage.

Is it serious?

Rheumatic fever can have serious consequences. The earlier the treatment, the less likelihood there is of any heart disease in later life.

Possible symptoms

- Fever.
- Swollen, painful joints.
- Blotchy, circular red rash on the trunk and limbs.
- Chest pain.
- Listlessness.
- Loss of appetite.

Areas affected

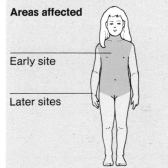

Early site

Later sites

What should I do first?

1 If your child has recently had tonsillitis or an ear infection, and complains of pain in his joints when he should be getting better, check to see if he has a fever.

Check for tenderness

2 Feel for swelling and tenderness by pressing on and around the major joints.

3 Look for a circular rash on your child's trunk and limbs.

Should I consult the doctor?

Consult your doctor immediately if you suspect rheumatic fever.

What might the doctor do?

☐ Your doctor will admit your child to hospital for bed-rest and medication.
☐ After he has recovered, your child will be given penicillin for many years to prevent a recurrence of rheumatic fever.

> **SEE ALSO:**
> **Otitis media,** *page 196*
> **Sore throat,** *page 220*
> **Tonsillitis,** *page 241*

Ringworm

Ringworm is a fungal infection of the skin and hair that shows itself as bald patches in the hair, and as round, reddish or grey scaly patches on the skin. As the infection spreads, the edges of the ring remain scaly, and the centre begins to look more like normal skin. Ringworm is usually contracted from animals, such as a household pet, or from other infected humans.

Is it serious?
Though not a serious disorder, ringworm is unattractive and irritating. Ringworm is also contagious and must therefore be treated promptly.

Possible symptoms
● Red or grey scaly rings on any part of the body, particularly warm, moist areas, and on the scalp, where they produce bald patches.
● Itchiness in the ringed areas.

What should I do first?

1 If your child is scratching, check all over his body for the distinctive rings of ringworm.

2 Do not try to treat it yourself and wash your hands after examining your child. Discourage him from touching the infected areas.

3 Keep your child away from school until you have visited the doctor.

Should I consult the doctor?

Consult your doctor as soon as possible as ringworm is contagious as well as irritating for your child.

What might the doctor do?

□ Your doctor will prescribe an anti-fungal cream for the skin and antibiotic tablets for the scalp. The tablets will have to be taken for at least four weeks.

What can I do to help?

□ Throw out any brushes, combs or headgear your child may have used while infected. Disinfectant will not destroy the fungi.
□ Keep your child's facecloth and towel separate from those of the rest of the family to avoid spreading the infection.
□ If your pet is a possible source of ringworm, take it to the vet for treatment as soon as possible.
□ Ringworm on the skin clears up quickly, but treatment of the scalp may take a couple of weeks. Get your child some form of headgear to hide the bald patches if he is bothered by them.
□ Always make sure that you and your child wash your hands carefully before and after touching the affected areas.

SEE ALSO:
Hair loss, *page 150*
Itching, *page 170*

Words in **bold** are A-Z entries

Roseola infantum

Roseola infantum is a relatively rare viral infection which causes **fever** and a **rash** in young children; it is contagious, and has symptoms that may be mistaken for **scarlet fever**. It starts with the sudden onset of a high fever which lasts for three days. As the fever subsides, a rash of flat red or pink spots appears, first on the trunk and then spreading to the limbs and neck. The rash fades after about 48 hours, with no other side-effects.

Is it serious?
Roseola infantum is not serious, though the temperature can rise high enough to cause a febrile **convulsion**.

Possible symptoms

● Fever with temperature of 39-40°C (102.2-104°F) for three days, with no apparent symptoms.

Sites of rash

Later sites

Early site

● Rash of separate, flat red or pink spots which appear first on the trunk and which spread to the limbs and neck, after the fever has subsided.

What should I do first?

1 Check your child's temperature. If it is high, try to reduce it with tepid sponging (*see page 31*).

2 Note where the rash starts and what part of the body it spreads to, if any.

Should I consult the doctor?

Consult your doctor as soon as possible for a definite diagnosis of the condition. Consult your doctor immediately if your child's temperature fails to come down after 48 hours or if your child has a febrile convulsion.

What might the doctor do?

☐ There is no specific treatment for viral illnesses, only treatments for the symptoms. Your doctor will advise you on how to reduce your child's fever and will recommend that you keep your child in bed until the rash appears.
☐ If your child has had a febrile convulsion before, your doctor may prescribe drugs to prevent possible convulsions.

What can I do to help?

☐ Take your child's temperature at regular intervals, and if it rises try to bring it down, first by tepid sponging and then by paracetamol elixir.

SEE ALSO:
Convulsion, *page 95*
Fever, *page 134*
Rash, *page 204*
Scarlet fever, *page 211*

Scabies

Scabies is an irritating, itchy rash caused by a tiny mite. The burrowing and egg-laying of these mites produce a rash which nearly always affects the hands and fingers, particularly the clefts between the fingers. It may also affect the ankles, feet, toes, elbows and the area around the genitals. When the eggs hatch, they are easily passed to another person by direct contact. They can also be picked up from bedding or linen that is infected with the mites.

Is it serious?

Scabies is not serious but it is contagious and could run through a family or a school class if not treated promptly.

Possible symptoms

● Intense itchiness.

Classic site of rash

● Fine, short lines that end in a black spot the size of a pinhead, most often found between the fingers.
● Scabs on the itchy areas.

What should I do first?

1 If your child is scratching a lot, look for the fine lines of the mites' burrows.

2 If you suspect scabies, keep your child away from school until you have administered the treatment.

3 Try to discourage your child from scratching. This may hinder the doctor's diagnosis and cause sores to form that could become infected.

Should I consult the doctor?

Consult your doctor as soon as possible if you suspect scabies or if your child is scratching a lot.

What might the doctor do?

☐ Your doctor will prescribe a lotion in sufficient quantity for the whole family to be treated.

What can I do to help?

☐ After thorough washing, you should paint the whole body below the neck with the lotion and leave to dry. Do not wash it off for 24 hours. To ensure disinfestation, repeat the procedure for a further 24 hours in a day or two.
☐ Carry out the treatment for other members of the family simultaneously.
☐ Launder or air all bedding and clothing to eradicate the mite. The mite does not live for longer than five or six days after it is removed from human skin.

SEE ALSO:
Itching, *page 170*
Rash, *page 204*

Words in **bold** are A-Z entries

Scarlet fever

Scarlet fever is one of the less common infectious diseases of childhood, even though it is caused by the widespread *streptococcus* bacterium (the same bacterium that causes **tonsillitis**). Scarlet fever is similar to tonsillitis, except that it produces a rash as well as a **sore throat**. The incubation period is one to five days, after which the symptoms manifest themselves. After three days of sore throat, inflamed tonsils, **fever**, **vomiting** and possibly abdominal pains because of swollen glands near the bowel, a rash of small spots that merge with one another appears on the chest and neck, and then the whole body. The rash may be itchy but is distinctive because it does not affect the area surrounding the mouth. The tongue may also be red and furry. The rash fades after five days, but the skin flakes off for up to two weeks.

Is it serious?
Scarlet fever is rarely serious. However, if your child is sensitive to the bacterium, the infection can cause inflammation of the kidneys (**nephritis**) or the joints and heart (**rheumatic fever**). However, these complications are rare.

Possible symptoms
- Sore throat.
- Inflamed tonsils.
- Fever, as high as 40°C (104°F).
- Vomiting.
- Abdominal pains.

Sites of rash

Early site

Later sites

- Rash of small spots starting on the chest and neck, then merging together over the whole body, except the area around the mouth.
- Strawberry-red patches on a furry tongue.

What should I do first?

Examine your child's throat

1 Check your child's throat to see if the tonsils are red and swollen

(*see page 241*). Check his tongue to see if it is furry with bright red patches.

2 Check your child's temperature to see if he has a fever. If he has, put him to bed and try to bring his temperature down with tepid sponging (*see page 31*).

3 Give your child plenty of cool drinks as well as giving paracetamol elixir to soothe his throat if he is in pain.

Should I consult the doctor?

Consult your doctor as soon as possible if you suspect scarlet fever.

Continued on next page ▶

S

Scarlet fever

◄ Continued from previous page

What might the doctor do?

☐ Your doctor will prescribe antibiotics or sulphonamides to minimize the severity of the illness and prevent complications. Your doctor will advise you about the complications that can follow a streptococcal infection, so that if certain symptoms occur after your child should have recovered you can consult your doctor immediately.

What can I do to help?

☐ Bed-rest is not usually necessary but keep your child warm and quiet.
☐ Scarlet fever is not generally a severe illness and your child should be well enough to return to school seven days after the onset of the symptoms.

Give frequent drinks

☐ Give your child plenty of fluids if he has lost his appetite, or if he has a sore throat that makes swallowing painful.
☐ Liquidize his foods if this makes swallowing easier for him.

SEE ALSO:
Fever, *page 134*
Nephritis, *page 187*
Rheumatic fever, *page 207*
Sore throat, *page 220*
Tonsillitis, *page 241*
Vomiting, *page 256*

Words in **bold** are A-Z entries

Scoliosis

Scoliosis is a sideways curvature of the spine, very often so slight that it is not observed until a child is approaching adolescence. The spinal deformity may be present from birth; it may be the result of injury to, or a weakness of, muscles in the back such as that caused by **muscular dystrophy**; or it may be the result of infection such as **tuberculosis** (now extremely rare) affecting the spine. Scoliosis can also develop at any time in otherwise perfectly healthy children and may be triggered off by a fast growth spurt, by one leg being longer than the other, or by poor posture. The condition is much more common in girls than in boys.

Is it serious?

Scoliosis should always be treated seriously. Early diagnosis is necessary to prevent deformity. Untreated, the condition can also affect the lungs, resulting in breathing difficulties.

Possible symptoms

● Looked at from behind, one shoulder is slightly lower than the other.
● Lopsidedness when your child bends forward.

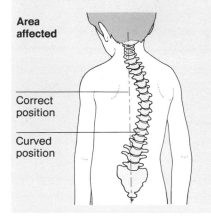

Area affected

Correct position

Curved position

What should I do first?

Ask your child to stand up straight with his heels together, then to bend forward from the waist. If there is a curvature, your child's back will remain curved sideways.

Should I consult the doctor?

Consult your doctor as soon as possible if you suspect scoliosis.

What might the doctor do?

☐ Your doctor may refer your child to an orthopaedic specialist who will monitor the curvature. Depending on the severity of the condition, the specialist may decide that it is necessary for your child to wear a back brace, perhaps for 23 hours a day, until he has stopped growing.
☐ Physiotherapy may be used to correct posture.

What can I do to help?

☐ Seek help from a scoliosis self-help group in your area; your doctor may be able to give you an address. If your child has to wear a brace, this can be a frightening experience. Communication with other parents experienced in coping with the problem may help.
☐ Treat the condition as casually as possible. Don't draw attention to it.

SEE ALSO:
Muscular dystrophy, *page 184*
Tuberculosis, *page 247*

Sickle cell anaemia

Sickle cell anaemia is an inherited condition caused by an abnormal form of haemoglobin in the blood. The inheritance is recessive; that is, both parents carry an abnormal gene but are themselves healthy. The risk of a child having sickle cell anaemia in such a family is one in four. The anaemia that results from the blood condition is not present at birth but develops in the first six months.

Haemoglobin is the protein contained in red cells in the blood. It picks up oxygen from the blood and carries it to various parts of the body. Sickle cell anaemia occurs when the inherited haemoglobin causes the red blood cells to become sickle-shaped as a result of abnormally low oxygen levels. In a child with this condition, the blood is less likely to clot efficiently and it flows through the blood vessels less smoothly than in a normal child. If it clogs the vessels, your child will experience pain in the area of the blockage, a worsening of anaemia, jaundice and an increased susceptibility to infections such as coughs and colds. It is almost exclusively people of African descent who are affected by this disease.

Possible symptoms

- Anaemia.
- Fatigue.
- Mild jaundice—yellowing of the the whites of the eyes.
- Pain in the limbs and abdomen, wherever blockages occur in the blood vessels.
- Susceptibility to infection.

What can be done to help?

Sickle cell anaemia does not affect a child's intelligence, and most children with this condition can attend ordinary schools. However, as your child may suffer an acute attack (known as a crisis) at school, when he will have severe joint and abdominal pain, his teachers should be alerted to the need to get immediate medical attention for him. The crisis will be treated with painkilling drugs.

A sickle crisis can be precipitated by strenuous activity, particularly in the cold and damp. It is essential for your child to be fully immunized against all infectious diseases and to take any prescribed vitamin supplements. As the condition is inherited, it is important for potential carriers to seek genetic counselling before deciding to have a baby. A blood test will show if the prospective parents are carriers of the disease.

S

FOR HELP AND ADVICE CONTACT:
Sickle Cell Society
c/o Brent Community Health Council
16 High Street
Harlesden
London NW10 4LX
01-451 3429

Words in **bold** are A-Z entries

Sinusitis

Sinusitis is an infection of the cheek and forehead sinuses. These are air-filled spaces grouped around the eyes and nose which make the skull bones light, and give the voice resonance. Infections of the sinuses are rare in babies because their sinuses are not fully developed, but in older children some degree of sinusitis often accompanies a **common cold**, **cough** or **sore throat**.

Because the sinuses are lined by the same mucus membrane as the nose, and are connected to the upper throat, infection in these areas can be easily spread to them. The sinuses also drain through small holes into the nose, and when your child has a cold the possibility of these holes becoming blocked and infected increases. You will know if your child's cold has developed into sinusitis if there is a yellow-green discharge from his nose.

Is it serious?

Sinusitis is not serious although it can become chronic if not treated efficiently and quickly.

Possible symptoms

- Yellow-green pussy discharge from the nose where previously there was a clear, runny discharge.
- Pain over the cheeks.
- Pain on moving the head.
- Slight fever.
- Blocked nose.

Affected areas

Frontal sinuses

Maxillary sinus

What should I do first?

1 If your child has a cold, cough or a sore throat, be on the look-out for a change in the colour of the nasal discharge.

2 Check to see if there is a **foreign body** lodged in your child's nose. The discharge will then be foul-smelling and stained with blood. Get medical attention immediately if you cannot remove the object easily.

Give menthol inhalations

3 If the cause is not a foreign object, relieve your child's blocked nose by giving him an inhalation of menthol crystals dissolved in boiling water. Take care your child doesn't knock over the bowl.

Continued on next page ▶

S

Sinusitis

◀ Continued from previous page

Should I consult the doctor?

Consult your doctor as soon as possible if the yellow-green nasal discharge continues for more than two days.

What might the doctor do?

☐ Your doctor will prescribe antibiotics to eradicate the infection. He may also prescribe special nose drops for your child to take whenever he has a cold, so that the sinuses keep draining, thus preventing a recurrence of sinusitis.
☐ If the infection persists, your child will be prescribed a prolonged course of antibiotics to prevent the sinusitis from becoming chronic.

☐ If sinusitis is recurrent, your doctor will refer your child to an ear, nose and throat specialist to see whether surgical draining of the sinuses is indicated.

What can I do to help?

☐ If your child complains of a headache or if he has a fever, give him paracetamol elixir.
☐ Continue giving your child menthol inhalations to relieve the symptoms of sinusitis.
☐ Don't overheat your child's bedroom. Try to keep the air cool and humid because a dry atmosphere makes the symptoms of sinusitis worse.

S

> **SEE ALSO:**
> **Common cold,** *page 90*
> **Cough,** *page 97*
> **Nose, foreign body in,** *page 189*
> **Sore throat,** *page 220*

Words in **bold** are A-Z entries

Sleeplessness

Sleeplessness may be a problem for parents when their child is very young. Your baby may sleep a less than normal amount from the first weeks of life: 12 hours instead of the accepted norm of 16-20 out of 24. These 12 hours may be taken in short, unpredictable bursts so that you never have more than a few hours consecutive sleep yourself. Sleepless babies are usually full of life, interested in everything that's going on, affectionate and sociable. As long as your baby is happy and cheerful when he's awake, he is normal and does not need medical attention.

The sleep patterns of toddlers can be very different. Some need to sleep for an hour or two during the day until they are four or five years old, while others need no daytime nap, and sleep only eight hours at night and wake early in the morning. Usually, however, a child that needed little sleep as a baby needs little sleep as a toddler. Providing a child can cope with school work and normal daily routine and is cheerful and bright, the sleep he takes is the amount of sleep he needs.

Is it serious?

Sleeplessness—that is, less than eight hours in a 24-hour day—is hardly ever serious, though it may seem serious and disruptive to parents.

What should I do first?

1 Face up to the fact of your baby's relative sleeplessness and sort out a shift system for the first months so that both parents don't become overtired.

2 If your baby wakes and cries in the night, go to him, comfort him and be cheerful. Try not to pick him up and take him into bed with you straight away, unless you think he is ill or frightened. If he continues to cry or call out, stay with him a while so that he doesn't feel that you are deserting him.

3 Have plenty of toys and books and a drink by your toddler's bed so that he can entertain himself if he wakes early.

Should I consult the doctor?

Consult your doctor as soon as possible if you are exhausted and the sleepless nights are affecting you or your baby's health.

What might the doctor do?

☐ If your baby is fit and well, but you are not, your doctor may prescribe a sedative for your baby to give you a break and to try to get him into a sleep routine.

What can I do to help?

☐ Make sure your baby's room is warm and snug.

☐ Try not to become resentful about your baby's wakefulness. Accept it as a fact of life and take practical steps to make sure you get enough sleep yourself. Sleep whenever your baby sleeps, get friends round to help look after the baby, look for support groups in your area.

☐ Take your baby to bed with you if you really want to; there is no danger of spoiling your baby by doing this.

☐ Never use bed as a punishment with an older child. Sleeping will then be associated with punishment, and this will make your child even less willing to go to bed.

☐ Never give your baby or child a sedative without your doctor's advice.

S

Sleepwalking

Sleepwalking, when a child wanders about the house while asleep, is a sort of "mobile dreaming". A sleepwalking child does not walk about with his eyes closed and his arms held straight out in front of him as is popularly supposed. His eyes will be open but he will be asleep; he won't see you and won't understand anything you say to him. Many children go through a short phase of sleepwalking but this soon passes. Sleepwalking may be associated with **nightmares** if your child is unduly troubled about something. If he has had frequent nightmares and you have tried to ignore them, he may be walking in his sleep to find you and seek reassurance.

Is it serious?
Sleepwalking is not serious unless your child is in physical danger, for example, from stairways or glass doors.

What should I do first?

If you find your child sleepwalking, don't try to waken him. Lead him slowly and gently back to bed.

Should I consult the doctor?

There is no need to consult your doctor unless sleepwalking becomes very frequent and you need reassurance that nothing is seriously wrong.

What might the doctor do?

□ Your doctor will question you about the frequency and nature of your child's sleepwalking and will ask you whether or not he has had any nightmares.
□ Your doctor may recommend that you and your child speak to a child psychiatrist to find the cause of the problem if your child is sleepwalking frequently.

What can I do to help?

□ Protect your child—for instance, by putting a barrier at the top of the stairway at night, and by making sure that no windows are left open.
□ Try to reassure your child if you think you know the underlying cause of the sleepwalking.

S

SEE ALSO:
Nightmares, *page 188*

Snake bite

Any bite from a snake, whether venomous or not, will be extremely frightening for your child. In Britain, the only venomous snake is the adder, recognizable by the zig-zag markings along its back. It is important to note the snake's markings wherever possible so that the correct anti-venom can be administered.

Is it serious?
A snake bite should always be treated as serious. Prompt treatment is necessary in case the bite was from a poisonous snake. However, deaths from snake bites are rare, even in countries where there are many poisonous snakes.

Possible symptoms

● Swelling and pain at the site of the bite.

Appearance of bite

● One or two puncture marks.
● Pain or numbness spreading through the rest of the limb.

What should I do first?

Mark the bite with a dressing

1 Clean the skin around the puncture mark and place a dressing over it. This will help to identify the wound when you get to hospital.

2 Get your child to the nearest casualty department. If possible, lay your child down flat as you do so. Don't raise the affected part above the level of the heart; this will only spread the venom.

3 Keep your child calm and still, and warm if he seems clammy and pale.

4 Don't apply a tourniquet or suck out the poison in cases of snake bite. This is now thought to be inadvisable.

Should I consult the doctor?

Take your child to the nearest casualty department or call an ambulance if your child has been bitten by a snake.

What might the doctor do?

☐ Your child will be given an anti-venom injection if the snake was recognized as, or thought to be, poisonous.
☐ There is always the risk of tetanus with a snake bite and your child will be given a tetanus toxoid booster.

What can I do to help?

☐ Give your child paracetamol elixir to ease the pain.
☐ If you are in an area where poisonous snakes are prevalent, seek advice as to whether you should keep an emergency anti-venom kit at home.

S

Sore throat

A sore throat is usually a symptom of an infection of the respiratory tract. With a baby or a young child, he may not be able to tell you about the raw feeling in his throat, but you will notice that he has difficulty swallowing. Sore throats most often occur because of inflammation of the tonsils (**tonsillitis**), caused by the *streptococcus* bacterium. Sore throats also occur with the **common cold** or **influenza** virus. If there is inflammation elsewhere, as there is in the larynx when your child has **laryngitis**, this can also give a raw feeling in the throat. If the glands in the neck are swollen, with **mumps**, for example, this may be felt by your child as pain in the throat.

Is it serious?
Most sore throats are not serious. However, if your child is allergic to the streptococcus bacterium and he has a streptococcal infection in the throat, this could have effects elsewhere in his body. Possible serious complications include **nephritis** and **rheumatic fever**.

What should I do first?

1 If your child complains of a sore throat, or if he has difficulty swallowing and is off his food, examine his throat in a good light, with his head held back and the tongue depressed gently with the handle of a clean spoon (*see page 241*). Ask him to say a long "aaah". This will open up the throat so that you can see if there is any inflammation.

Check for swollen glands

2 Run your fingers down either side of your child's neck and under his chin to check for any swelling in the glands—the glands will feel like large peas under the skin.

3 Take your child's temperature to see if he has a fever.

4 As the sore throat is most likely caused by an infection, keep your child away from school until you have seen your doctor.

Should I consult the doctor?

Consult your doctor as soon as possible. Streptococcal infection of the throat should be treated promptly to avoid complications.

What might the doctor do?

☐ Your doctor will examine your child to determine the cause of the sore throat. If it is a streptococcus bacterium, your doctor will prescribe antibiotics.

What can I do to help?

☐ Soothe your child's sore throat with cold drinks or hot lemon drinks.
☐ Give your child plenty of liquids. If he isn't eating because it hurts to swallow, liquidize foods where possible.

SEE ALSO:
Appetite, loss of, *page 55*
Common cold, *page 90*
Influenza, *page 166*
Laryngitis, *page 172*
Mumps, *page 182*
Nephritis, *page 187*
Rheumatic fever, *page 207*
Scarlet fever, *page 211*
Tonsillitis, *page 241*

S

Words in **bold** are A-Z entries

Spina bifida

In a child born with spina bifida, the bones of the spine (the vertebrae) which normally protect the spinal column fail to join up properly, leaving a gap, so that in extreme cases the nerves of the spinal column are exposed. The condition most commonly affects the lower region of the spine and can be relatively minor—with just a dimple, or a brown, hairy mole growing from the bottom of the spine—or very serious, when the spinal cord is underdeveloped and the gap in the spine is covered by a large red membrane instead of skin. The symptoms reflect the severity of the condition. These may range from no symptoms at all, except for the skin markings, to complete paralysis of the lower limbs and incontinence. With a moderate to severe form of spina bifida, the development and function of your child's lower body will never be quite normal and he may be physically stunted, and walk with a limp. Nine out of ten spina bifida babies also have hydrocephalus—a condition in which excessive fluid accumulates in the brain. Spina bifida is one of the most common congenital disorders.

Possible symptoms

- Part of the spinal cord exposed.
- Dimple or brown, hairy mole at the base of the spine.
- Swelling over part of the spine— covered by skin or large red membrane.
- Paralysis of the lower body.
- Excessively large head.
- Incontinence.

What can be done to help?

Severe cases of spina bifida are recognized at birth. The degree and extent of paralysis will be assessed as soon as possible by a paediatrician, and a brain scan will be performed to see if excessive fluid is present on the brain. In very severe cases, the paediatrician may have to tell the parents that their child will be paralyzed below the waist, and that there could be mental retardation as well. Surgery can be carried out to correct the skin defect and prevent infection, but this will not restore function to the spinal cord. A drainage valve operation can also be performed to control the hydrocephalus. If no action is taken in such severe cases, the babies usually die peacefully within weeks of birth.

Less severe cases are referred for surgery and then a programme of rehabilitation and physiotherapy.

Checks will be made at frequent intervals on bladder control, kidney function and the development of hip joints.

If there is a family history of spina bifida, it is important to make a special search for this during pregnancy. This can be done by ultrasound scanning and measuring the alphafetoprotein levels in the mother's blood, and, if necessary, in the amniotic fluid. If the tests are positive, you will be given the option of terminating the pregnancy.

S

FOR HELP AND ADVICE CONTACT:
Association of Spina Bifida and Hydrocephalus
Tavistock House North
Tavistock Square
London WC1 9HJ
01-388 1382

Splinter

A splinter is a tiny slither of material that becomes embedded in or under the skin. It may be wood, metal, glass, a thorn or a prickle. Generally, it is hardly ever necessary to get medical help; most splinters can be removed at home.

Is it serious?

A splinter is rarely serious. However, splinters that cause deep wounds, particularly if they do not bleed much, can be serious because they carry the risk of **tetanus** infection.

What should I do first?

1 Find out from your child, if possible, what material is embedded in the skin. If it is glass, the entire surface of the splinter will be capable of cutting into your child's flesh, so don't try to remove it yourself; seek medical aid.

Sterilize the tweezers

Pull out splinter

2 If the splinter is not of glass and the end is sticking out of the skin, remove it with tweezers. Sterilize them first by passing the ends through a flame. Allow them to cool, then distract your child so that he doesn't flinch too much when you gently pull out the splinter.

3 If the splinter is under the skin, sterilize a sharp sewing needle with a flame or by standing it in some surgical spirit or antiseptic lotion for a few minutes. Place a piece of ice over the splinter area so that the skin is lightly numbed, then use the sterile needle to gently break the skin's surface and expose the splinter. Once the end of the splinter is free, pull it out with a sterilized pair of tweezers.

4 Clean the area with soap and water and apply an antiseptic cream. Don't put a plaster on unless your child asks for one.

5 If you experience any difficulty while trying to remove a splinter, abandon the attempt and obtain medical help.

Should I consult the doctor?

Consult your doctor immediately if the splinter is glass, if it is deep in the skin, if it's contaminated with garden material (which increases the risk of tetanus), or if you cannot remove it easily yourself.

What might the doctor do?

☐ If the splinter is a piece of glass, or if it is deep in the skin, your doctor will remove it under a local anaesthetic.
☐ If there is any garden material in the wound, your doctor may give your child a tetanus booster injection.

> **SEE ALSO:**
> **Tetanus,** *page 236*

Words in **bold** are A-Z entries

Sprain

A sprain is the tearing of the tough, strap-like structures (ligaments) that support a joint and limit its movement. The sprain usually occurs because of overstretching or a sudden twisting action which wrenches the joint beyond its normal movement. The tearing causes bleeding into the joint, which results in swelling, pain and a bad bruise. (If only a few fibres of a ligament tear, it is known as a strain.)

The most common sites of a sprain are the ankle, knee and wrist. Because the ligaments are near to the skin's surface in these joints, and there is little but hard bone beneath them, swelling shows rapidly and your child will not be able to take any weight on the sprained joint.

It is rare for young children to suffer a sprain because their joints are so supple. Sprains are, however, quite common in the six to 12 age group.

Is it serious?
A sprain is painful but not serious, though it can be difficult to determine without an X-ray whether the injury is a sprain, a **broken bone** or a dislocated joint.

Possible symptoms

- Swelling and tenderness.
- Pain when the affected joint has to bear any weight.
- Bruising.

Common site of sprain

Ligaments

What should I do first?

1 If the affected joint or limb is not misshapen (which could indicate a dislocation or fracture), lay your child down and raise the injured part.

2 Apply a cold compress to reduce the swelling.

3 Support the joint with a firm crepe bandage applied over a thick wad of cotton wool. Check the bandage regularly to make sure that subsequent swelling has not made it too tight.

4 Encourage your child to rest the joint for at least 24 hours.

Should I consult the doctor?

Consult your doctor immediately if there is intense pain and the affected joint or limb is misshapen, suggesting a dislocation or fracture. Consult your doctor as soon as possible if, after 48 hours, the swelling has not subsided or if your child still complains of severe pain and cannot bear any weight on the injured part.

What might the doctor do?

□ If your doctor suspects a dislocation or fracture, your child will be referred to a hospital casualty department.
□ If the injury is a sprain, your doctor will strap the damaged joint with a firm bandage.

> **SEE ALSO:**
> **Broken bone,** *page 70*

S

Squint

It is quite common for the eyes of newborn babies to move independently of each other until the age of eight to ten weeks. At about this time, the baby's eyes should become permanently aligned. If this doesn't happen, and one or both eyes wander, this is known as a squint or crossed-eyes. This condition is most commonly caused by an imbalance of the eye muscles. It may also be associated with other vision defects such as long or short sight. The brain compensates for the wandering eye by blocking out what is seen by it.

Is it serious?
A squint that persists is serious because the child could lose sight from that eye.

Possible symptoms

Common form of squint

● Eyes appear to be looking in different directions.

What should I do first?

Checking for squint

If you think that your baby's eyes wander out of focus, check this by getting him to follow your finger or a colourful toy. See if both eyes track the object together or if one eye wanders to one side.

Should I consult the doctor?

Consult your doctor as soon as possible if the squint persists after your baby is three months old.

What might the doctor do?

☐ Your doctor will treat the condition by blacking out the strong eye with a pad or patch. This forces the muscles of the wandering eye to work and become

stronger. The treatment usually corrects the laziness in the eye within four or five months.
☐ If your child is older, an eye specialist will teach your child a series of simple eye exercises to help to strengthen the eye muscles.
☐ If your child's squint is associated with some vision defect, and spectacles are required, you will be referred to an optician.
☐ If the squint persists, surgery may be performed to correct muscular imbalance. This will not be contemplated until your child is at least two years old.

What can I do to help?

☐ Have your child's eyes checked annually.
☐ If you are concerned about your child's eyes, ask to be referred to an ophthalmologist for another opinion.

SEE ALSO:
Vision problems, *page 253*

Words in **bold** are A-Z entries

Stammering

Stammering is a speech disorder in which the flow of words is interrupted while the child struggles to start a word. It is perfectly normal in a child who is learning to speak, when excitement, a profusion of ideas and the inability to form sentences properly may result in jerky speech. Nearly all children grow out of this phase by the time they reach school age. If stammering continues beyond this time, there is nearly always an underlying emotional problem such as fear, anxiety or tension—usually caused by parental concern. Stammering does tend to run in families.

Is it serious?

Stammering is not serious and can be controlled, if not cured. However, drawing unnecessary attention to the stammer may make your child feel self-conscious and worsen the problem.

What should I do first?

1 Resist the temptation to give your child the word you think he needs. Give him plenty of time to express himself.

2 Check to see if there is any cause for anxiety or stress in your child's life and do your best to deal with it.

Should I consult the doctor?

Consult your doctor as soon as possible if your child is obviously embarrassed and upset by the stammering, and it is causing him to contort his lips, tongue and face when he tries to express himself.

What might the doctor do?

☐ Your doctor may reassure you that the stammer will soon disappear.
☐ Your doctor may refer your child to a speech therapist for assessment and therapy. If therapy is started early on, there is a very good chance of eliminating the stammer completely from your child's speech.

What can I do to help?

☐ Your child needs your help to prevent him losing confidence in himself. Never ridicule or draw attention to your child's stammering. Try to be open and frank about discussing it and never show embarrassment.
☐ If your child is old enough to understand, discuss with him the possibility of therapy. Ask him if he would like professional help and see how he responds. He may be quite happy to live with his stammer.
☐ Don't push your child or interrupt him when he's talking. If he asks for help with a word, then give it.
☐ Suggest that your child imposes a rhythm when speaking and that he speaks slowly to accentuate the rhythm of his sentences. Stammerers don't stammer while they are singing or reciting poetry.

225

Sticky eye

Sticky eye is a mild eye infection that is quite common in the first week of a baby's life. It is nearly always due to a foreign substance getting into the eye during delivery, possibly a drop of amniotic fluid or blood. Your baby's eye will ooze pus and when he wakes from sleep, the eye will be gummed up with it.

Is it serious?
Sticky eye is not serious. There is no danger to your baby's eyes, but sticky eye should be treated promptly to prevent the more serious infection of **conjunctivitis** from developing.

Possible symptoms

● Pus coming from the inner corner of one or both of the eyes.
● Eyelashes stuck together after sleep.

What should I do first?

Wipe from the corner of the eye downwards

1 Wash both eyes with warm, boiled water, using a clean piece of cotton wool for each eye. Start on the outside corner of the eye and move downwards.
2 Put your baby down to sleep with the infected eye uppermost. The other eye may otherwise become infected from the sheet.

Should I consult the doctor?

Consult your doctor immediately if your baby's eyeball is red. This could be conjunctivitis. Consult your doctor as soon as possible if the sticky eye does not improve within 24 hours.

What might the doctor do?

☐ If there is an infection, your doctor will prescribe eye drops or an eye ointment to apply to the eye three or four times a day.

What can I do to help?

☐ Bathe your baby's eyes frequently, whenever you notice a discharge.
☐ Change his bed linen regularly to avoid contaminating his eyes.

SEE ALSO:
Conjunctivitis, *page 92*

S

Words in **bold** are A-Z entries

Stings

Most stings, whether from insects or jellyfish, cause only local irritation and pain. In the rare cases where there is a severe allergic reaction to a sting, shock may develop (*see page 293*). This is known as *anaphylactic shock*. Bee and wasp stings make a small puncture hole in the skin; bees leave their stings behind but wasps rarely do. Jellyfish stings cause a localized burning sensation.

Are they serious?

A sting is rarely serious. However, if it causes an allergic reaction with severe swelling leading to loss of consciousness; if it is in the mouth or throat, where swelling could lead to breathing problems; if it is caused by a Portuguese man-of-war jellyfish sting; or if your child is stung by a number of insects (in which case the amount of poison in his body could be more than he can cope with), then it should be treated as an emergency.

Possible symptoms

● Small puncture mark, with or without the sting left behind.
● Localized swelling and irritation.
● Red swelling with pieces of jellyfish still adhering to the skin.
● Breathing difficulties.
● Signs of shock—rapid pulse, clammy and pale skin, shortness of breath, sweating and faintness.

Appearance of bee sting

What should I do first?

Calm your child and keep him as still as possible to slow down the poison's rate of spreading.

If your child is stung by a bee or wasp

Scrape off sting

1 If the sting is still in the skin, scrape it off with the blade of a knife or a fingernail. Avoid squeezing the sac at the top of the sting because this will force more poison into your child's body.

2 To reduce the pain and swelling, apply a cold compress of diluted vinegar for wasp stings and bicarbonate of soda and water paste for bee stings. Don't rub the area; just lay the compress on top.

If the sting is in the mouth or throat

1 If the sting is visible, remove it with a pair of tweezers. Avoid squeezing the sac at the top of the sting because this will force more poison into your child's body. Give your child cold water to drink or a cube of ice to suck. If not visible, seek medical aid.

2 If the area swells quickly, place your child in the recovery position (*see page 285*) and get medical help immediately.

Continued on next page ▶

S

Stings

◀ *Continued from previous page*
If your child is stung by a jellyfish

Wipe off bits of jellyfish

1 Use dry sand to wipe away any bits of the jellyfish.

2 Wash the area with water or soap and water if available.

3 Relieve the pain and irritation with calamine lotion or ice.

Should I consult the doctor?

Take your child to the nearest casualty department if he has an allergic reaction, if he has been stung more than once by an insect, or if he has been stung by a Portuguese man-of-war jellyfish. Consult your doctor immediately or go to the nearest casualty department if he develops any symptoms of shock (*see page 293*), has breathing difficulties, or if your child has been stung in the throat or mouth and you can't remove the sting, or if the area is swelling.

What might the doctor do?

☐ The hospital doctor will treat your child for shock.
☐ If your child has suffered an allergic reaction to a sting, your doctor may prescribe antihistamine tablets or cream, depending on the severity of the reaction. Your doctor may also give your child a series of desensitizing injections to prevent the same reaction in future.
☐ Your doctor will remove the sting from your child's mouth if you've been unable to do so, and will control any swelling in the area.

What can I do to help?

☐ Make up an emergency pack of antihistamine medication if your child suffers an allergic reaction to insect stings. Carry it with you on holidays and outings.
☐ Keep a proprietary brand of aerosol sting reliever with you on picnics and outings. The quick relief of pain and itching will reduce any fear your child may build up about insects like wasps or bees.
☐ Have a bracelet or medallion engraved for your child to wear stating that he is allergic to stings and should be given immediate medical treatment.

S

Stye

A stye is a pus-filled swelling on the margin of the eyelid. It is caused by the inflammation of one of the hair follicles from which the eyelashes grow, and it nearly always appears on the lower eyelid. It usually comes to a head and bursts within four or five days. Styes are encouraged by rubbing and pulling at the eyelashes and may be associated with a general irritation of the eyelids known as **blepharitis**. Styes are not highly infectious, but they can be conveyed from one eye to the other.

Is it serious?
A stye is usually harmless and can be treated at home.

Possible symptoms

Common site

● Swollen, sore red area on the eyelid, which enlarges to become pus-filled.

What should I do first?

1 If the spot on the eyelid is merely red and sore, leave it alone and discourage your child from touching or rubbing it. If the stye is painful and unsightly, keep the eyelid still with a pad of gauze or a clean, ironed handkerchief held loosely in place with a bandage.

2 If the stye is pus-filled and painful, apply a warm compress, or a ball of cotton wool squeezed out in hot water, for a few minutes every two or three hours. This will soothe the pain and bring the stye to a head.

3 Once the stye has come to a head, your aim is to release the pus and ease the pain. If you can see the eyelash at the centre of the stye, try to pull it out gently with a pair of tweezers. If it won't come out, leave it, and continue with the warm compresses. As soon as the eyelash comes out, the pus will drain away and the stye will get better quickly. Bathe the pus away with warm water and cotton wool.

4 Note whether the eyelids are red-rimmed, with dandruff-like flakes clinging to the eyelashes. This may be blepharitis.

Should I consult the doctor?

Consult your doctor as soon as possible if the home treatment does not improve the stye within four or five days, or if the eyelid becomes generally swollen, or if the stye is accompanied by blepharitis.

What might the doctor do?

☐ If there is an infection of the eyelid or the eye itself, your doctor will prescribe an antibiotic ointment or eye drops. If the stye is accompanied by blepharitis, your doctor may prescribe an ointment to clear it up.

What can I do to help?

☐ Keep your child's facecloth and towel separate from those of the rest of the family to avoid spreading any infection.
☐ Wash your hands before and after treating the stye and discourage your child from touching the area.

S

> **SEE ALSO:**
> **Blepharitis,** *page 66*

Sunburn

Sunburn is inflammation of the skin caused by excessive exposure to the ultra-violet rays in sunlight. It is always due to misjudgement or carelessness on the part of the parent. The best cure is prevention. Even adults should give all but deep olive or black skins a chance to acclimatize to the sun and toughen up. This must be done gradually and it is necessary to be strict with children who may not appreciate the dangers. Your child's sunburn can result in tender and damaged skin that may blister or peel off. Even in mild sunshine, the effects of the sun can be increased if you are near water, snow or sand, where the rays are reflected off the bright surface.

Is it serious?
Sunburn can be serious if a large area of the skin is involved. The skin may lose its ability to regulate body temperature so that your child's temperature soars and **heatstroke** results.

Possible symptoms
- Red, hot, tender skin.
- Blisters.
- Itchiness prior to peeling skin.

What should I do first?

Apply calamine lotion

1 Apply a soothing lotion such as calamine, or a cold compress, to any tight, red skin to cool it down and reduce irritation.

2 When you're inside don't put any clothing on the sunburned areas; leave them exposed to the air. Cover sunburned areas when you are outside.

3 If blisters appear and your child appears to be in some pain, give him paracetamol elixir.

4 Take your child's temperature to see if he has a fever. If his temperature is over 39°C (102.2°F) consult your doctor immediately and try to reduce the fever with tepid sponging (*see page 31*)

5 Keep your child out of direct sunlight for at least 48 hours.

Should I consult the doctor?

Consult your doctor as soon as possible if blisters form on your child's sunburnt skin and he is feverish and unwell. Consult your doctor immediately if your child has a fever but his skin is dry and he seems confused and drowsy. This could be heatstroke, which should be treated as an emergency.

Continued on next page ▶

S

Words in **bold** are A-Z entries

Sunburn

◀ *Continued from previous page*

What might the doctor do?

☐ In a mild case of sunburn, your doctor may prescribe a soothing cream.
☐ If blisters have formed and your child is feverish, your doctor may prescribe an anti-inflammatory cream to help the skin to heal more quickly.
☐ If your child is suffering from heat-stroke, your doctor will treat this accordingly.

What can I do to help?

☐ Draw the sheets on your child's bed tightly so that nothing scratches his tender skin.
☐ To prevent sunburn, keep all but the toughest parts of your child's skin covered up for the first few days of bright sunlight. From then on, apply a total sunblock lotion to all the exposed parts of his body.

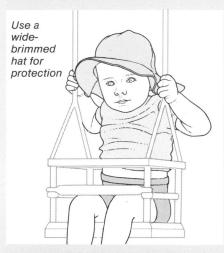

Use a wide-brimmed hat for protection

☐ Cover your child's lips and nose with a sunblock and protect the nape of his neck with a wide-brimmed hat.
☐ Remember to apply the sunblock again after your child has been swimming.

☐ Increase exposure to sun by 10 minute increments only each day.
☐ Keep a check on your child's skin, even after the first few days when he should be acclimatized to the conditions. If his skin is starting to burn, cover him up immediately.

SEE ALSO:
Heatstroke, *page 158*

S

Teething

Teething is the term used to describe the eruption of a baby's first teeth. Teething usually begins at about the age of six or seven months, with most of the first teeth breaking through before your baby is 18 months old. Your baby will produce more saliva than usual and will dribble; he will try to cram his fingers into his mouth and chew on his fingers or any other object that he can get hold of. He may be clingy and irritable, have difficulty sleeping, and he may cry and fret more than usual. Most of these symptoms occur just before the teeth erupt. It is important to realize that the symptoms of teething do not include bronchitis, nappy rash, vomiting, diarrhoea or loss of appetite. These are symptoms of an underlying illness, *not* teething.

Is it serious?
Teething and the symptoms associated with teething are never serious.

Possible symptoms

- Increased saliva and dribbling.
- Desire to bite on any hard object.
- Irritability and increased clinginess.
- Sleeplessness.
- Swollen red area where the tooth is being cut.

Order of appearance
1 1st incisors
2 1st incisors
3 2nd incisors
4 2nd incisors
5 1st molar
6 1st molar
7 Eye
8 Eye
9 2nd molar
10 2nd molar

What should I do first?

Feel your baby's gums

If you can't work out why your child is so irritable, and he has no other symptoms of illness, feel his gums. If a tooth is coming through, you will feel a hard or sharp lump and the gum area will be swollen and red.

Should I consult the doctor?

You should not need to consult your doctor unless your baby has other symptoms which cannot be attributed to teething, or you are unduly worried.

What might the doctor do?

Your doctor will give you advice on how to cope with the symptoms of teething and will perhaps prescribe a mild analgesic to be used for a short time to relieve the irritation.

What can I do to help?

☐ Nurse your baby often. A teething baby needs your comfort and closeness. Don't think that the arrival of teeth means a necessary speeding-up of the weaning process. Babies with teeth can still be breastfed with no discomfort to the mother.
Continued on next page ▶

Words in **bold** are A-Z entries

Teething

◀ Continued from previous page

Give your child a carrot to chew

☐ Distract your child with a chilled teething ring (never freeze the ring or your baby may get **frostbite**) or a piece of carrot or apple—something with a firm texture. Stay with your baby so that he doesn't choke on the food.

☐ Try not to resort to analgesics such as paracetamol elixir if possible. Over the course of the teething process, doses of such painkillers could become too large. Only use analgesics on your doctor's advice.

☐ Rub the swollen gum with your finger. Try to avoid teething jellies that contain local anaesthetics as these have only a temporary effect and they can cause an allergy.

☐ If your child refuses food, encourage him to eat by giving him cold, smooth foods such as yogurt, ice cream or jelly.

T

SEE ALSO:
Crying, *page 101*
Frostbite, *page 138*
Sleeplessness, *page 217*

Temper tantrums

Temper tantrums are normal in children between the ages of two and four years. They arise because the child hasn't acquired the judgement to match his will, nor has he the linguistic skills to argue or to explain what he wants. Clashes with parents tend to become frequent towards the end of the second year, leading to the time known as the "terrible twos". Tantrums take many forms, but usually the child throws himself on the floor, kicking and screaming, banging his feet against the walls or perhaps holding his breath with frustration. The child's actions show no regard for his own safety and he can easily hurt himself on hard objects.

Are they serious?
Temper tantrums are not in themselves serious, though they may happen at inconvenient times and in embarrassing situations. Even if your child holds his breath until he becomes blue in the face, he will not be able to harm himself. There is an automatic reflex which forces the body to take a breath when it is running short of oxygen, and this cannot be overriden by willpower.

What should I do first?

1 Stay calm. Even if your child's anger affects you, don't let him see that you are upset. Your child can easily catch your mood.

2 Ignore your child as much as possible. Walk away, but don't go out of sight. A tantrum loses much of its effect if there is no audience. However, move sharp pieces of furniture and breakable objects so that no harm can come to your child.

3 If this doesn't work, try holding your child on your lap while he calms down. He may fight to get away or he may realize that comfort and sympathy are really what he wants.

Should I consult the doctor?

There is usually no need to consult your doctor about temper tantrums. If your child continues to throw tantrums after the age of five, however, or if you are finding them difficult to cope with, ask your doctor for advice.

What might the doctor do?

☐ Your doctor will ask you about the frequency and nature of the tantrums and whether they are accompanied by other behavioural problems. Your doctor may refer you to a child psychiatrist for further assessment.

What can I do to help?

☐ Remember that the tantrums are directed against you. Your child is trying to gain your attention. Tantrums can be difficult to deal with in a public place when your child may sense that he will succeed. But if you show that the tantrums never succeed, they should stop.

☐ Try to anticipate problems and forestall clashes with distraction tactics. As your child grows up, he will be better able to tolerate delays and accept compromises.

☐ Don't ask your child why he is angry during a tantrum. He won't be able to reason with you.

☐ Don't slap your child to bring him out of a breath-holding attack. Just leave him and it will end naturally.

T

Testicles, undescended

The testicles grow and develop inside the abdomen, near the kidneys. Shortly before a boy is born, they move down or "descend" into their normal position in the bag of skin called the scrotum.

Position of testicles

Undescended testicle

Descended testicle

Scrotum

For testicles to develop normally at adolescence and produce sperm, it is necessary for them to hang outside the body. This is because sperm production can proceed only at a temperature that is slightly below the body's internal temperature. If the testicles—or, more usually, one testicle —fail to descend, sperm will not be produced normally, nor will the hormone testosterone (which produces male characteristics such as a deeper voice and body hair). Theoretically, one descended testicle could be sufficient to produce sperm and male hormones, but if your son's testicles have failed to descend by the age of five or six, the problem should probably be corrected surgically.

Are they serious?
Undescended testicles are not serious and they cause no health problems in childhood.

What should I do first?

When a baby boy is born, a paediatrician will examine his testicles to see if they have descended. If not, you will be advised of the fact and reassured that they may descend naturally. If your baby's testicles did not descend at birth, feel for them occasionally in the scrotum. If they have descended, they will feel small— each about the size of a pea. Warm your hands before you do this, otherwise the testicles may temporarily retract into the abdomen.

Should I consult the doctor?

Your doctor will be aware of your baby's problem and will check the scrotum regularly.

What might the doctor do?

☐ Your doctor will probably advise waiting until your son is five or six years old before taking action. If by this time the testicles have failed to descend, your doctor will refer you to a surgeon who will discuss with you when the operation to lower the testicles should be performed.

What can I do to help?

☐ Try to stay with your child in hospital when he has the operation to lower his testicles.
☐ Keep your son quiet and calm when he returns after the operation. If he engages too soon in any boisterous play, he could easily damage the scrotum.

235

Tetanus

Tetanus is a serious bacterial infection caused by the bacterium *clostridium tetani*. The bacterium is commonly found in farm and garden dirt, gravel and rusty metal and usually enters the body through a cut which could be caused by anything from a rose thorn to a sharp piece of metal. The bacterium, which thrives in the low-oxygen environment created by a deep cut, makes a poison or toxin that causes the muscles of the body to go into spasm (uncontrollable contraction). The jaw muscles are often affected first, hence the common name for the illness, lockjaw. This is followed by spasm of muscles throughout the rest of the body. These symptoms of tetanus can occur any time from a week to several months after the wound was sustained.

Possible symptoms

- Muscle stiffness and cramp, at first around the jaw and mouth.
- Sore throat.
- Difficulty in swallowing or breathing.

Tetanus is entirely preventable if your child has a course of injections within the first five years of life, updated every five years. Because of this programme, tetanus is very rare.

Is it serious?

Tetanus is very serious. Sometimes the breathing muscles go into spasm, and even with intensive care this can result in death.

What should I do first?

1 Always examine any wound your child receives to see if it is deep and dirty. Clean the wound thoroughly with an antiseptic solution or soap and water, removing the dirt where you can.

2 Take your child to your doctor or the nearest casualty department for a tetanus booster injection if more than six months have elapsed since your child last had a tetanus injection.

3 If your child complains of muscle stiffness, especially of the jaw and neck, get medical attention at once.

Should I consult the doctor?

Consult your doctor immediately or take your child to the nearest casualty department if your child has a deep cut from a possibly contaminated source, if six months have elapsed since his last tetanus injection, or if he develops symptoms of tetanus.

What might the doctor do?

☐ The doctor will clean a deep or dirty wound and give your child a booster injection if he is already immunized. If your child is not immune, an injection of anti-tetanus globulin will be given to provide immediate protection against the poison.

☐ If tetanus develops, the treatment includes a course of antibiotics and nursing in an intensive care unit. The child's breathing is supported by a respirator for the time it takes the disease to run its course, which may be several weeks.

What can I do to help?

☐ All babies should receive a course of three tetanus injections (usually as part of the "triple vaccine", DTP) in the first year. This provides a good immunization against the toxin. Booster injections are needed every five years to maintain protection.

T

Words in **bold** are A-Z entries

Thalassaemia

Thalassaemia is a form of genetically inherited anaemia. It occurs mostly in people from the Mediterranean area but it can also affect people from India and South-east Asia. Thalassaemia can be passed on to a child if both parents carry the faulty gene (or trait). The parents themselves may not be anaemic but there is a one in four chance that their child will suffer from the disease. If he does, his body cannot make normal haemoglobin, the substance in the blood which makes the red cells red and carries oxygen through the body. The problem reveals itself when the child is about three months old with symptoms of severe anaemia: fatigue, breathlessness and pallor; he will become increasingly inactive. The child will have difficulty feeding, and his abdomen will become swollen as the spleen and liver enlarge.

Possible symptoms

- Fatigue.
- Breathlessness.
- Pallor of the lips, tongue, hands, feet and other parts.
- Loss of appetite accompanied by a swollen abdomen.

What can be done?

Your doctor will take a blood sample for testing. If a disease such as thalassaemia is suspected, your child will be referred to hospital for more blood tests. If thalassaemia is confirmed, blood transfusions will usually be necessary—perhaps every six to eight weeks—to prevent your child from being incapacitated by severe anaemia.

Later in childhood, your child may need an operation to remove his spleen. This will reduce the need for such frequent transfusions. There is a problem if your child has to have too many transfusions: iron can build up in the body and damage the liver, pancreas and heart. This "iron overload" is the major threat of the disease and many sufferers have died in their teens; with new treatment, however, prospects are better. Many children with thalassaemia now receive injections of a drug which helps the body to get rid of the iron. In some cases this treatment is carried out overnight by means of a continuous injection into the skin.

A child with thalassaemia should lead as normal a life as possible. There should be no need to restrict physical activity, but he will need support and encouragement with the repeated transfusions. Ask your doctor or the hospital to put you in touch with other families with a similar problem so that you can learn how others cope.

If you are from a race particularly susceptible to this disease, ask your doctor to carry out a blood test on both you and your partner before you conceive, in order to find out if one or both of you might be a carrier of the thalassaemia trait.It is now possible to test the fetus at an early stage in pregnancy to detect thalassaemia so that a termination of the pregnancy can be offered.

> **FOR HELP AND ADVICE CONTACT:**
> **United Kingdom Thalassaemia Society**
> **107 Nightingale Lane**
> **London N8**
> *01-348 0437*

Thrush

Thrush is an infection caused by the fungus *candida albicans*. Under normal circumstances, this fungus is kept under control by other bacteria that also live in the intestines. If the balance is disturbed— for example, when your child is on antibiotics or his natural resistance is low because of illness — the fungus can overgrow, causing infection in any part of the gastro-intestinal tract. Thrush most often affects the mouth, causing white patches to appear on the tongue, roof of the mouth and inside the cheeks. It can also affect the anus. In babies, anal thrush is sometimes confused with **nappy rash** because it forms red patches with little red spots within them. It does not, however, respond to the usual self-help treatments.

Is it serious?
It is rare for thrush to give rise to serious symptoms, but as it does not respond to self-help treatment, you should get medical advice.

Possible symptoms
● Creamy yellow or white frothy patches inside the cheeks, on the tongue and the roof of the mouth which become raw or bleed when wiped off.
● A pimply red rash around the anus.

What should I do first?

Wipe white patches

1 If your child refuses to eat, check his mouth for any white patches. Try to wipe them off with a clean handkerchief. If they don't come away easily or if they leave raw patches underneath, or bleed, your child probably has oral thrush.

2 Avoid giving your child spicy foods and cool all cooked food to lukewarm. Natural yogurt is the best food to give until you have consulted your doctor.

3 Change your baby's nappies frequently. The fungus may be in his stools and this could give rise to thrush around the anus.

Should I consult the doctor?
Consult your doctor as soon as possible if you suspect your child has thrush.

Continued on next page ▶

Thrush

◀ *Continued from previous page*

What might the doctor do?

☐ Your doctor will prescribe a liquid anti-fungal medication to be dropped on to the affected area in your child's mouth if he has oral thrush.

☐ Your doctor will prescribe an anti-fungal cream if there is a rash around the anus.

What can I do to help?

☐ Feed your child with mild, liquidized foods if he has oral thrush.

☐ Keep your child's hands clean so that the infection does not spread from the anus to the mouth, or vice versa.

Leave your baby's bottom exposed

☐ Leave your baby's bottom exposed to the air as much as possible if he is still in nappies.

SEE ALSO:
Nappy rash, *page 185*

Tic

A tic in a child is an habitual, jerky movement of the body or face that can become a mannerism. It is not the result of neuralgia as are the facial tics seen in elderly people. The commonest tics in children are slight twitching of the eye or the corner of the mouth, wiggling the nose or blinking. Other habits include tossing the hair back off the forehead, fiddling with the hair, clearing the throat and sniffing; even head banging can be seen as a tic. Tics of all kinds are usually transient and they often appear when a child is particularly stressed or fatigued and disappear when the child settles back to normal. In young children, some sort of tic is fairly common and is not usually indicative of any problem.

Is it serious?
A tic is not serious, although it can be irritating.

Possible symptoms
● Habitual, jerky movements of parts of the face or body.

What should I do first?
Don't over-react to a tic; you may increase your child's anxiety and make it worse. Play it down and pretend not to notice, even though it may be irritating to you.

Should I consult the doctor?
Unless the tic is interfering with everyday life, or it is causing a problem at school, you really should not need to consult a doctor.

What might the doctor do?
☐ If you do seek advice, your doctor will reassure you that there is no longterm problem.

What can I do to help?
☐ A tic is nearly always worse when a child gets tired, so make sure he has plenty of rest.
☐ Learn to control your irritation so that you don't increase your child's tension.
☐ If your baby is a head banger, make sure he isn't left alone to get bored. Put bumper pads around his cot so that he can't hurt himself.

Words in **bold** are A-Z entries

Tonsillitis

Tonsillitis is an acute infection of the tonsils usually caused by the *streptococcus* bacterium, but sometimes by a virus. Positioned on either side of the back of the throat, the tonsils form the body's first line of defence by trapping and killing bacteria, thus preventing them from entering the respiratory tract. In the process, the tonsils themselves can become infected and inflamed, causing the symptoms of a **sore throat**, **fever** and swollen glands. The adenoids, positioned at the back of the nose, are nearly always affected as well. Babies under the age of one rarely suffer from tonsillitis; the infection occurs mainly among children of school age, when the relatively large tonsils and adenoids are exposed for the first time to infectious microbes. As resistance to the infection increases and the adenoids become smaller, so attacks of tonsillitis should lessen. Most children cease to suffer from tonsillitis around the age of ten.

Is it serious?
Tonsillitis is not serious unless repeatedly accompanied by **otitis media** which could lead to permanent deafness. There are also the rare complications of **nephritis** and **rheumatic fever.**

Possible symptoms
● Sore throat, possibly bad enough to cause difficulty in swallowing.

Area affected

Enlarged tonsils

● Red and enlarged tonsils, possibly covered in yellow spots.
● A temperature of over 38°C (100.4°F).
● Swollen glands in the neck.
● Mouth-breathing, snoring and a nasal voice when the adenoids are affected.
● Unpleasant breath.

What should I do first?

Check for enlarged tonsils

1 If your child complains of a sore throat or you notice that he has difficulty eating, examine his throat in a good light, with his head held back and the tongue depressed gently with the handle of a clean spoon. Ask him to say a long "aaah". This will open up the thoat, and a second or two should be enough for you to see whether his tonsils are red, enlarged or covered with yellow spots.

2 Take your child's temperature to see if he has a fever.

Continued on next page ▶

Tonsillitis

◀ *Continued from previous page*

Check for swollen glands

3 Check to see if your child's glands are swollen by running your fingers down the sides of his neck and under his chin—swollen glands will feel like large peas under the skin.

4 If your child is old enough, ask him if he has earache. In a young child, note whether he pulls or rubs one of his ears. Check the ear to see if there is any discharge.

5 Give him plenty of cool drinks to soothe his throat.

Should I consult the doctor?

Consult your doctor as soon as possible if you suspect tonsillitis.

What might the doctor do?

☐ Your doctor may take a throat swab (which is quite painless), to be sent to a laboratory for identification of the organism that is causing the infection. Your doctor may prescribe antibiotics if a bacterial infection seems likely. There is no specific medication for viral tonsillitis.

☐ Your doctor will examine your child's ear and eardrum to check for any ear infection. If there is any sign of infection, antibiotics will be prescribed.

☐ If your child suffers from frequent attacks of tonsillitis, or if enlarged adenoids are causing recurrent middle-ear infections, you may be referred to a specialist to see whether the tonsils and adenoids should be removed. The circumstances under which the operation might be performed would take the following into account:

a *Age* The operation is seldom performed before a child is four years old.

b *The onset of tonsillitis* The length of time that your child has been suffering from recurrent attacks of tonsillitis or earache is important. Most doctors would wait two years before deciding to operate.

c *Effect on the child* Tonsillectomy is advisable if the attacks are so frequent that they affect your child's education because he is absent from school so often, or if his health is deteriorating because he cannot eat well.

What can I do to help?

☐ Treat your child as you would for a fever. Bed-rest is not necessary but keep him in a warm room.

☐ Keep your child's fluid intake up by offering regular drinks.

☐ Liquidize your child's foods if he finds swallowing difficult, but don't force him to eat. Give him his favourite foods, especially those that slip down easily like ice cream or yogurt.

☐ Never give your child a gargle for a sore throat. This has been shown to spread infection from the throat to the middle ear.

SEE ALSO:
Earache, *page 121*
Fever, *page 134*
Nephritis, *page 187*
Otitis media, *page 196*
Rheumatic fever, *page 207*
Sore throat, *page 220*

T

Words in **bold** are A-Z entries

Toothache

Toothache is the pain which results when a tooth is decaying. The decaying process erodes the outer protective coatings of the tooth and bores through to the nerves in the soft centre, causing pain, particularly when anything cold, hot or sweet touches the tooth. Tooth decay (or dental caries) and gum disease are caused by plaque. This is a thin film of saliva and food residue in which bacteria grow. The bacteria thrive in the presence of sugar in the mouth—for example, in the form of refined white sugar, the sugar in dried fruits or even honey—which is one of the reasons why sugar in the diet is so harmful. Teeth can become resistant to the action of bacteria and sugar if they contain fluoride or if they are painted or coated with fluoride as they would be if regularly brushed with a fluoride-containing toothpaste. This is one of the main ways to prevent tooth decay along with good oral hygiene and regular dental check-ups. It is important that children do not lose their first teeth through tooth decay, or a complication of tooth decay— a **gum boil**—in which the root of the tooth also decays. The permanent tooth may come through misaligned if a gap is left for too long while the new tooth is developing.

Is it serious?
Toothache is not serious as long as it is treated immediately. If untreated, a gum boil may erupt, causing damage to the underlying permanent tooth, or loss of a second tooth.

What should I do first?

1 If your child complains of pain in the jaw, **earache**, or throbbing, stabbing pains in the mouth, tap his teeth gently with a small metal spoon to see if this identifies the source of the pain.

2 Give your child paracetamol elixir to relieve the pain until you can visit the dentist.

Heat may ease pain

3 Put a hot-water bottle covered in a cloth or towel against your child's cheek to relieve the pain.

4 Do not apply oil of cloves or anaesthetic jellies as this can cause damage to the gum around the tooth.

Should I consult the doctor?

You don't need to consult a doctor, but you should consult your dentist immediately for an emergency appointment.

What might the dentist do?

☐ Your dentist will examine the tooth to determine the extent of the damage. The tooth may only need to be drilled and filled, but if there is a gum boil the dentist will drain the pus from the abscess. If there is no possibility of saving the tooth, it will be extracted, probably under a general anaesthetic, depending on the age of your child.

T

Continued on next page ▶

Toothache

◀ *Continued from previous page*

What can I do to help?

Use fluoride toothpaste

☐ Prevent tooth decay. Use fluoride toothpastes and, depending on the level of fluoride in your local water supply, use fluoride tablets or drops in your child's drinks. Your dentist can provide you with information.

☐ Prevent the development of a sweet tooth by restricting your child's sugar intake. Don't give him sweets, cakes and biscuits, and avoid canned foods and fizzy drinks, which often have a surprisingly high sugar content.

☐ Brush your child's teeth yourself once a day or supervise the brushing up until the age of six or seven.

☐ Once your child is over the age of four, take him for a dental check-up every six months. Get him used to the dentist from an early age so that the prospect holds no mystery or terror for him.

☐ Encourage your child to drink plenty of water after eating sweet foods. The water will immediately wash much of the sugar off his teeth.

☐ Ask your dentist about fissure sealing. When your child is about seven or eight, his permanent back teeth can be sealed with a plastic coating to prevent plaque from getting into the biting surfaces.

SEE ALSO:
Earache, *page 121*
Gum boil, *page 148*

Words in **bold** are A-Z entries

Toxocariasis

Toxocariasis is a rare infection caused by the toxocara **worm** that lives in the intestines of some cats and dogs. The eggs of the worm are passed out in the animal's faeces and if a child plays on ground contaminated with the faeces and then puts his hands into his mouth, he may ingest the eggs. The eggs hatch and the worms burrow through the intestinal wall into the body and are carried in the bloodstream to the lungs and other parts of the body. They are then coughed up from the lungs; if swallowed, they develop in the child's intestines, so setting up a reinfestation cycle. Children show few specific symptoms of the disease.

Is it serious?

Toxocariasis is rarely serious in children, although in rare cases a worm may lodge in the eyes, causing blindness.

Possible symptoms

- Loss of appetite.
- Slight fever.
- Bouts of abdominal pain.
- Loss of sight.

What should I do first?

If your child has a mild infestation, you may not even be aware of it. If he suffers from unexplained fever and abdominal pain, it is wise to seek medical advice.

Should I consult the doctor?

Consult your doctor as soon as possible if you suspect that there is something wrong with your child, particularly if you have a pet, or if your child has played on land where animals defecate regularly.

What might the doctor do?

☐ Your doctor will examine your child and take a sample of his stools or blood for laboratory examination.
☐ If evidence of worms is found, your doctor may prescribe a special anti-parasite drug or he may advise you to keep your child away from all animals or possibly contaminated areas for six months while the worms die off.

What can I do to help?

☐ Encourage your child to wash his hands after playing with animals.
☐ Worm your dog or cat regularly.
☐ Train your pet to use its own toilet area well away from places frequented by the family.
☐ Disinfect any area where your children play if the dog or cat has fouled it.
☐ When you go to a public park, keep to the areas where dogs are not permitted.

SEE ALSO:
Worms, page 261

Travel sickness

Travel sickness occurs when the balance organs in the ear are upset by movement. When this sensation of movement doesn't correspond with what the eyes see, it causes confusion in the brain. The problem can result if a child rides a roller coaster or swings at a playground as well as being in a car, boat or plane. Symptoms range from a slight queasiness to **vomiting** and faintness. Children tend to suffer from travel sickness more than adults, though why is not known; most outgrow it by adolescence.

Is it serious?
Travel sickness is not serious, but it is inconvenient. With a young child there is a risk that prolonged vomiting could cause **dehydration**.

Possible symptoms

- Nausea.
- Vomiting.
- Pale, clammy forehead.
- Weakness or dizziness.
- Fainting.

What should I do first?

1 If your child complains of feeling sick, looks pale, or becomes abnormally quiet while you are travelling, check whether his forehead feels cold and clammy.

2 Tell your child to close his eyes, and lay him down if possible. This should minimize the confusing signals being received by the brain.

Should I consult the doctor?

Consult your doctor if your child suffers from travel sickness on even short journeys, or if proprietary brands of travel-sickness medicine do not help.

What might the doctor do?

☐ After questioning you about the symptoms and their frequency, your doctor may prescribe a drug such as an antihistamine, though some antihistamines can have side-effects such as **drowsiness**.

What can I do to help?

☐ Don't make a fuss before you travel. This can make your child more excited and apprehensive.
☐ Prevent travel sickness by giving your child a travel-sickness medicine before you start the journey. There are several good over-the-counter medications available from the chemist.
☐ Give your child a small snack before setting out. Don't let him travel on either an empty or a full stomach.
☐ Take plenty of drinks with you, or check that they will be available en route, to prevent the possibility of dehydration through vomiting. Fresh drinks can also reduce the feeling of nausea.
☐ Carry suitable "sick bags" (strong brown paper bags are best) in case of vomiting.

> **SEE ALSO:**
> **Dehydration,** *page 108*
> **Drowsiness,** *page 117*
> **Vomiting,** *page 256*

Words in **bold** are A-Z entries

Tuberculosis

Tuberculosis (TB) is a disease that causes chronic ill-health. It is caused by bacteria, and, if left untreated, can destroy large areas of an affected organ. It most commonly affects the lungs, but can also affect the kidneys and the membranes covering the brain and spine (*meninges*). The disease can take many forms because it is capable of travelling through the bloodstream and affecting any organ in the body. This makes it difficult to diagnose. Tuberculosis has been almost completely eradicated in Great Britain by means of a pasteurization programme for milk and tuberculin testing of the national dairy herd (cows are the commonest carriers of the disease); by a mass X-ray programme to pick up chest tuberculosis in its early stages; by skin testing and vaccination of all adolescents; and by improved drug treatment. However, immigration from areas where TB is still common has recently caused an increase in the number of cases. If a healthy child becomes infected by an adult, this first infection (the primary lesion) hardly ever progresses to anything serious, because the body forms a strong resistance to the tuberculous organism and prohibits its spread by walling it off within a chalky coating. If the child remains healthy and doesn't become reinfected with tuberculosis, there may never be any effects of the disease. If,

Possible symptoms

- Tiredness.
- Weight loss through loss of appetite.
- Persistent, dry cough with blood and pus in the sputum if the lungs are affected.
- Headache, fever and coma if the meninges are affected.

however, there is a period of malnourishment and illness, the primary lesion may break out of its chalky coating and spread through the blood to affect other organs.

The symptoms of this secondary phase of the disease depend on the organ that is affected. A child may merely be tired and lose his appetite, or, as in the case of TB infection in the lungs, the child will have a dry cough which eventually contains pus and blood.

Is it serious?

Tuberculosis is a serious disease if left untreated. However, there is an efficient public health programme that traces contacts of known carriers of the disease. This means that children who have had contact with someone suffering from tuberculosis are likely to be traced and tested for the disease before serious problems occur.

What should I do first?

It is extremely unlikely that you would suspect that your child had tuberculosis from any of the symptoms. However, if you hear of anyone who has tuberculosis and your child has been in contact with them, or if you are advised by the public health authorities that your child may have been in contact with a known TB sufferer, contact your doctor immediately.

Should I consult the doctor?

Consult your doctor immediately if you think your child has been in contact with someone with tuberculosis, or if you are worried about your child's general health or a persistent, dry cough.

Continued on next page ▶

Tuberculosis

◀ Continued from previous page

What might the doctor do?

A skin test will be arranged

□ Your doctor will arrange for your child to have a skin test to see if there is an active TB infection or not. If there is, your child will have an X-ray and sputum and urine tests to find out which organs the TB is affecting. In the majority of cases, TB can be adequately managed at home. Antibiotics will be prescribed, but rest and a good diet are also essential. Your child will need to be away from school for some months. There will be periodic check-ups after the treatment is finished to make sure the TB does not flare up again. At the end of two years, your child should be completely cured.

□ Your doctor will ask you for all known contacts of your child so that they can be traced and checked as a possible source of the infection.

What can I do to help?

□ Administer the drugs regularly and keep your child happy and as involved in normal life as is possible.

□ Make sure your child gets plenty of rest.

□ Arrange for a friend to come and play with your child regularly. After the drug treatment is started, your child will no longer be contagious and can safely play with friends.

SEE ALSO:
Cough, *page 97*
Meningitis, *page 177*

Words in **bold** are A-Z entries

Umbilical cord infection

After birth, the umbilical cord, which joins the baby to the placenta, is clamped and cut close to the baby's body. It then withers and the remaining stump drops off, usually within ten days of birth. You will be advised to clean the navel area and umbilical stump daily since it may become contaminated with urine. The stump will have become infected if it weeps, crusts over, discharges pus or appears red or swollen.

Is it serious?
Infection of the umbilical cord is rarely serious and is easily treated.

Possible symptoms

- Redness and swelling of the umbilical area.
- Umbilical stump weeps fluid which then crusts over.
- Pussy discharge.

What should I do first?

Check the stump at every nappy change for signs of infection. If the area seems to be getting red, contact your doctor or midwife.

Should I consult the doctor?

Consult your doctor as soon as possible if the stump shows any signs of infection. Consult your doctor or midwife if you are worried about the umbilical cord.

What might the doctor do?

☐ Your doctor will probably prescribe an antibiotic cream or powder to apply to the cord several times a day. He will also give you advice on daily hygiene.
☐ If your doctor thinks that infection is spreading along the cord and into your baby's body, your baby will need to be admitted to hospital for treatment with antibiotics.

What can I do to help?

Clean area thoroughly

☐ Clean the stump and surrounding area thoroughly at every nappy change. Gently wipe around the stump with a piece of cotton wool soaked in surgical spirit.
☐ There are anti-infective powders available from the chemist which can be sprinkled on the stump—ask your midwife for advice.
☐ Place a piece of sterile gauze between the cord and the nappy, or fold the nappy below the cord, to prevent urine from contaminating the navel area.
☐ Put a little salt in your baby's bath water to promote healing. Dry the navel area thoroughly afterwards.
☐ Allow the stump to fall off naturally. Never pull or twist it in an attempt to remove it.

Urinary tract infection

A urinary tract infection can affect any part of the urinary tract. This includes the kidneys, the bladder and the urethra (the tube leading from the bladder to the outside). In most cases, the part infected is the lining of the bladder, and the condition is known as cystitis.

Girls suffer from such infections more often than boys because the female urethra is shorter, thus making it easier for infecting microbes to reach the bladder. Young girls sometimes do not clean themselves thoroughly after using the toilet, and if they wipe their bottom from back to front instead of front to back this may bring faecal material near the urethral opening, which could cause infection. Rarely, a minor structural abnormality of the urinary tract is to blame. The most common symptoms of infection are pain on passing urine and the need to pass urine frequently.

Is it serious?
A urinary tract infection is serious.

Possible symptoms

- Pain or burning sensation on passing urine.
- Frequent urination, which can lead to bedwetting where previously the child was dry at night.
- Fever.
- Unpleasant-smelling and/or cloudy urine.
- Low abdominal pain.
- Low back pain.

The urinary system

Male   Female

| Kidney |
| Ureter |
| Bladder |
| Urethra |

What should I do first?

1 If your child complains of pain when passing urine, check his temperature to see if he has a fever.

2 Check his urine to see if it is cloudy or unpleasant-smelling.

3 Give your child plenty of fluids to keep his kidneys flushed out.

4 Place a hot-water bottle against the back is he is suffering from low back pain.

Should I consult the doctor?

Consult your doctor immediately if your child complains of pain on urination.

What might the doctor do?

☐ Your doctor will examine your child and take a sample of his urine for laboratory examination to identify the type of organism causing the infection. Your doctor will then prescribe the appropriate treatment, usually a course of antibiotics.

☐ If the infection recurs, your doctor may refer your child to a paediatrician for full investigation to see if there is a minor anatomical abnormality.

What can I do to help?

☐ Show your daughter how to wipe herself from the front backwards after using the toilet so that her urethra is not contaminated by her faeces.

SEE ALSO:
Bedwetting, *page 63*
Fever, *page 134*

Words in **bold** are A-Z entries

Vagina, foreign body in

A little girl is naturally curious about her vagina and she will investigate it with her fingers or perhaps something else. Fortunately it is rare for a foreign body to become lodged in a child's vagina, despite such exploration. If, however, there is a foreign body in your child's vagina, there may be symptoms of local soreness and tenderness or, after a day or two, an unpleasant-smelling, blood-stained discharge from the vagina. A discharge with itchiness, especially around the anus, may be an infestation of **worms**.

Is it serious?
Any discharge from the vagina, or soreness of the genital area, should be treated by a doctor, but is rarely serious.

Possible symptoms
● Soreness or tenderness around the vagina.
● Unpleasant-smelling or blood-stained discharge.

What should I do first?
1 Ask your child if she or a playmate has tried to push anything into her vagina.
2 Check your child's stools for tiny, thread-like worms.

Should I consult the doctor?
Consult your doctor as soon as possible if you notice any inflammation or discharge.

What might the doctor do?
☐ Your doctor will examine your child to try to determine whether the symptoms are the result of a foreign body being pushed into the vagina. If he thinks there is something there, he may refer you to a paediatric or gynaecological specialist who will perform an internal examination. The specialist will remove the foreign body, treat any infection with antibiotics and prescribe an ointment to relieve soreness or itching.

What can I do to help?
☐ Don't make too much fuss about the incident. It is important that your child doesn't develop an obsession about her genitalia that may affect her in later life.
☐ Discourage your child from using any instruments when playing "doctors and nurses".

SEE ALSO:
Worms, *page 261*

Verruca

A verruca is a wart on the sole of the foot that has been pushed up into the foot by the pressure of walking. It is highly infectious and is spread by direct contact with surfaces where infected feet have been, such as communal swimming pools, showers and gymnasiums. It takes about two years for the body to build up resistance to the wart virus (after which, the warts usually disappear naturally), but because a verruca can be spread easily and because it can be painful, treatment is advisable.

Is it serious?

A verruca is never serious but it can cause pain and discomfort, depending on where it appears on the sole of the foot.

Possible symptoms

Classic appearance of verruca

- White or brown, flat lump on the sole of the foot.
- Pain when walking or standing on the foot.

What should I do first?

1 Wash your child's feet and leave them to soak in warm water to soften the skin.

2 With a clean scalpel (available from the chemist) pare away thin layers of the softened verucca very gently. It is always wiser to take off too little rather than to draw blood.

3 Apply a proprietary brand of wart treatment, obtainable from a chemist. Don't apply the wart treatment to healthy skin. To avoid this, use a corn plaster or a piece of ordinary plaster, with a hole the size of the verruca cut out of it, to protect the surrounding areas. After putting on the lotion, cover the verruca with a sterile dressing and plaster.

4 Repeat the procedure every day until the verruca has disappeared.

Should I consult the doctor?

Consult your doctor as soon as possible if the verruca is painful or if the verrucae are increasing in number, or if self-help treatment fails.

What might the doctor do?

☐ Your doctor may refer you to a special wart clinic under the supervision of a dermatologist. The verruca will be removed either by treatment with a freezing agent such as liquid nitrogen, or by being burned off or scraped out under a local anaesthetic.

What can I do to help?

☐ Cover the verruca with a secure plaster whenever your child goes barefooted; this should prevent the spread of the virus.
☐ Discourage your child from scratching the verruca. He could infect himself elsewhere.

SEE ALSO:
Warts, *page 257*

Words in **bold** are A-Z entries

Vision problems

Most vision defects are due to a fault in the eye itself and are not the result of disease or injury. Babies are rarely born totally blind and routine check-ups during a child's pre-school years should detect any defect that could later lead to problems of vision.

Cross-section of eye

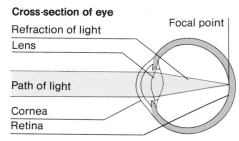

Many defects are caused when the light entering the eye does not focus properly on the retina. If the eyeball is too long from front to back, the images of distant objects will be focused in front of the retina and will appear blurred; near objects will be seen clearly. This is known as short sight. If the eyeball is too short from front to back, the images of both near and far objects will focus behind the retina. All images will be blurred, but near objects will be the worst. This is known as long sight. Short sight usually develops in late childhood and tends to run in families and a child

with a parent who is short-sighted should be regularly tested. Long sight is generally present at birth, and can cause eye fatigue as your child strains to focus on objects close to him. Both long and short-sightedness can be easily corrected with glasses.

Colour blindness is another common condition, especially in boys, and it too tends to run in families. True colour blindness, when everything appears grey, is rare; what most people refer to as colour blindness is in fact an inability to distinguish between reds and greens. There is no treatment for this condition but it does not interfere greatly with everyday life.

A **squint** is the other common eye problem. If your baby is under three months old and one or both eyes seem to wander slightly, there is no need to worry. However, if the squint persists, you should seek medical advice.

Are they serious?
Vision problems can be serious if they go untreated. Eyes need constant exercise and stimulation to keep them healthy, and a disused eye, as occurs in a squint, will deteriorate rapidly. However, early treatment, generally with glasses, occasionally with an operation, should correct most problems.

What should I do first?

Get your baby to track object

1 Although your baby will have regular sight tests, you can check

his vision yourself when he's about three months old. Dangle a familiar object about 20 cm (8 in) from your baby's face and move it slowly to one side. Your baby's eyes should track the object.

2 Be on the alert for any changes in the appearance of your child's eyes, such as the development of a squint, when both eyes do not follow an object together.

3 Be responsive to signs that your child cannot see clearly—if, for
Continued on next page ▶

Vision problems

◀ *Continued from previous page*
example, he is always bumping into furniture or is not able to follow the trajectory of a ball that is thrown to him.

4 Get another eye test done if your child does not co-operate with the doctor at a regular check-up, and the test is not carried out thoroughly for any reason. Often a child who is unable to do the test will cover up the disability with bad behaviour.

Should I consult the doctor?

Consult your doctor as soon as possible if you suspect any defect in your child's vision or notice any change in the appearance of his eyes, if your child complains of sore eyes and rubs his eyes a lot for no apparent reason or if your child's school performance is poor for no obvious reason (your child may be having difficulty following his teachers because of some vision problem and may be misbehaving or not concentrating during his lessons because of it).

What might the doctor do?

☐ Your doctor will check your child for sharpness of vision. Your child will be asked to read the letters on a card placed 6m (20ft) away from him. Each eye will be tested separately. A child under three years old will be asked to match figures or pictures placed in front of him with the same object held up for him by the doctor.
☐ Your doctor will check the general condition of your child's eyes with an ophthalmoscope to see if there is any internal eye disorder. If treatment is necessary, your child will be referred to an optician or an ophthalmic surgeon. In most cases, suitable glasses will be prescribed and fitted.

What can I do to help?

☐ Get glasses with plastic lenses—they are lighter to wear and don't break.
☐ Help your child to cope with teasing from his playmates by emphasizing the benefits of being able to see clearly.
☐ Keep a spare pair of glasses as children tend to break frames often.
☐ Teach your child how to keep the lenses clean, and encourage him to clean them daily.
☐ Be firm with your child to make sure he wears his glasses as often as the doctor instructs him to, particularly in the early weeks when he is still getting used to them.

Tie elastic to secure glasses during play

☐ Tie a piece of elastic round the back of your child's glasses so that they stay on during active play.

SEE ALSO:
Squint, *page 224*

Vomiting

See also page 256

Consult your doctor immediately if your child continues to vomit over a six-hour period; if vomiting is accompanied by diarrhoea or a fever; or if the vomiting is accompanied by any other symptoms such as earache.

Accompanying symptoms

Common causes

Accompanying symptoms	Common causes
Your baby often brings up a little milk during or after a feed, but seems contented, feeds well and is gaining weight.	This regurgitation of a little milk—possetting—is normal and harmless.
Your baby is less than ten weeks old and has more than once vomited forcibly during, or immediately after, a feed.	He could have **Pyloric stenosis**, *page 203.*
Your baby seems well and hungry but vomits during, or immediately after, his feed.	Solids given before he can chew properly may be the cause. Until your baby is six or seven months old, give puréed foods.
Your baby has a runny or blocked nose, snuffly breathing or a cough.	A **Common cold**, *page 90,* can make your baby vomit if he swallows a lot of the mucus it produces. A **Cough**, *page 97,* may also make him vomit.
Your bottlefed or weaned baby, or child, seems unwell and has passed frequent, watery stools.	**CONSULT YOUR DOCTOR IMMEDIATELY** Your baby may have **Gastroenteritis**, *page 139.* An older child may have **Food poisoning**, *page 136.*
Your child seems unwell, looks flushed and feels hot.	An infection is the most likely cause. See **Fever**, *page 133.*
When travelling, your child seems pale and quiet and complains of nausea.	**Travel sickness**, *page 246,* is the most likely cause.
Your child complains of a severe headache on one side of his forehead.	He could have **Migraine**, *page 178.*
Your child has abdominal pain around the navel and to the lower right side of his groin.	**CONSULT YOUR DOCTOR IMMEDIATELY** Your child could have **Appendicitis**, *page 53.*
Your baby is in severe pain and is passing stools that contain blood and mucus, resembling redcurrant jelly.	**CONSULT YOUR DOCTOR IMMEDIATELY** Your baby could have a bowel blockage known as **Intussusception**, *page 169.*
Your child cannot bend his neck forward without pain and turns away from bright light.	**CONSULT YOUR DOCTOR IMMEDIATELY** Your child may have **Meningitis**, *page 177.*

V

Vomiting

Vomiting is the violent expulsion of the contents of the stomach through the mouth. A baby may posset up small quantities of curdled milk after a feed but this should not be confused with vomiting. Vomiting has many causes (*see page 255*), but in the majority of cases there is little warning and after a single bout your child should be comfortable and back to normal. Vomiting can be a symptom of a specific disorder of the stomach such as **pyloric stenosis**, or a symptom of an infection, such as an ear infection. It frequently accompanies a **fever**, and even the **common cold** can cause vomiting if your child swallows enough nasal discharge to irritate his stomach. If your child has a bad cough, this can also cause him to vomit up food that he has recently eaten. Other causes of vomiting include **appendicitis**, **meningitis**, **migraine** headaches, **food poisoning** and **travel sickness**. Some children vomit because of excitement and anticipation but this is usually limited to toddlers.

Is it serious?
Vomiting should always be taken seriously because it can rapidly cause **dehydration**, particularly in a baby or young child.

What should I do first?

1 Put your child to bed and place a bowl for him to vomit into within easy reach.

2 Give your child frequent, small amounts of liquid, preferably cold water with a pinch of salt and 5 ml (one teaspoonful) of glucose added, every 10-15 minutes.

3 Check your child's temperature to see if he has a fever too.

4 Keep your child cool by wiping his face with a cool, damp cloth.

5 Get him to brush his teeth to take away the taste.

Should I consult the doctor?

Consult your doctor immediately if your child continues to vomit over a six-hour period; if vomiting is accompanied by diarrhoea or a fever over 38°C (100.4°F); or if the vomiting is accompanied by any other worrying symptoms such as **earache**.

What might the doctor do?

☐ Your doctor will diagnose the cause of the vomiting and treat your child accordingly. He will also make sure that there is no danger of dehydration.

☐ Your child may be admitted to hospital to be given fluids intravenously if he is in danger of becoming dehydrated.

What can I do to help?

☐ Give your child plenty of his favourite drinks, but dilute any fruit juices and don't give him milk.
☐ Feed your child bland foods when the nausea and vomiting have passed. Reintroduce solid foods slowly.

SEE ALSO:

Words in **bold** are A-Z entries

Warts

Warts are small benign lumps caused by the wart virus. They are made up of an excess of dead cells that protrude above the surface of the skin. They can appear singly or in alarming numbers over all parts of the body, including the face and genitals. If they occur on the soles of the feet, they are known as **verrucae**. It takes about two years for the body to build up a resistance to the wart virus, and after that time warts usually disappear spontaneously. Warts are spread by direct contact with an infected person.

Are they serious?
Warts are neither serious nor painful.

Possible symptoms

● Hard lumps of dried skin that appear spontaneously and grow singly or in clusters anywhere on the body.
● Small black dots within the lumps (these are blood vessels and not dirt).

What should I do first?

1 If your child has a wart, check the rest of his body for others.

2 Try ignoring the warts; they will go away of their own accord.

Apply a corn plaster to protect the healthy skin from wart solution

3 If your child wants the warts removed or they appear on a part of the body where they would easily infect other people, try the patent wart cures from your chemist. These work by the application of a weak acid solution to the wart and the daily removal of the resulting burnt skin. You should follow the manufacturer's instructions carefully and avoid applying the solution to healthy skin.

Don't use patent wart cures on warts that appear on the face or genitals. You may cause scarring.

Should I consult the doctor?

Consult your doctor as soon as possible if you are unsure whether the lumps are really warts. Any growth or lump on your child's skin which you are uncertain about should be checked by a doctor. Consult your doctor as soon as possible if the warts continue to multiply, or appear on the face or genitals and you want them removed.

What might the doctor do?

☐ Your doctor may advise you to ignore the warts, or refer you to a hospital dermatologist. If your child has to attend a special wart clinic, be prepared for frequent visits and some discomfort for your child. Methods of wart removal include cauterization and surgical removal.

SEE ALSO:
Verruca, *page 253*

Wax in the ears

Some wax in the external ear canal is quite normal. It is produced by glands in the skin of the canal to protect the ear from dust, foreign bodies and infections, and it appears as golden-brown or rust-coloured waxy crumbs. The wax is usually moved along and out of the canal by chewing movements of the jaw, but in some children an excess of wax is produced as a response to chronic **otitis media** or a dusty environment. Very occasionally wax may collect, dry and block the ear canal, leading to a temporary reduction in hearing.

Is it serious?
An excess of wax is not serious, although it may affect the hearing temporarily until the plug of wax is removed.

Possible symptoms
● Visible build-up of wax in the ear canal.
● Partial deafness.
● Feeling of fullness in the ear or a ringing sound.

What should I do first?

Check your child's ears regularly for wax build-up. Dislodge the wax only if it is at the opening of the ear canal and can be lifted out easily. Never poke anything, even a cottonwool swab, into the ear canal.

Should I consult the doctor?

Consult your doctor as soon as possible if you cannot remove the wax easily, or if your child seems to be having trouble hearing.

What might the doctor do?

□ After examining your child's ears with an otoscope, your doctor may syringe his ears with warm water to wash out the wax. This is a painless, though uncomfortable, procedure.
□ If the wax is hard and compacted, your doctor may prescribe ear drops to soften and dissolve the wax. You may have to return to have your child's ears syringed a few days later if the drops have not dislodged the wax.

What can I do to help?

□ Insert the ear drops just before your child's bedtime. Lay your child across your lap, or on his side on a bed, and drop the required amount into the ear canal. Ensure he lies still for two minutes so that the drops don't drain out of the ear.
□ After inserting the ear drops, make an ear plug from cottonwool and leave it in your child's ear overnight. The wax may come out with the ear plug in the morning. If it doesn't, you may have to return to the doctor to have the ear syringed.
□ Be on the alert for a possible blockage in the future. The tendency to produce an excess of wax is inherited, and blockage may recur after your child has a **common cold** or other respiratory tract infections.

> **SEE ALSO:**
> **Common cold,** *page 90*
> **Deafness,** *page 107*
> **Otitis media,** *page 196*

Words in **bold** are A-Z entries

Whooping cough

Whooping cough is one of the most dangerous childhood diseases, especially in babies under 12 months of age. It is caused by the bacterium *bordatella pertussis*, which causes the airways to become clogged with mucus.

Whooping cough begins as an ordinary cold with a cough. The coughing becomes severe, with spasmodic coughing bouts which make it difficult to breathe. When your child does manage to draw breath during a coughing bout (which can last up to a minute), there is a characteristic whooping sound as air is drawn in past the swollen larynx. The breathing difficulties are even greater for babies, who may never develop the technique of whooping to get air into their lungs, an inability which can prove fatal. Sometimes **vomiting** occurs after a coughing bout. The coughing phase of whooping cough can last for up to ten weeks. The risk of developing a secondary infection, such as **pneumonia** or **bronchitis**, is high after this illness.

Whooping cough is once again on the increase because parents are failing to immunize their children following the recent controversy surrounding the vaccination's possible side-effects. How-

Possible symptoms

- Cold symptoms of a fever, runny nose, aches and pains.
- Excessive coughing, with a characteristic "whoop" as the child struggles to draw breath.
- Vomiting after a coughing bout.
- Sleeplessness because of the coughing.

ever, medical opinion still holds that it is better for your child and for the community if the vaccination programme is continued, though there are some babies who should be placed in a special category and not immunized (for example those with epilepsy in the family). Ask your doctor's advice.

Is it serious?

Whooping cough is a serious disease, especially in babies, who may become dangerously short of oxygen during a coughing bout. If vomiting is severe, there is also the danger of **dehydration**. A severe attack of whooping cough can damage the lungs and cause recurrent bronchial infections.

What should I do first?

1 If your child's cold fails to improve and his cough worsens, put him to bed and get medical attention.

2 If you suspect your baby has whooping cough, consult your doctor immediately.

3 If you suspect your child has whooping cough, do not send him back to school or nursery school until you have seen your doctor.

Hold a bowl for your child

4 If your child is having a long coughing bout, sit him up and hold him so that he is leaning slightly forward. Hold a bowl nearby so that he can spit up any phlegm into it.

Continued on next page ▶

Whooping cough

◄ *Continued from previous page*

Should I consult the doctor?

Consult your doctor immediately if you suspect whooping cough.

What might the doctor do?

☐ Your doctor may prescribe antibiotics to reduce the severity of the cough and limit the infectiousness of the child. However, whooping cough is difficult to diagnose during the pre-liminary stage of the disease, and medication must be taken early to do any good. Your doctor may need to take a throat swab from your baby to diagnose whooping cough because babies rarely whoop.

☐ Your doctor will keep a close check on a baby with whooping cough and if the disease is severe will probably recommend hospital admission to prevent dehydration and to administer oxygen quickly if this should become necessary.

☐ Your doctor will make sure that you know how to hold your child during a coughing attack, and will show you how if you are unsure. He may advise you to raise the foot of your baby's cot and put your baby to sleep on his stomach.

What can I do to help?

☐ During a coughing bout hold your child as you've been shown and keep him calm. Panic will make the breath-lessness worse. Hold a bowl under his chin and encourage him to spit up the phlegm into it. This helps to clear the airways.

☐ Put bowls in all the rooms in the house so that he can spit up any phlegm or vomit without worrying about getting to the toilet in time. Clean these bowls in boiling water to prevent the spread of infection.

☐ If your child vomits after a coughing bout, give him small meals and drinks afterwards. This gives him a better chance to keep some food and liquids down and therefore to keep his strength up.

☐ Don't let your child play boisterously while he's recuperating. Exertion will bring on a coughing bout quickly and leave him exhausted.

☐ Keep your child away from cigarette smoke.

☐ Sleep in the room with him so that he is never alone during a coughing bout.

☐ Don't give your child any cough medicines without your doctor's advice.

☐ If, after the whooping cough has cleared up, your child seems unwell and is breathing with difficulty, contact your doctor immediately in case there is a secondary infection, such as pneumonia or bronchitis.

☐ Don't worry if your child "whoops" when he next catches a cold. This is not a return of the disease; your child is simply repeating a habit learned during all those coughing bouts.

> **SEE ALSO:**
> **Bronchitis,** *page 73*
> **Dehydration,** *page 108*
> **Pneumonia,** *page 200*
> **Vomiting,** *page 256*

Words in **bold** are A-Z entries

Worms

There are a number of worms that can live in the human body but the most common in temperate climates is the threadworm. The worm usually enters the body as eggs in contaminated food which then hatch in the intestine and develop into adults in 15 to 28 days. The female worms then lay more eggs around the host's anus, which causes **itching**, especially at night. If your child scratches himself, he can easily pick up the eggs and, by putting them into his mouth, start off the whole cycle again. Threadworms, which are 2-13mm ($1/16$-$1/2$ in) long, are harmless, but they can produce unpleasant symptoms, like the itching around the anus. Threadworms are highly infectious and all the family should be treated simultaneously.

Roundworms are rare but are most likely to infect children in areas where sanitary conditions are poor; they are more common in tropical climates. These parasites are long—10-15cm (4-6in)—and resemble a white earthworm. The eggs are swallowed with contaminated food or drink and, after hatching in the intestine, the worms lay eggs which are sometimes excreted in the stools. Your child will appear undernourished and he will fail to thrive.

Are they serious?
Worms are not usually serious and are easily treated.

Possible symptoms

Threadworms
● Itching around the anus, usually at night.

Appearance of worms

● White thread-like worms in the stools.
● Sleeplessness caused by intense itchiness.

Roundworms
● Failure to thrive.

Appearance of worm

● White worms in the stools.

What should I do first?

1 If your child is scratching his bottom, inspect the area about an hour after he has gone to bed. This is when the adult female usually comes out to lay eggs. The worm will look like a tiny piece of white thread.

2 Alternatively, inspect your child's stools for the numerous worms.

3 If you have recently been travelling in areas where infections with roundworm are common, and your child seems unwell and malnourished, inspect his stools for the larger roundworm.

W

Continued on next page ▶

261

Worms

◀ *Continued from previous page*

Should I consult the doctor?

Consult your doctor as soon as possible if you find any worms. Consult your doctor as soon as possible if you've been in an area where roundworm is common and your child is not thriving.

What might the doctor do?

☐ Your doctor will prescribe a simple treatment, usually in the form of a pleasant-tasting, soluble powder to be taken by the whole family.
☐ If your child has a roundworm, your doctor will prescribe a drug to be taken by mouth which will paralyse the worm. He will also prescribe a laxative so that your child can pass the worm easily in his stools.

What can I do to help?

☐ Follow the instructions for the medication carefully. The bowel motions may be loose for 12 hours afterwards so you may be advised to give the medication early in the morning.
☐ Repeat the dosage for all the family after two weeks. One dose of medication usually kills the worms but a follow-up dose will kill off any eggs that were not yet hatched when the first dose was taken.
☐ Be meticulous about hygiene. The eggs can be picked up under the fingernails and reingested.
☐ Make sure your child wears pyjamas or pants at night so that when he scratches, his hands don't come into direct contact with his anus.

SEE ALSO:
Itching, *page 170*
Toxocariasis, *page 245*

Safety

Safety around the home

Most accidents occur at home, and over half are to children under the age of five. Many are preventable, so you should take the time to look around your home and make sure that you minimize the chances of an accident occuring, both by altering the layout and position of items in your home, and by training your child. Teach your child self-protection from an early age by making him aware of the dangers. He will not fully understand your instructions at first, and he will probably forget them soon afterwards, but, with persistence, the message will get through. As your child gets older, he will begin to understand the logic of your advice, and will start to do as you say.

However, when your child is young, and cannot understand reasoning, there are certain simple, strict rules which should be observed at all times. Such rules would include: never touching electric sockets and never playing with sharp objects.

General safety tips

● Never leave your child alone for long: no matter how busy you are, always keep a check on what your child is doing and where he is. Be especially cautious at the end of the day, when you will be tired and possibly preoccupied with the family get-together.
● Check all your electrical cords: they are dangerous if frayed or split and should be replaced immediately.
● Teach your child that radiators and towel rails are hot to touch. Cover them with towels or seal them off with furniture if necessary.
● If you keep a gun in the house, never leave it loaded. Lock it away and lock the cartridges away in a separate container. Television films have made guns more familiar to children and they are now much more likely to use them as part of their play.
● Whenever you give your child medicines, read the label to check that you are administering the correct dosage.
● Make safe all upper storey windows by fitting either bars or safety catches, depending on the style of window. Don't leave any furniture beneath the window— your child may climb up and attempt to open or lean out of the window.
● Fit safety film to large areas of glass that your child could fall against, such as French windows and patio doors.
● If you have smooth tiled or wooden floors, use a special polish to make the surface non-slip. Don't let your child run around in stockinged feet.
● Put safety covers on all unused electric sockets throughout the house.
● Keep emergency numbers by the telephone, especially if you are out and your child has a babysitter.
● When visiting grandparents or friends who have no children, check around the house for possible problems, especially if children don't often visit. Breakable items or sharp objects may have been left in accessible places and cleaning chemicals may not have been put out of reach. Never be complacent; always presume that your child will find trouble if he tries.

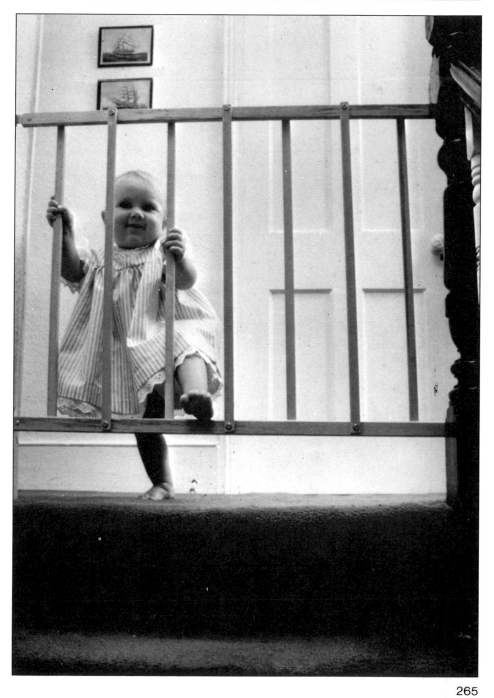

Kitchen

The kitchen is very often the focal room for the whole household and as such is often full of the bustle of the family. It is potentially dangerous for a number of reasons: from the cooking itself (boiling water and hot fat); from cooking utensils (knives and hot pans) and from the fact that you are preoccupied with food preparation and may not be paying full attention to your child.

Buy special safety guards for your cookers. Point saucepan handles away from the front of the cooker so that your child cannot grab the handle and pull the contents on to himself. When possible, use the back rings.

Keep your iron in a safe place, out of your child's reach; a wall-mounted iron rest is ideal.

Never leave objects near the edges of work surfaces; tuck them well back.

Attach safety catches to all cupboards and drawers that contain dangerous substances.

Clean out your pet's bowls after use, or keep them out of reach.

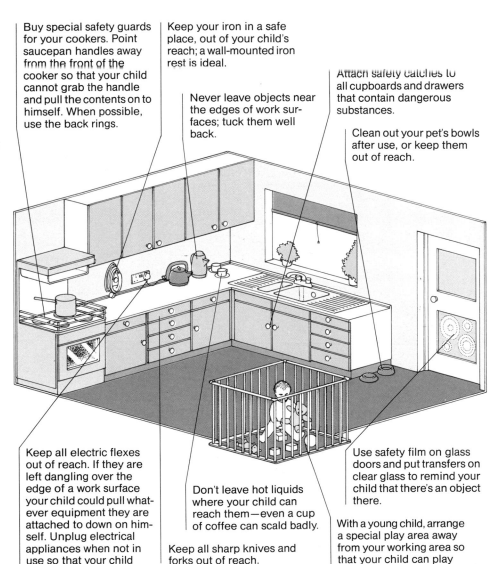

Keep all electric flexes out of reach. If they are left dangling over the edge of a work surface your child could pull whatever equipment they are attached to down on himself. Unplug electrical appliances when not in use so that your child cannot start them by accident.

Don't leave hot liquids where your child can reach them—even a cup of coffee can scald badly.

Keep all sharp knives and forks out of reach.

Use safety film on glass doors and put transfers on clear glass to remind your child that there's an object there.

With a young child, arrange a special play area away from your working area so that your child can play near you without becoming a safety hazard.

Kitchen

Highchairs

Until your child is old enough to sit at the table, a highchair is the most suitable and comfortable way of feeding him. Highchairs are available in a variety of designs, but there are certain safety features that you should look out for, no matter what style you opt for. Choose one which is stable, with widely spaced legs. If the tray is removable, there should be a strong enough lock or clasp to hold it in position while the chair is being used. There should be special clips at either side for attaching a safety harness and this should always be used when your child is in the highchair. Never leave your child unattended in the highchair.

Make sure your floor is non-slip and free of grease; mop up any spills.

Don't store uncooked meat next to cooked meat—one can contaminate the other. Don't store open tins in the fridge; put the remainder into a clean container.

Gastroenteritis can be a real risk for a bottlefed baby so sterilize all equipment carefully—milk is a favourite breeding ground for bacteria. Never leave a prepared feed standing at room temperature, or keep the remains of the last feed for the next.

Secure a swinging or self-closing door when your child is around—he could easily catch his fingers or be knocked over.

Keep a fire extinguisher and fire blanket in case of fire.

Don't use tablecloths if you have a toddler. Even a crawling baby can pull a cloth and bring the table's contents on to his head. Keep all items in the centre of the table.

Place the highchair out of the way of doors and thoroughfares, and well away from work surfaces.

If your child is going through a stage where he rummages through the bin, be very careful with sharp-edged cans. Always put a tin lid back inside the can and squeeze the sides together.

Bedroom

An awareness of safety in the bedroom is especially important in the first year of your baby's life because this is probably the room where your child will spend most of his time—either sleeping, being nursed or being changed.

Buy a sturdy cot with rounded edges. If the cot has a movable side rail, make sure it has strong clasps so that your child cannot release it and get his fingers caught. Make sure the mattress can be positioned low enough so that even if your child stands, he cannot get out.

Don't leave open electric or gas heaters in your child's room when he's asleep or unattended.

Have all your baby's changing equipment close to the changing mat, but never above it in case something falls on the child. Never leave your child alone on the mat in case he rolls off.

Use wall-mounted or ceiling lights rather than those with trailing flexes.

Don't use a pillow in your baby's cot; if you want to raise his head, put a pillow under the mattress. Always use a safety mattress—one that has specially designed air holes which minimize the risk of choking by allowing any vomit to drain away through them.

Firmly attach mobiles, out of your child's reach.

Buy non-flammable night-clothes and bedding.

Don't have any lightweight furniture in your child's room—he may topple it over on to himself. Try to buy round-edged furniture.

Bathroom

Your child is most at risk from falls and poisoning in the bathroom. Electrocution is also a potential danger, but improved building regulations now mean that no power points other than shaver sockets are installed in bathrooms. Only wall-mounted heaters should be used, and these should be positioned high and out of reach. Portable electric heaters should *never* be taken into the bathroom. Never leave a child under the age of three alone in the bath: he could go under the water.

Install a childproof medicine cabinet. Don't put it above the toilet—your child could climb up to it. Keep all medicines in childproof containers and remember, 50 aspirins can kill a child.

Keep cosmetics out of reach, especially those in aerosol cans.

Use safety film on a glass shower door. In case of accident, the glass will be held in place and will not splinter.

Use a non-slip mat if you have a tiled or polished floor.

Keep all toilet-cleaning chemicals and the toilet brush locked away—don't be tempted to tuck them behind the toilet itself.

Use a non-slip bathmat.

Use a special toilet seat and step for your toddler so that there is no risk of his slipping off the seat.

Keep the toilet lid closed and never mix cleaners with bleach as this gives off toxic fumes.

Sitting room

Much of day-to-day living goes on in the sitting room as well as the kitchen. One of the problems for parents trying to childproof their sitting room is not only how to make it safe for their child, but how to preserve valuable and much-loved objects from the child. Initially, it's probably easier to keep breakables out of reach, but, with time, repeated warnings should work.

If you have an open fire, always use a fireguard when the fire is lit to prevent your child from falling into the flames.

Keep all breakable items out of reach.

Keep the television in such a position that the back cannot be touched. It's also advisable to keep any recording, video or stereo equipment out of reach.

Make sure that carpets and rugs are in good condition, with no holes or turned up edges which could act as trip wires.

Use safety film on French windows or patio doors.

Don't leave anything belonging to your child above the fireplace or on a windowsill; he may try to climb up to get at it.

Make sure that none of your houseplants is poisonous.

Keep permanent flexes pinned to the skirting board, and position long flexes where they cannot be tripped over or played with by putting them behind furniture or under carpets.

Don't leave hot drinks, alcohol, cigarettes, matches or lighters where your child can get at them. Don't place heavy objects on low tables.

If you have any sharp-edged table tops and there is a risk that your child could run into them, fit plastic safety corners.

Hall and stairs

The two major dangers in halls and stairways are the stairs themselves and the possibility that your child could run out of the front door and on to the street. Until your child has the balance to come down a step at a time holding on to the banister, train him to come down the stairs on his bottom. Always stop him from going outside unless he is accompanied by you.

Make sure the banister supports are close enough together to prevent your child sticking his head between them and running the risk of getting it stuck, or of a young child falling through.

Have a stair-gate at the top and/or bottom of the stairs to prevent your child from climbing up or tumbling down. Stop him if he tries to climb over the gate.

Keep all breakable items, and the phone, out of reach.

Make sure that the front door closes properly so that there is no risk of your child being able to pull the door open and escape on to the street.

Keep stairs well lit and keep the stair carpet well maintained to minimize the risk of anyone tripping and falling.

Keep your child's toys as tidy as possible so that no one can trip over them.

If you've got polished floors, don't let your child run around in socks. He could easily fall and hurt himself.

Garden

The garden can be a dangerous place for a child, not only because it provides the means of escape on to roads, but also because of the machinery that is used to maintain it. There is the added danger, especially for toddlers, that some garden plants are themselves poisonous but nevertheless look like sweets. Although rarely fatal if eaten, they can produce unpleasant effects, ranging from skin to stomach irritation. Never let your child play unattended; keep him away from sharp or prickly plants like roses, and stop him from playing with earth—it may be contaminated with chemicals, or have bits of glass and animal dirt in it. If you have an area in the garden where you keep your car, make sure you know *exactly* where your child is before your start up the engine and move off.

Attach childproof locks to any gates.

Erect a climbing frame on grass so that any falls are cushioned. Keep all play equipment well maintained—check wood for splinters, ropes for fraying and chain links for good joins.

Cover a pram with a safety net to prevent any cat smothering your child.

Pull up mushrooms and fungi as soon as they appear.

Keep all paved areas and steps in good condition and de-moss them regularly to prevent falls.

Cover drains with wire mesh.

Empty the paddling pool as soon as your child has finished playing with it. Fit any water-collecting devices with a close-fitting lid so that your child cannot fall inside.

Garden

Poisonous plants

Skin irritation
Bleeding heart
Daphne
Poison ivy
Poison oak
Christmas rose
Foxglove

Mouth and throat irritation
Daphne

Jack-in-the-pulpit
Buttercups
White bryony

Stomach irritation
Daphne
Ivy
Wisteria
Belladonna lily
Christmas rose
Daffodil

Hyacinth
Iris
Sweetpea

General poisoning
Rhododendron
Crocus
Hydrangea
Larkspur
Lily of the valley
Laburnum

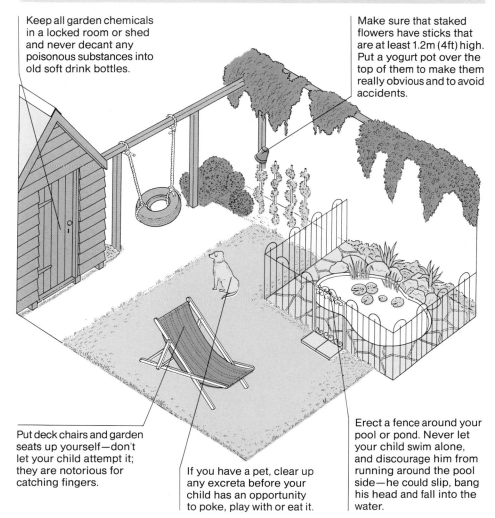

Keep all garden chemicals in a locked room or shed and never decant any poisonous substances into old soft drink bottles.

Make sure that staked flowers have sticks that are at least 1.2m (4ft) high. Put a yogurt pot over the top of them to make them really obvious and to avoid accidents.

Put deck chairs and garden seats up yourself—don't let your child attempt it; they are notorious for catching fingers.

If you have a pet, clear up any excreta before your child has an opportunity to poke, play with or eat it.

Erect a fence around your pool or pond. Never let your child swim alone, and discourage him from running around the pool side—he could slip, bang his head and fall into the water.

Road safety

After the home, most accidents to children occur on the street. It is therefore most important that, from an early age, your child is taught the rules of the road—where it is safe to cross, how to judge distances, where to play safely. The road codes may differ slightly between busy city streets and quiet country lanes, but wherever you are, talk to your child while walking or driving, and explain what you are doing and why.

Never be complacent about your child's road sense: keep reminding him of the rules. Even up to the age of twelve, children may have difficulty interpreting road safety; they may always regard a pedestrian crossing as safe, even with fast-approaching traffic; they may be distracted and not think before stepping out on to the road; they will certainly not be able to judge the speed of on-coming traffic, or hear an unseen car.

The green cross code

● Find a safe place to cross, such as a pedestrian crossing, subway or controlled lights.
● Stop at the kerb, look in both directions and listen for traffic.
● If traffic is coming, let it pass.
● Look in both directions again and, when nothing is coming, walk across the road. Keep looking and listening while you cross.

Encourage your child to press the button at pedestrian crossings.

Never push a pram out into the traffic without first checking that there is no traffic coming. Some parents forget that the pram sticks out in front of them by at least 1 metre (3ft).

Make the kerb the safety line and make it clear to your child that he's not to cross it without holding your hand.

Teach your child to wait at pedestrian crossings until the cars stop for him.

Beware of strangers

At frequent intervals, remind your child of the dangers of talking to strangers. Make up your own code word so that should you have to send a friend or neighbour to pick up your child, this word can be used. Tell your child never to go with anyone unless they use the code, no matter what the pretext.

When crossing with a pram and an older child, make sure you hold on to the walking child, too. When you know you can trust him not to run away, he can hold on to the side of the pram.

Road safety

Points to remember

Never allow your child to play or cycle on the pavement near a busy road. Unless you live in a very quiet road with few parked cars, don't let your child play in the road. Instead, encourage him to play in a garden or park.

Never let your child play on the pavement near a blind kerb.

Stress that your child must never chase a ball, pet or friend out on to the road without first stopping to look and listen.

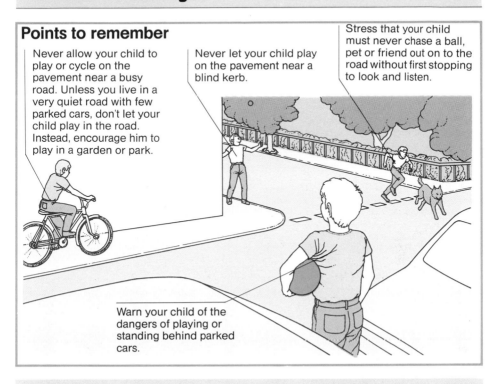

Warn your child of the dangers of playing or standing behind parked cars.

Pram safety

When you go out with a pram, never put heavy shopping bags over the handles— they could easily tip it backwards. Instead, buy a pram with a basket underneath. When you park a pram, always put on the brakes, but also point the pram in such a way that even if the brakes failed, it wouldn't roll into the road. Never leave a child unattended, and never tie a dog to the pram.

If the pram is collapsible, make sure that there's a safety lock to prevent it collapsing suddenly.

There should be a safety strap and side buckles for the separate attachment of a safety harness.

Make sure the pram is stable, with a base wide enough and sturdy enough not to tip over easily.

There should be good brakes.

Car safety

The safety laws for children travelling in cars differ from country to country, but whatever they are, you should never allow a child under ten to travel in the front passenger seat. Children are very often more vulnerable than adults in cars because their parents assume that a child travelling in the back is not in danger. This is false. On collision, a child who is not secured in a belt or special seat will be thrown forcefully against the seat or passengers in front, or worse still, through the windscreen. Apart from this basic feature of car safety, there are certain rules that you should observe to make travelling with your child as safe as possible. These are illustrated, below. Even once you have stopped the car, you should still be vigilent: for example, never leave your child unattended, even briefly.

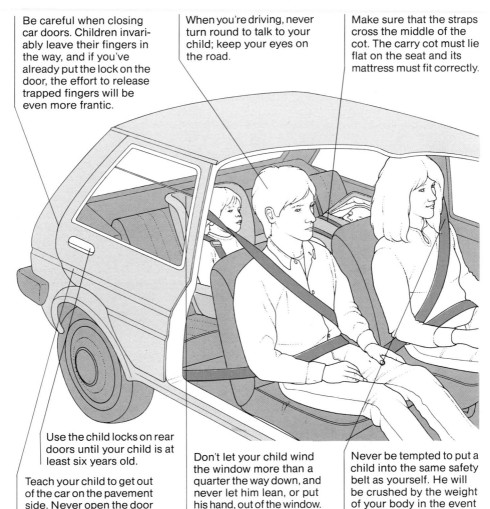

Be careful when closing car doors. Children invariably leave their fingers in the way, and if you've already put the lock on the door, the effort to release trapped fingers will be even more frantic.

When you're driving, never turn round to talk to your child; keep your eyes on the road.

Make sure that the straps cross the middle of the cot. The carry cot must lie flat on the seat and its mattress must fit correctly.

Use the child locks on rear doors until your child is at least six years old.

Teach your child to get out of the car on the pavement side. Never open the door on the traffic side, even on the quietest street.

Don't let your child wind the window more than a quarter the way down, and never let him lean, or put his hand, out of the window.

Never be tempted to put a child into the same safety belt as yourself. He will be crushed by the weight of your body in the event of a crash.

Car safety

If your child is under the age of eleven, or weighs less than 36kg (80lb), a regular seat belt is not the right safety device for him. His pelvic bones are not sufficiently developed to protect the internal organs from the pressure of the belt In the case of a crash. Your child should, instead, be restrained in a special car seat or safety harness. Whatever design you select, make sure that it is approved by the national standards authority, and that you have it properly installed. A baby in a carry cot should be secured to the back seat with restraining straps to prevent the cot from sliding across the back seat, and the straps should be bolted to the car frame. Car seats should also be bolted to the frame. Once your child has grown out of his car seat, he can be strapped in with a safety harness and raised on a booster seat so that he can see out of the window but remain safe.

Safety for babies

Until your baby is old enough to sit up and support his own weight, he will have to travel in either a carry cot, or a special back-facing baby seat. The latter is buckled into an adult safety belt and faces backwards so that, in an accident, any force is exerted against the baby's back and not his pelvis.

Safety for older babies and toddlers

Once your child can support his head and can sit well on his own, he should go into a car seat. By the time he's about three, or weighs more than 18kg (40lb), he can use a special safety harness, with or without a booster seat. Safety seats come in several styles and sizes—it's important to find the one that best suits your child by shopping around and trying your child out in the ones available.

Carry cot with child restraint straps

Adjustable car seat

Car seat with protective shield

Moulded car seat

Booster seat with safety harness

Playthings

Although there are now much tougher laws governing the safe production of toys, and the awareness of manufacturers is greatly improving, every year children are hurt and even killed by the toys that they play with. When buying toys or equipment for your child, try to buy those approved by the national safety authority (this will be indicated somewhere on the item by a symbol or number). If in doubt, contact your local consumer association.

Any household is potentially lethal for a child because there is so much that is new to be explored—a couple of minutes away from your child and he could have found that shirt button you lost, swallowed it and choked. *Never* give your young child anything to play with that is so small that he might swallow it by accident, or push it up his nose, or into his ear, Make sure there are no sharp edges or projections on any toys, and avoid those made of thin, rigid plastic. On soft toys and animals, check that the eyes and nose, bells and ribbons are well secured and that they cannot be pulled off. Toys are often marked suitable for a certain age— follow these guidelines, and always supervise your child while he's playing if he's under one year old.

Toys and objects
Examine toys carefully before you buy or give them to your child. Smooth-edged, hand-sized, or bigger, toys are safest until your child is old enough to know not to put objects into his mouth. Before giving him household objects to play with, check them over carefully for cracks, sharp bits and splinters. Don't let your child play with pens or other long objects which he could accidentally poke into his eye.

Baby walker
Select a walker with a wide base for stability. Avoid the X-type of walker —these collapse easily and can trap fingers. Keep an eye on where your child moves to in his walker, especially if you have any steps or ledges. Babies can build up quite a speed in the walker, and if they hit a raised thresh-old, even a carpet ledge, they can tip over, or be catapulted out of it.

Baby walker

Paints and pencils
Always give your child non-toxic, edible paints, pencils and crayons to play with. (For your own peace of mind, use non-spill paints, too.)

Baby bouncer
Make sure that your child is secured properly into the seat part of the bouncer, and that the clamp at the top is securely fastened to the door frame.

Baby bouncer

Sports and pastimes

Whatever sport or pastime your child takes up, you should ensure that he is properly equipped for it and that he is taught the sport's basic rules for safety. For example, if he's skateboarding or BMX bike-riding, make sure he goes to the specially set-up areas rather than on the road, and that he wears as much protective equipment as necessary. For example, get him to wear the helmet, knee-pads and gloves that are necessary. Almost every child learns to swim and ride a bike, and safety tips for these pastimes are given, below.

Bicycle safety

Children under ten should only ride their bikes in the garden, parks or special areas. They should never ride on the road, not even when crossing it. Nor should they be allowed to ride on the pavement as they are a hazard for pedestrians, especially when going around corners. When you buy your child's first bike, buy one with stabilizers at the back. This will allow him to gain confidence and general bike sense, without having to worry about falling off.

Saddle
Adjust the saddle so that your child can sit astride the bike with both feet touching the ground.

Brake blocks
Check the brake blocks regularly, and, if they show signs of wear, change them yourself or take the bike to a repair shop.

Carrier
If your child has a carrier on the back, tell him it's not to be used to carry friends on. They could easily topple over.

Mudguards
Make sure that the mudguards are firmly attached to the frame and are in no danger of slipping into the wheel spokes.

Tyres
Keep the tyres firmly pumped up.

Water safety

The most important element in water safety is your child's ability to swim. Enquire at your local swimming baths about mother and baby groups, and take your child to the nearest pool as often as possible, both to get him accustomed to the water and to encourage him to learn. Never let your child play in or near water without supervision. When you are at the seaside, or swimming in a lake or river, always heed local advice about swimming conditions: never swim when the red flag is flying, no matter how competent your family is at swimming. At the beach, always keep a close eye on your child, no matter how old, and don't let your child play alone with a lilo—it's very easy for either currents or wind to pull your child out from the shore. Because children have less subcutaneous fat than adults, they get cold quickly, so keep swimming times short.

Playground safety

All children get bored playing in their own or a friend's garden, and if there's a playground in your area, they are bound to want to visit it, especially if it's an adventure playground. Part of the adventure of an adventure playground is the sense of danger. However, you must try to help your child to understand his limitations and be cautious. The bravado that comes from being with friends who act like daredevils can easily lead to accidents. Playgrounds usually have special areas for younger children and toddlers. You should keep to these areas if you have young children, as older children play more boisterously.

Check that roundabouts have smooth surfaces and that they move round easily. Tell your child never to put his feet underneath the roundabout.

Make sure your child has non-slip soles on his shoes and that he is wearing sturdy jeans.

Climbing frames should be built on grass or sand to break falls, they should be completely stable.

Discourage your child from throwing sand in the sandpit. Sand in the eyes can scratch the surface of the eye and cause an injury. Make sure that the sandpit is too shallow for your child to bury himself.

Slides should be no higher than 2.5m (8ft) high, preferably constructed on an earth mound so that any fall is broken. The slide should be of one smooth, continuous piece —not jointed panels.

Swings should be surrounded by a fence to prevent children running in front of, or behind, them and being knocked over. Until your child can hold on properly, always use the box type of swing.

First aid

Dealing with an accident

Children are prone to accidents because they are naturally inquisitive and often unaware of danger. Although most accidents are relatively minor, it is important that you are familiar with life-saving first-aid techniques so that you know what to do in the event of a serious accident. Knowing the right way to deal with the situation will not only enable you to act quickly and efficiently but it will also help you to stay calm. The calmer you are, the more you can comfort your child and the more you will be able to help him.

On pages 290 to 300 I have described the immediate action and treatment for several emergencies such as choking, unconsciousness, electric shock, serious bleeding, shock, drowning, burns; other injuries are covered in the A-Z section of the book.

Priorities

Whatever injury your child has sustained, if he is unconscious you must do the following:

1 Make sure that he is breathing (*see page 284*) and if he is not, begin mouth-to-mouth ventilation (*see page 286*) before you attend to any other injury.

Note *If your child is breathing, his heart will also be beating.*

2 You should stop any severe bleeding (*see page 292*).

3 Only when steps one and two have been dealt with should you treat any other injuries.

Examining your child

1 If your child is unconscious but breathing and his injury is not immediately obvious, examine him very carefully from head to foot. Try and keep his head tilted back to keep his airway open (*see opposite*). If possible, get someone else to support his head while you examine him.

2 Always compare one side of his body to the other side, or one limb to the other. Move him as little as possible; slide your hand under his back or his head to make sure there is no sign of bleeding. Treat any injury you find.

Multiple injuries

Your child may have suffered several injuries, and the correct treatment of one may interfere with the treatment of another. If this is the case, treat the injury you consider to be the most serious, then treat the others as correctly as you can.

Calling for help

Your child will need to be taken to the nearest casualty department following any accident resulting in unconsciousness, difficulty in breathing or injuries such as bleeding, broken bones or burns. You should always call an ambulance if your child needs a stretcher for a broken leg or spine injury, for example, or if you are on your own and first aid needs to be continued on the way to hospital. However, if speed is very important and there is another adult available who can drive you to hospital, it may be faster if you sit in the back of the car with your child and continue first aid while the other adult drives.

When you ring for an ambulance, give the control officer as much information as possible. He will want to know the extent of your child's injury, the cause of the injury if it is known and probably the age of your child. Also describe any landmarks that will help the ambulance get to your house, especially if it is difficult to find.

Resuscitation

Everyone needs a constant supply of oxygen to survive—permanent brain damage can result after only three minutes without oxygen. If your child is unconscious and not breathing you may still be able to save his life by taking over his breathing and blood circulation. Resuscitation is the term used to describe the combination of techniques used to revive someone who is unconscious and not breathing. These techniques include: Opening the airway (*see below*), Breathing for your child (*Mouth-to-mouth ventilation, see page 286*), and Circulating his blood (*External chest compression, see page 288*).

It is *always* worth starting resuscitation and you should keep going until a doctor arrives or your child starts to breathe again on his own.

OPENING THE AIRWAY

The airway consists of the passages between your child's mouth and nose and his lungs. If your child is unconscious, particularly if he is lying face upwards, breathing may be difficult. Air may not be able to get through to his lungs because: the tongue has fallen back and blocked the windpipe; the head has tilted forward narrowing the top of the windpipe; fluid or vomit has collected at the back of the throat and is unable to drain.

> **IMPORTANT**
> **Keep your fingers and hand well away from the soft tissues under a child's chin and along his neck.**

What should I do?

1 Lay your child on a firm surface. Place one hand on the child's forehead and one hand under the back of his neck. Press very gently on the forehead and tilt the head back. It is in the right position when you can see straight down his nostrils.

2 Place two fingers of one hand on your child's chin and lift his jaw up so that his chin juts forward. The tongue will come forward with the jaw, thus opening the airway. Check breathing (*see overleaf*).

Opening the airway for babies and small children

Babies have very short necks and soft windpipes and if you tilt the head back too far you can easily block the airway.

1 Lay your child on a firm surface. Place one hand on the child's forehead and press very gently to tilt his head slightly.

2 Support the jaw by placing two fingers of the other hand on the BONY part of the chin. Check breathing (*see overleaf*).

Resuscitation

CHECKING BREATHING

If your child is unconscious, before you do anything else you must make sure he is breathing. Open the airway as described on the previous page just in case the tongue has fallen back and blocked the air passages, then check his breathing as described below.

What should I do?

1 With his head tilted back, place your ear as near to his mouth and nose as possible and look along his chest at the same time.

2 If he is breathing, you will see his chest moving and you will hear and feel his breath against your face.

3 If he is not breathing, try clearing the airway as shown right.

> **IMPORTANT**
> If your child is breathing, even slightly, leave well alone, do not try to give him mouth-to-mouth to try to increase the breathing rate. Just turn him into the recovery position as shown opposite and keep checking his breathing.

CLEARING THE AIRWAY

If your child is not breathing after you have tilted his head back, take a look inside his mouth, to see if there is something blocking the airway.

What should I do?

1 Turn your child's head to one side and quickly but carefully run your index finger around the inside of his mouth; hook out anything you find.

2 Be very careful not to push anything further down his throat. If you think your child has choked on something, *see page 294.*

3 Check your child's breathing again, see left.

> **IMPORTANT**
> With a young baby, do not put your finger in his mouth unless you can see the foreign body clearly and you are sure there is no risk of pushing it back down his throat. It is much better to hold him upside down and slap his back (*see page 294*).

What should I do next?

● If your child is now breathing, place him in the recovery position (*see opposite*). Remember, if he is breathing, his heart will be beating.

● If your child is still not breathing, you must begin mouth-to-mouth ventilation immediately (*see page 286*).

Resuscitation

THE RECOVERY POSITION

If your child is unconscious but breathing, place him in this position while you are waiting for the doctor or ambulance. It keeps your child's tongue well forward and allows any fluid or vomit to drain freely from his mouth, allowing him to breathe without choking. Immobilize any broken bones (*see page 71*) before turning him.

The method shown below assumes that your child is lying on his back. If he is lying on his side or his front you may only need to move his head back and bring his uppermost leg and arm up as shown in the last step to prevent him rolling on to his face.

Positioning your child

1 Turn your child's head towards you and tilt it back slightly to open the airway. Place the arm nearest you by his side and, keeping his fingers flat, slide his hand under his buttock.

2 Lay your child's other arm across his chest and bring his furthest leg across the near one at the ankle.

3 Kneel beside your child, level with his chest. Grab his clothing at the hip and, supporting his head with the other hand, pull him towards you until he is resting against your knees. Re-adjust the position of his head to make sure it is well back and he can breathe easily.

4 Bend the upper arm and the leg up to support the child and prevent him rolling on to his face. Make sure that your child's other arm is free and leave it lying parallel to his back to prevent him rolling on to his back.

> **IMPORTANT**
> **You should never leave an unconscious child on his own, even when he has been placed in the recovery position. Try to get another adult to call for the ambulance while you stay with him.**

Resuscitation

MOUTH-TO-MOUTH VENTILATION

This is the resuscitation technique to use if you find your child unconscious with no signs of breathing (*see pages 283-84*). It is also known as rescue breathing. You should start this wherever you find your child. If, for example, he is in the water, start rescue breathing there. If for any reason you cannot put your mouth over your child's mouth, you can close off his mouth and breathe into his nose. If he is very small it may be easier to place your mouth over his mouth and nose together (*see opposite*).

What should I do?

1 Tilt your child's head back to open the airway and if necessary clear the airway (*see pages 283-84*).

2 Support your child's jaw with one hand, taking great care not to rest your hand on his neck because you can

close off the windpipe. Pinch your child's nostrils shut with two fingers of the other hand.

3 Take a deep breath. Open your mouth wide and seal your lips around your child's mouth.

4 Breathe gently but firmly into his mouth, blowing from your lungs not just your mouth, until you see his chest rise. Look along your child's chest—you should see the chest fall again if you have been successful.

IMPORTANT
If your child's chest has not risen, check that:
1 The head is in the correct position (*see page 283*); you should be able to see straight down his nostrils.
2 You are pinching the nostrils shut and that your mouth is forming an air-tight seal around his mouth.
Try again and if you are still not successful try giving him back slaps as described for choking (*see page 294*).

Resuscitation

5 Repeat the breathing procedure three more times as quickly as possible; wait for the chest to fall between each breath. Then check your child's heartbeat (*see overleaf*).

6 **If your child's heart is beating,** continue rescue breathing at a rate of 15-20 breaths per minute until he can breathe by himself. As soon as he is breathing on his own, place him in the recovery position (*see page 285*) while you wait for the ambulance.

7 **If your child's heart is not beating,** START EXTERNAL CHEST COMPRESSION NOW (*see page 288*).

Mouth-to-mouth for babies and small children

Although the basic breathing techniques are the same, you have to take the baby's smaller size into account when giving mouth-to-mouth ventilation. Because the gap between the nose and mouth is so small you may find it easier to place your mouth over his mouth and nose together. Also you'll only have to breathe a small amount of air into his lungs, at a slightly faster rate of 20 breaths per minute, so do not breathe too hard.

1 Lay your child on his back. Tap the soles of his feet to make sure he really is unconscious. If there is no reaction, tilt his head back slightly by pressing on his forehead and support-ing his chin with your fingers (*see page 283*). Do not tilt the head too far.

2 Slide one hand under his back to support him and keep his head back, and put your mouth over his mouth and nose together. Breathe out gently until his chest rises. Repeat three more times as quickly as possible then check heartbeat as above.

IMPORTANT
If you cannot inflate the lungs, check that the airway is open. If you still cannot force air in, hold him upside down and give him back slaps (*see page 294*).

Resuscitation

EXTERNAL CHEST COMPRESSION

This resuscitation technique is used in conjunction with mouth-to-mouth ventilation when a child is unconscious and not breathing and his heart is not beating after you have started mouth-to-mouth. Chest compression is important because if the heart is not beating, the oxygen you breathe into your child will not get to the body tissues and permanent brain damage can occur after only *three minutes* without oxygen.

Checking for the heartbeat

To find out whether your child's heart is beating, check the pulse in the carotid arteries—the arteries that supply blood to the brain.

1 Find the front of your child's windpipe (*see page 18*) and slide the pads of three fingers across into the groove between it and the large muscle in the neck, just below the jaw and in line with the earlobe. Don't use your fingertips because they have a pulse of their own.

2 Feel for about five seconds. If you cannot feel anything, the heart has stopped beating.

What should I do?

1 If your child's heart has stopped beating, lay him on a hard surface and kneel beside him facing his chest. Find his breastbone (the bone that runs down the centre of his chest, *see page 13*). Feel for the top in the groove between the collar bones, then find the centre of the breastbone by measuring the bone with both hands as shown.

2 Place the heel of one hand over the lower half of the child's breastbone, keeping your fingers off his ribs. Position yourself so that your shoulders are directly over the child's breastbone. Depress it 2.5-3.5 cm (1-1½ in), then release the pressure.

Resuscitation

3 Complete five compressions at a rate of about 80-100 compressions per minute (count "one-and-two-and-" as you go). Then stop and give your child one breath of mouth-to-mouth ventilation (*see page 286*).

IMPORTANT
It is important to follow these instructions very carefully because if you press too hard you could crush your child.

---

4 Continue giving five compressions followed by one breath of mouth-to-mouth for about a minute, then stop and check the carotid pulse again.

5 If the heart is still not beating, continue giving him five compressions followed by one breath of mouth-to-mouth but stop to check the pulse at least every three minutes.

6 As soon as you can feel a pulse again STOP PUMPING. Continue giving your child mouth-to-mouth until the ambulance arrives or he starts breathing again.

External chest compression for babies and small children

The sequence of steps for giving chest compression to babies and small children under the age of about two is the same as for large children, but the hand position is slightly different and you must use less pressure.

1 Lay your baby on a hard surface such as a table and support the head and back by placing one hand under his back and grasping the top of his arm.

2 Imagine a straight line across the child's chest between his nipples and place two fingers of the other hand on the centre of the line. Depress the breastbone 1.5-2.5 cm (½-1 in) then release the pressure.

3 If your baby is too large for you to depress the breastbone easily with your fingers, do not put your hand under his back. Use the heel of one hand to depress the breastbone.

4 Give five compressions to one breath of mouth-to-mouth as for large children, checking the pulse after one minute and again every three minutes.

Dealing with unconsciousness

The danger of unconsciousness is that the normal reflexes, such as coughing, that prevent a child choking while he is asleep do not work properly or do not even work at all.

Head injury (*see page 153*), shock (*see page 293*), electric shock (*see page 299*), choking (*see page 294*), convulsions (*see page 95*), diabetes (*see page 110*) and epilepsy (*see page 127*) can all result in unconsciousness.

If your child regains consciousness or has been unconscious only for a very short time, he must still be seen by a doctor, even if he appears to be alright. If the unconsciousness was caused by a head injury, your child will need to have a skull X-ray to make sure there is no fracture.

Levels of unconsciousness

Your child may pass through various stages of unconsciousness before becoming completely unconscious. The same will apply as he regains consciousness. At first he may appear very confused; he may then lapse into a stupor, when he will behave as if he is drunk, and then a coma, when he will become completely unconscious. Because of this, it is essential that you remain with the child all the time, and if possible send another adult to telephone for an ambulance. Watch your child carefully and note any changes in his state of awareness. This information may help the doctor decide what treatment to give him later.

What should I do?

1 Shake your child gently by his shoulders or pinch his earlobe. Question him, asking him if he is alright. Give him about 10 seconds to respond.

2 If your child does not respond, tilt his head back (*see page 283*) and check to see if he is breathing (*see page 284*).

Dealing with unconsciousness

3 If he is breathing but is making snoring or gurgling sounds, there may be something blocking the airway. Clear the airway (*see page 284*).

4 If he is breathing, keep his head tilted and examine him from head to foot; treat any injuries such as broken bones. Then turn him into the recovery position (*see page 285*). If there is any fluid coming from your child's ear, position him so that he is lying on the affected ear; the fluid can then drain away. Place a pad under the ear.

5 If your child is still not breathing you must start mouth-to-mouth ventilation (*see page 286*) and external chest compression if necessary (*see page 288*).

IMPORTANT
Any child who has been unconscious or who has a head injury must be seen by a doctor. Do not give a child who has been unconscious anything to eat or drink before he is seen by a doctor.

Dealing with an unconscious baby

The procedure for treating an unconscious baby is the same as for an older child except that you should tap his feet to establish whether he is really unconscious; he is unconscious if there is no response.

You should also remember that when opening the airway you must not tilt a baby's head back as far as for an older child; puff gently into the mouth when giving mouth-to-mouth; and apply only gentle pressure when giving external chest compression.

Dealing with bleeding

Bleeding happens when any of the vessels that carry blood around the body are cut or torn. It can be external, and therefore visible, or internal and not visible (*see opposite*). Serious bleeding should be treated as an emergency because, if too much blood is lost from the child's circulatory system, there will not be enough left to supply the body cells with oxygen, and shock can result (*see opposite*). Treat the child as described below and constantly reassure him.

What should I do for minor injuries?

Most small cuts and grazes can easily be dealt with at home. Hold the affected area under gently running cold water, wash it with ordinary soap and water, then protect the injury with a plaster (*see page 103*).

What should I do for severe bleeding?

1 As soon as you see that your child is injured, apply pressure directly on to the wound to compress the ends of the damaged blood vessels. At the same time, raise the affected area above the level of his chest (heart). This slows down the flow of blood to the injured area by making it flow uphill and keeps the vital organs supplied with blood.

2 If your child is not already lying down, help him to lie down, keeping the affected area raised and maintaining pressure on the wound.

3 If you have a first-aid box near you, place a wound dressing (*see page 35*) or a pad and bandage over the wound. If not, use any clean *non-fluffy* material near at hand and secure it with a scarf, tie or similar material. Tie the ends in a knot directly over the pad on the wound to maintain pressure.

4 Get your child to a casualty department as soon as possible because he may need stitches. Either call an ambulance or get another adult to drive you there while you sit with your child, continuing first aid if necessary.

Dealing with a foreign body or broken bone

1 If there is something sticking out of your child's wound, do not press directly on it. Raise the affected part and press the area above and below the object or bone end.

2 Never remove a foreign body from your child's wound because it may be plugging it, preventing bleeding, and you may cause more damage when pulling it out.

Dealing with shock

Shock in this context does not mean that your child is suffering from fright. Medical shock is a potentially fatal condition that can occur if blood pressure becomes severely lowered after a loss of body fluids such as blood, or if the heart is not working properly. None of the vital organs can function if they do not get enough blood.

Shock can be caused by serious bleeding, severe burns, electric shock, or dehydration following profuse vomiting or diarrhoea. Shock can also be caused by a severe reaction to an insect bite, such as a bee sting, or some medicines, when it is known as anaphylactic shock. The treatment is always the same.

Even if your child is not suffering from any of the symptoms and signs listed below, but he is bleeding or badly burnt, for example, there is a possibility of shock developing. Treat him as described below and right and get him to hospital as quickly as possible.

Possible symptoms

If your child is suffering from shock, he may show some or all of the following symptoms:
- Pale, blue/greyish skin (this is particularly noticeable just inside his lips and under his fingernails).
- Rapid, weak pulse.
- Shallow, fast breathing.
- Cold, clammy skin.
- Sweating.
- Dizziness.
- Blurred vision.
- Restlessness.
- Thirst.
- Unconsciousness.

What should I do?

1 Reassure your child. Treat any bleeding and move him as little as possible.

2 Lay him down on a blanket on a flat surface, raise his legs so that they are higher than his chest (heart) and support them on cushions or pillows. Loosen any tight clothing, particularly around his neck, chest and waist and turn his head to one side.

3 Keep your child comfortably warm, cover him with a blanket if he is cold but do not let him get too hot. Never use a hot-water bottle or an electric blanket to warm him because they cause blood to come to the surface of the body, taking it away from the vital organs.

If your child is unconscious

Turn your child into the recovery position immediately (*see page 285*). Watch his level of consciousness (*see page 290*) and check his breathing rate (*see page 284*) every few minutes until the ambulance arrives or you can get to a doctor.

Internal bleeding

This can happen if, for example, an internal organ is damaged in an accident or a large bone such as the thigh-bone or pelvis is broken. If your child develops any of the symptoms listed left, without obvious injury, if he complains of severe pain in the chest or is unusually quiet after an accident, treat as above and get him to hospital quickly.

Dealing with choking

Small children are liable to choke because they may eat something they cannot chew properly, and because they have a habit of putting small objects in their mouths. You must act quickly because, if the object is not removed, breathing could stop.

Possible symptoms

- Coughing.
- Grasping of the throat.
- Blueness in the face—the blood vessels in the neck and face may stand out.

4 Continue the back slaps until the object is cleared. Then either hook the object out with your finger—be very careful not to push it back down his throat—or ask your child to spit it out.

What should I do?

1 If your child is coughing, encourage him to keep coughing hard and do not interfere.

2 If he is not coughing, quickly lay him head down across your thigh.

3 Support him so that his head is lower than his chest and give him four slaps on the upper part of his back between his shoulder blades.

Dealing with a choking baby

If your baby is choking on something you must act very quickly to clear the blockage.

1 Pick him up immediately and place him face down on your forearm, supporting his head and neck with your hand.

2 Hold your baby so that his head is lower than his chest and give him four quick slaps between his shoulder blades. Continue slapping his back until the blockage is cleared.

3 If you can see the foreign body in your child's mouth try to remove it, but be very careful not to push it back down his throat again. Never probe his mouth (*see page 284*) if you cannot see the object.

Dealing with drowning

You can help your child only if you are safe. Don't jump into the water if you can throw him a life-belt or reach him with your arm or a pole. If your child is not breathing you must start mouth-to-mouth ventilation immediately, even if you are in the water. However, to do this while dragging a child to safety can be quite difficult; you need to be a strong swimmer.

Very young children can go into a state of "underwater hibernation" and hold their breath for amazingly long periods of time so never give up mouth-to-mouth, keep going until an ambulance or doctor arrives. Do not try to drain water from your child's lungs if he is not breathing—he will cough it up when he starts to breathe again.

Remember, water does not have to be deep to drown a child. He can drown in only 5cm (2in) of water, so never leave your child unattended when he is outside near water or when he is in the bath. Also, if your child is immersed in cold water for any length of time, there is a danger of hypothermia (*see page 300*).

What should I do?

1 *If your child is conscious,* get him out of the water as quickly as possible, cover him with dry clothing while you get him into the house or the nearest shelter, then replace his wet clothes with dry ones to prevent hypothermia.

2 *If your child is unconscious,* check to see if he is breathing. If he is not breathing, start mouth-to-mouth ventilation (*see page 286*) even while he is still in the water. Get him out of the water and continue mouth-to-mouth until help arrives, even if your child has been submerged for a long time.

3 If your child is unconscious but breathing, get him out of the water, place him in the recovery position (*see page 285*) and cover him with anything readily available, such as a coat or a blanket, to keep him warm but don't take off his wet clothes. Keep checking his breathing and level of consciousness and be prepared to start mouth-to-mouth if his breathing stops.

4 Wait for the ambulance to arrive. However, if it will be quicker, you can get another adult to drive you to the nearest casualty department while you sit in the back with your child and continue giving mouth-to-mouth.

Dealing with burns

Burns need urgent treatment because of the risk of infection and because of the risk of shock (*see page 293*), following the loss of body fluid.

Burns can be divided into two main types: superficial and deep. Superficial burns involve damage to the surface of the skin, deep burns involve the whole thickness of the skin. If more than one tenth of the body's surface—an area roughly the size of the child's abdomen—is burned, even superficially, shock will occur.

The most important thing to remember is that only small, superficial burns can safely be treated at home (*see page 77*). If you are in doubt consult the doctor.

IMPORTANT
If one tenth, or more, of your child's body is injured, call an ambulance immediately. Treat your child as described for shock and prevent the burned area from coming into contact with the ground by laying him on a sheet of *non-fluffy* material.

What to do if clothing is on fire

If your child's clothing is on fire, first stop him running about in a panic because this will fan the flames. Secondly, because flames rise, you must get him down on to the floor with the flames uppermost. Put the flames out as quickly as possible, then treat any burns.

1 If there is a bucket of water nearby, douse the flames with water. However, do not use water if the clothes have been set on fire by an electric heater and the child is still near the heater—you will electrocute yourself (*see page 298*).

2 If you have no water, smother the flames by covering your child with a coat or blanket made of a NON-flammable material. Do not use a synthetic material because it will melt on to his skin, intensifying the burn.

3 As a last resort, lie down on top of your child but make sure that you lie right down on top of him because a tunnel of air will develop in the smallest gap and fan the flames, setting your clothes on fire as well.

Dealing with burns

What should I do?

1 Remove your child from the source of danger, breaking any electrical contact if necessary (*see page 298*). Reassure him: burns can be very painful and your child will be frightened.

2 Cool the affected area immediately; this stops the heat damaging your child's skin any more. Hold the affected area under cold running water for as long as the child can stand it—at least 10-20 minutes. If a large area is burned, put the child in a cool bath or cover him with a cold wet cotton or linen sheet (it must not be fluffy).

3 Carefully cut away and remove any clothes soaked in boiling fluid or chemicals, making sure that you do not burn your fingers.

4 Cover the injury with a gauze dressing that is larger than the area covered by the burn. If you have no suitable dressings in your first-aid box, you can protect a large burn on a hand or foot by placing a clean plastic bag over it.

5 While you are waiting for the ambulance or are taking your child to hospital, treat your child as described on page 293 to prevent shock.

> **IMPORTANT**
> **1 Never put any fats, ointments or lotions on a burn.**
> **2 Never break a blister caused by a burn.**
> **3 Do not use plasters to cover a burn, or cover it with anything fluffy such as cotton wool because it may stick to the injury.**
> **4 Be very careful about immersing very young children in cold water for too long because it can cause hypothermia (*see page 300*).**

Dealing with chemical burns

1 Put the affected part under cold running water as quickly as possible and for as long as your child can stand it—about 10-20 minutes—to wash the chemicals off. Hold your child so that the contaminated water can drain away without touching any other part of his or your own skin.

2 While you are washing the chemicals off, very carefully remove any contaminated clothing, then treat as for burns, above.

Dealing with electric shock

Contact with household electricity can cause burns and the shock may cause unconsciousness or even stop your child's breathing and heartbeat. If your child is still in contact with the electricity, you must switch off the power source or break the electrical contact (see below) *before* touching him, otherwise you will electrocute yourself.

Contact with electricity can also result in burns. Although these burns look small, they are often deep. In addition, there may be a burn not only where the electricity enters your child's body but also where it leaves the body. There is a serious risk of infection, so it is essential that all electrical burns, however small, are seen by a doctor.

Breaking electrical contact

If it is not possible to switch off the source of power, you must break the contact immediately. Find something that will not conduct electricity, such as a broom or plastic tube, and push your child's limb away from the electricity. Make sure that your hands and whatever you use are dry and that you are not standing on anything wet or metal.

What should I do?

1 When the contact is broken, examine your child carefully—if you find a burn, check to see if there is another burn on the other side of the limb.

2 Cool any burns by placing the affected area under a cold tap for 10-15 minutes (*see page 297*). Cover the burns with dressings and get your child to the nearest hospital casualty department.

3 Treat your child for shock (*see page 293*) while you are waiting for the ambulance or being driven to hospital.

If your child is unconscious

When you have broken the electrical contact, check your child's breathing and begin resuscitation if necessary (see *Dealing with unconsciousness, page 290*). If your child is unconscious, but breathing, turn him into the recovery position to keep his airway open (*see page 285*) and treat any burns or other injuries.

Dealing with poisoning

If your child has eaten something poison-ous, or something that you think may be poisonous, find the container if there is one and read the list of ingredients. Ring your local poison centre, your doctor or the nearest casualty department imme-diately and tell them what you think your child has swallowed. They will probably be able to tell you whether the substance is poisonous and what you can do while waiting for the ambulance or being driven to hospital.

Possible symptoms

● Vomiting and diarrhoea.
● Burns around his mouth if he has taken a corrosive poison.
● Convulsions for no apparent reason.
● Empty or open container known to have held a poison or medicine lying near your child.
● Poisonous plant or berries in his hand or near him if he is unconscious.

What should I do?

1 Quickly ask him to tell you, or point to, what he has taken because he may lose consciousness.

2 Keep a sample of what you think your child has taken, for example a few leaves or berries, or the empty bottle or can. If he has eaten some pills, keep the container even if it is empty because it will help the doctor decide what treatment to give him.

3 If your child has taken some form of corrosive poison such as bleach, caustic soda or weed-killer, NEVER try to make him sick. Anything that burns the gullet going down will burn the gullet again coming up. Give your child sips of cold water or milk to drink to cool the burns and get him to hospital as soon as possible.

4 If you are absolutely positive that your child has NOT TAKEN A CORROSIVE POISON, you can try to make him sick by tickling the back of his throat with your finger or by giving him one spoonful of syrup of ipecac or a glass of salty water. However, do not make him sick if he is unconscious, having a fit or is very confused.

If your child is unconscious

Call an ambulance immediately or get another adult to drive you to the nearest hospital casualty department while you give first aid in the back of the car.

1 Place your child in the recovery position and treat him as described in Dealing with uncon-sciousness (*see page 290*).

2 Keep checking breathing and watching for any change in his level of consciousness.

3 If it becomes necessary to give your child mouth-to-mouth venti-lation (*see page 286*), take great care not to get any of the poison on your mouth. Try to wash the poison off his face before you start and, if necessary, push your child's lips together and breathe into his nose.

Dealing with hypothermia

Hypothermia is a dangerous condition that can develop if your child's body temperature drops below 35°C (95°F). It is potentially fatal because the functions of the vital organs such as the heart, liver, lungs and intestines will slow down and eventually stop.

The symptoms are not always easy to see so you have to be on the lookout. It is worth keeping a low-reading thermometer so that you can check for low body temperature. Remember, a child's body can lose heat just as quickly through wet clothing as through being in water if the surrounding temperature is very low.

3 An older child can be put in a bath of water that feels warm to the inside of your wrist or your elbow.

4 If your child is conscious, give warm, NOT HOT, sweet drinks.

5 Take your child's temperature every half hour or feel the temperature of his skin. Continue these warming procedures until the doctor arrives or you are sure your child's body temperature is back to normal.

6 If your child's temperature does not begin to rise, get him to a hospital casualty department by ambulance or by car as soon as possible.

Possible symptoms

- Severe shivering.
- Very cold skin, particularly areas that are usually warm.
- Skin may look pale, even blue.
- Drowsiness and loss of strength.
- Slurred speech.
- Confusion.
- Temperature below 35°C (95°F).

IMPORTANT
You must warm your child *gradually.* ***Never*** **use a hot-water bottle or an electric blanket because it will take blood away from the body core to the surface so that more heat will be lost and this can result in shock (***see page 293***).**

What should I do?

1 If your child is out of doors, put something dry on top of his wet clothes and carry him to the nearest shelter or into the house.

2 Remove his wet clothing as soon as he is in a warm room and put on some dry clothes. Wrap him in a blanket alongside someone else. Call your doctor immediately.

Hypothermia in babies

Very young babies lose heat relatively easily when sleeping in a room that is not warm enough or if outside without adequate clothing when it is cold.

Possible symptoms
- Cold skin—don't be misled into thinking your baby's alright if his skin looks bright pink and healthy.
- Drowsiness and floppiness—these are danger signs.

What should I do?
Call your doctor immediately. While you are waiting, get into bed or a sleeping bag with your baby to rewarm him gradually with your body heat.

Bandaging techniques

Try to get your child to help because it will take his mind off his injury. When applying a roller bandage to secure a dressing or support a muscle or joint injury, always start below the injury and work up the limb because the bandage will lie flatter and therefore provide more support (*see overleaf*). Always leave your child's fingertips or toes exposed so that you can check the circulation in the affected area after applying the bandage.

Checking circulation

1 Press one of the exposed fingernails until it turns white, then release the pressure. The nail should become pink again immediately.

2 If colour does not return quickly, or the fingers look blue or feel cold, remove the bandage immediately and start again.

SLINGS

These are used to support an injured arm or the arm on the injured side if your child has a chest injury. Use a triangular bandage as described below. If you do not have one in your first aid kit, you can use a piece of material or a scarf about 1m (1yd) square, folded in half diagonally.

Applying a sling

1 Sit your child down and place his arm across his chest so that his wrist is slightly higher than his elbow.

2 Fold the long edge (base) of a triangular bandage up to make a hem and slide the bandage up through the gap between your child's elbow and his chest. Keep the base parallel to his side and carry the top end over his shoulder and round to the front on the injured side.

3 Still supporting your child's arm, carry the lower end of the bandage up and over his arm and tie the ends together in the hollow above his collar bone using a reef knot.

4 Fold the corner of the bandage at the elbow back and bring the point forward; pin it to the front of the sling.

5 Check the circulation in your child's fingers and, if necessary, adjust or reapply the sling.

Bandaging techniques

LEG/ARM BANDAGES

1 Unroll the bandage slightly and hold it so that the rolled part is upper-most. Working from the inside of the leg or arm outwards, place the end of the bandage on the limb below the injury and make a straight turn around the limb to secure the end of the bandage.

2 Then work up the limb, making spiral turns so that each layer covers about two-thirds of the previous turn. Finish off with a straight turn and secure the end with a safety pin.

3 If you have not got a safety pin, leave about 15cm (6in) hanging free —enough to wind once around the limb. Cut down the centre of the piece of bandage and tie a knot at the bottom of the split. Wrap the ends around the limb and tie off on the other side.

ANKLE/HAND BANDAGES

1 Raise and support your child's foot. Unroll a few centimetres of the bandage. Holding the rolled part, roll uppermost, in one hand, and working from the inside of his leg outwards, make one straight turn around his ankle.

2 Take the bandage diagonally across your child's foot to his big toe, round under the ball of his foot and up at the base of his little toe. Make two straight turns around the ball of the foot.

3 Take the bandage up and across his foot to his ankle, round the ankle and diagonally across his foot to the toes. Continue these figure-of-eight turns so that each layer covers two-thirds of the previous layer until his foot is covered.

4 Finish off with one straight turn around the ankle and secure the bandage with a safety pin or tie the ends, *as left.*

5 To bandage a hand, support the affected hand injured side upper-most and bandage as above.

Personal records

Growth charts

Your child will grow and put on weight at his own rate, so while it is interesting to plot his development, do not become obsessive or anxious about it. It is only in the first few months of a baby's life that weight gain should be watched closely, and it will be monitored at your clinic. After this stage, it is regularity of weight gain which is most important.

To use the chart, first weigh your baby. Then go along the bottom axis until you find his age. Look up the vertical axis until you reach your baby's weight. The point where the two axes meet will give you an idea of your baby's progress in comparison to an average figure.

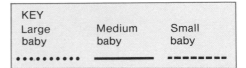

KEY		
Large baby	Medium baby	Small baby
●●●●●●●●●●	——————	– – – – –

Immunization

The aim of immunization is to protect both individuals and communities from infectious diseases. Every parent should therefore take steps to have their child properly immunized. Even if a disease has been eradicated, it is still necessary to continue immunizing against it to prevent its re-emergence.

Immunization works by preparing the body to repel infection. The body usually has to have an infection once before its defences are capable of responding against it. Immunization does this for us—by means of injection, drops in the mouth or scratching of the skin. The substance introduced into the body is called a vaccine, and the method for doing so is known as vaccination or inoculation.

Most vaccination programmes start at about four months, and you should receive a card asking you to attend your doctor's practice or clinic. Remember to keep a record of dates and types of vaccination (see page 308), along with a record of your family's medical history. This is necessary to help your doctor determine whether or not your child should have a particular vaccination. For instance, children with a family history of tuberculosis may well be advised to have a BCG injection in the first year of life. Similarly, children who suffer from convulsions, who have a family history of epilepsy, or who have a long standing heart or lung disease may be advised not to have a measles or whooping cough vaccination. Always ask your doctor's advice.

It is quite common for a small red bump to develop at the site of an inoculation. If, however, your child becomes irritable or develops a fever, or if you notice the development of a high-pitched scream, and certainly if your baby has a convulsion, get in touch with your doctor.

The chart (below) outlines the commonly recommended immunizations of childhood. The guide to infectious fevers (see page 306) lists the symptoms and treatment for some of the most common childhood illnesses; it also lists preventive measures, where applicable. If you think your child has contracted an infectious fever, always contact your doctor to confirm the diagnosis.

Disease	Time	Reaction	Protection
Diphtheria, whooping cough (pertussis), tetanus Also known as DTP or triple vaccine	Injections at 3, 5-6 and 9-11 months; repeat diphtheria and tetanus at 5 years	Child may become feverish; the site of the injection may be sore	Tetanus must be repeated every five years to provide continuing protection
Polio	Oral vaccine at 3, 5-6 and 9-11 months, repeat at 5 and 16-18 years	None	Has to be repeated to provide continuing protection
Measles	Injection at 14 or 15 months	Child may become feverish and have a slight rash	Not known how long protection from vaccination lasts
German measles (Rubella)	Injection for girls between 10 and 14 years	Child may complain of sore joints	Not known how long protection from vaccination lasts
Tuberculosis (BCG)	Injection at 13 years, if protection needed	The site of the injection may be sore and stiff	Lifelong

Infectious fevers chart

Disease	Incubation Period	Symptoms
Chickenpox (see page 82)	7-21 days	Groups of spots that quickly develop into intensely itchy blisters. These appear in crops every three or four days, usually starting on the trunk, then spreading to the face, arms and legs. The spots are usually accompanied by headache and fever.
German measles (see page 141)	14-21 days	Slightly raised temperature, a rash of tiny pink or red spots which starts behind the ears, spreads to the forehead and then to the rest of the body, and enlarged glands at the back of the neck.
Measles (see page 176)	8-14 days	The first signs are a runny nose, dry cough, headache, fever with a temperature as high as 40°C (104°F), white spots inside the mouth and on the linings of the cheeks (Koplik's spots); also, the eyes may be red and sore. These symptoms are then followed by a brownish-red rash, which starts behind the ears and spreads to the face and torso.
Mumps (see page 182)	17-28 days	Swelling and soreness of the glands at the sides of the face, just below the ears and beneath the chin, painful swallowing, dry mouth, fever and a headache. In boys, the testes may be swollen and painful; girls may experience lower abdominal pains.
Roseola infantum (see page 209)	7-14 days	A fever with a temperature of 39-40°C (102.2-104°F) for three days, with no other symptoms. As the fever subsides, a rash of separate, flat, red or pink spots appears, first on the trunk, then spreading to the limbs and neck.
Scarlet fever (see page 211)	1-5 days	Sore throat, inflamed tonsils, fever with a temperature as high as 40°C (104°F), vomiting, abdominal pains, rash of small spots starting on the chest and neck, then merging over the body, except the area around the mouth, and strawberry-red patches on a furry tongue.
Whooping cough (see page 259)	5-14 days	Slight temperature, runny nose, slight cough, which develops into a compulsive cough accompanied by whooping breath.

Treatment	Complications	Immunity	Prevention
Relieve itching with calamine lotion. If your child develops a fever, reduce it by tepid sponging (see page 31), then by paracetamol elixir.	In rare cases, chickenpox may cause encephalitis (see page 125) or be complicated by Reye's syndrome.	Lifelong	None
If the child's temperature rises above 38°C (100.4°F), give him paracetamol elixir.	None to your child, but fetal damage could occur in a pregnant woman who comes into contact with your contagious child.	Lifelong	Inoculation for girls between the ages of 10 and 14.
Try to reduce your child's temperature with tepid sponging (see page 31), then by paracetamol elixir. Prophylactic antibiotics.	In rare cases, otitis media (see page 196), pneumonia (see page 200), and encephalitis (see page 125).	Lifelong	Inoculation at about 14 or 15 months.
Try to reduce your child's temperature with tepid sponging (see page 31), then by paracetamol elixir. Liquidize food if eating is painful and give your child plenty to drink.	In rare cases, encephalitis (see page 125) and meningitis (see page 177).	Usually lifelong	None
Try to reduce your child's temperature with tepid sponging (see page 31), then by paracetamol elixir.	Possible febrile convulsions.	Usually lifelong	None
Try to reduce your child's temperature with tepid sponging (see page 31), then by paracetamol elixir.	Rare, though scarlet fever can cause inflammation of the kidneys (nephritis, see page 187) or of the joints and heart (rheumatic fever, see page 207).	Lifelong	None
Antibiotics, which must be given early to be effective.	Very rare nowadays, although there's a possibility of bronchitis (see page 73) or pneumonia (see page 200).	Lifelong	Inoculation at 3, 5-6 and 9-11 months.

Records

The charts, below, are designed to help you keep track of any events concerning your family's health. It is important to keep records to ensure that you stay up to date with immunizations, and to provide reliable information in the future.

Birth record

	First baby	Second baby
Baby's name		
Date of birth		
Time of birth		
Place of birth		
Height		
Weight		
Blood group		
Problems during pregnancy		
Type of delivery		
Problems with delivery		
Postnatal problems		

Family medical history

Mother's birth date

Illnesses

Father's birth date

Illnesses

Family allergies and chronic conditions

Records

Illness, injury and allergy record
First child

Illnesses	Injuries	Allergies

Second child

Illnesses	Injuries	Allergies

Immunization record

	First child Date/Age	Second child Date/Age
Diphtheria, whooping cough, tetanus		
Diphtheria, tetanus boosters		
Polio		
Polio boosters		
Measles		
German measles		
Tuberculosis		

Telephone numbers

Doctor/Paediatrician	Dentist
Health centre	Late night chemist
Health visitor	Family planning clinic
Local hospital	Police

Glossary

Words in **_bold italic_** denote glossary entries.

Abscess
A localized collection of **_pus_** that gathers as part of the body's way of fighting an **_infection._**

Acute
A term applied to short attacks of a disease or pain.

Allergen
A substance—often as common as house dust, grass pollen, animal fur, or a particular food—which is harmless to most people, but which provokes an allergic reaction in certain individuals. Such substances are also called antigens.

Allergy
Abnormal reaction of the body to substances called **_allergens._** These are harmless to most people, but certain individuals develop a sensitivity to them. **_Antibodies_**, usually produced by the body's defence system to fight infection, react to the allergen causing the allergy, resulting in a variety of symptoms.

Anaemia
A type of blood disorder in which the oxygen-carrying power, or the number of, mature, healthy cells of the blood is diminished. Lack of **_haemoglobin_**, the oxygen-carrying agent in the blood, brings about a shortage of oxygen in the body's tissue. Characteristic symptoms of anaemia are pale skin, especially at the tips of the fingers, on the lips and tongue and around the eyes.

Anaesthetic
A drug used to bring about temporary loss of sensation and hence remove pain. General anaesthetics induce unconsciousness and are usually administered by anaesthetists, either in the form of injection or through inhalation. Local anaesthetics are usually given as injections and remove sensation from only a limited area.

Analgesic
A pain-relieving drug. The one most frequently given to children is paracetamol. It is available as a syrup, or elixir, for very young children. Junior aspirin has been withdrawn from the market because of serious side-effects, and no form of aspirin should ever be given to a child under 12 except under strict medical supervision.

Anaphylaxis
A very severe, general allergic reaction (see **_allergy_**). Symptoms can range from attacks of asthma and flushing, to collapse and unconsciousness. Where there is severe allergic reaction, caused by a sting for instance, shock may develop. This is known as anaphylactic shock.

Antenatal
Literally, before birth; refers to a condition or event during pregnancy.

Antibiotic
A drug used to fight bacterial infection. A prescribed course of antibiotics should always be completed, even if the illness is cured; future treatment with the drug may face greater bacterial resistance if the course is not finished.

Antibodies
Agents of the body's defence system, produced by white blood cells in order to combat an **_infection_** or foreign agent such as grass pollen (see **_allergy_**).

Anticoagulant
A drug used to stop the blood clotting.

Anticonvulsant
A drug used to prevent or end convulsions, often in the treatment of epilepsy. Sudden withdrawal from the drug may itself precipitate a convulsion.

Antifungal
A drug used to treat fungal infections, such as those that affect hair, skin, nails or mucous membranes.

Antigen see **_Allergen_**

Antihistamine
A drug used to counter the effect of a **_histamine,_** a chemical produced by the body as a result of an inflammatory and allergic reaction (see **_allergy_**).

Antiserum
A **_serum_** prepared from the blood of a person (or animal) whose defence system has been stimulated to fight an infecting agent or foreign protein, such as snake venom. When given, the antiserum protects against the infecting agent or foreign protein through the **_antibodies_** contained within it.

Antitoxin
A substance, produced by the body or injected into it, that nullifies the effects of a **_toxin_**, a poisonous substance produced by **_bacteria_** and some plants and animals.

Glossary

Autoimmune
The word given to a defect in the body's defence system against disease. This defect causes the body to manufacture *antibodies*, normally produced to combat infection, which attack and harm the body's own healthy tissue.

Bacteria
A group of organisms, some of which are harmless and some only harmful when they multiply too quickly. Certain bacterial infections can be controlled by *antibiotics*.

Benign
The term used to describe unnatural growth that is, nevertheless, harmless to surrounding tissue and which will not return once removed.

Biopsy
The process by which a small piece of body tissue is removed for analysis. It is often used to determine if an unnatural growth is *malignant* (cancerous) or *benign* (harmless).

Bolus
Ball of chewed food, as it passes from the mouth to the stomach.

Bronchodilator
A drug which widens bronchial passages, and is used in the treatment of asthma. The drug is taken either by nasal inhalation, or orally through a spray.

Carcinogen
A substance that causes or promotes cancer.

Cauterization
The process by which tissue is destroyed, using either a red-hot instrument or a chemical. Warts and other skin growths are often treated in this way.

Cerebral
Relating to the structure and workings of the brain.

Chromosomes
Microscopic strands which are present within the nucleus of every cell. They carry the genetic information needed to determine the characteristics of an individual. There are normally 46 chromosomes in each cell. Abnormal numbers or formations of chromosomes are found in sufferers of certain diseases, such as Down's syndrome.

Chronic
A term describing a condition that has lasted, or is expected to last, for some time, while not necessarily being life-threatening. Chronic conditions tend to get better or deteriorate slowly.

Cilia
Minute hairs lining the surface of mucous membranes, for example, in the nose. Their waving movement serves a cleaning purpose, clearing dust particles, mucus, and *bacteria*.

Congenital
A term applied to a disease or condition present at birth.

Cyanosis
A blueness of the skin, caused by lack of oxygen.

Cyst
An abnormal fluid-filled swelling.

Dermatologist
A doctor who specializes in treating diseases of the skin.

Dialysis
A treatment for kidney failure. Waste products, usually excreted by the kidney, are removed either by cleansing the blood on a dialysis machine (haemodialysis), or by cleaning the peritoneal cavity (peritoneal dialysis) in the abdomen.

Diuretic
Any substance that increases water excretion and therefore urine production, thus lowering the body's fluid content.

Drip
The common name for an intravenous infusion (see *intravenous*). Liquid substance, whether blood, saline or *plasma*, is passed from an elevated sterile container through a vein and into the body. The rate of flow is controlled by the rate of dripping through a transparent container.

Dys-
A prefix meaning difficult, painful and/or abnormal. For example, dyslexia (difficulty in learning to read or spell).

Electroencephalogram (EEG)
A recording of the electrical impulses of the brain, using a painless process called electroencephalography. It involves placing metal plates on the head which record the impulses graphically.

Embolism
The sudden blockage of a blood vessel, caused by a blood clot or other foreign solid (known as an embolus).

Endocrinologist
A doctor who specializes in

Glossary

the study of *hormones* and the diseases caused by their disorders.

Endoscope
An instrument enabling a doctor to look into a body cavity, usually the oesophagus, stomach or duodenum. Photographs and tissue samples can also be taken, and some small growths removed, with an endoscope.

Endoscopy
The procedure in which an *endoscope* is used.

Enema
Liquid injected into the rectum, usually to produce a bowel movement or for diagnostic purposes; also the name for this process. The technique is sometimes used to give an *anaesthetic* to a baby or small child, or to give drugs to a child who is vomiting, because the walls of the bowel are so absorbent. An enema should be given only on doctor's orders.

Excretion
The removal of the body's internal waste matter by natural processes, such as urination, sweating and exhalation.

Febrile
Characterized by fever and a high temperature, as in a febrile convulsion.

Follicle
Most commonly, a tiny cavity on the body's surface.

Gammaglobulin
A type of blood protein that includes *antibodies*. Obtained from donated

blood, gammaglobulin can be used in the prevention of infections such as hepatitis.

Haematologist
A doctor who specializes in the treatment of diseases of the blood, bone marrow, and lymph glands.

Haematoma
A collection of blood under the skin or deep in the tissues.

Haematuria
Blood in the urine, either visible to the naked eye or under a microscope.

Haemoglobin
The oxygen-carrying agent in the blood. It is present only in red blood cells, giving the blood its colour.

Haemorrhage
Bleeding, either externally (from the skin or an orifice) or internally (within a body cavity).

Heaf test
A method of determining tuberculosis *immunity*, using an extract of TB *bacteria*. The extract is applied through a series of light punctures of the skin on the forearm, in the shape of a ring. If the ring becomes a single red patch in about three days, the subject of the test is immune.

Histamine
A chemical released into the body when an allergic or inflammatory reaction takes place (see *allergy*); the most common results are redness, swelling and itching.

Hormone
A chemical released by special (endrocrine) glands

into the bloodstream. It regulates the activities of certain body organs and tissues.

Hyper-
A prefix meaning "high" or "above" an expected norm. For example, hyperactive (active above the expected norm).

Immuno system
The body's own defence system against disease, enabling it to recognize and destroy invading *microbes* (minute *bacteria*, viruses or fungi invisible to the naked eye) or foreign tissues, through the white blood cells' production of *antibodies.*

Immunity
Resistance to a disease, developed either by the body's *immune system* when an infection is contracted, or through purposeful intervention, as in vaccination.

Immunization
The process by which the body is prepared, by inoculation, to repel infection.

Incubation period
The interval (usually measured in days) between the time a disease is caught—when the germs enter the body—and when symptoms begin to appear.

Infection
A type of illness caused by *microbes*—minute *bacteria*, viruses or fungi invisible to the naked eye—invading the body and multiplying within it.The microbes may clog up blood vessels and ducts, and also produce harmful waste products.

Glossary

Inflammation
A painful, red swelling which is warm to the touch. Inflammation is the body tissue's reaction to a variety of injuries (physical blows, infection, autoimmune disease).

Inoculation
The introduction of a *vaccine* into the body.

Intravenous
Within, or inserted into, a vein.

Laxative
A type of drug used to ease and increase the frequency of bowel movements. Laxatives should be given to a child only on doctor's orders.

Lumbar puncture
The procedure for taking a sample of fluid from the base of the spine by inserting a needle. This is done under local anaesthetic. The fluid is analyzed in order to diagnose certain diseases, particularly those affecting the nervous system, such as meningitis.

Lymph
A colourless liquid which contains white blood cells. Lymph flows in channels, taking nutrients to, and removing waste products from, local cells. The white blood cells in lymph are an important part of the body's defence system against infection.

Malignant
A term applied to a cancerous growth which is likely to spread, and recur, even after removal. A malignant growth is sometimes impossible to eradicate totally.

Membrane
A thin lining or covering tissue of various organs and cavities of the body.

Meninges
The three layers of *membrane* protecting the brain and spinal cord. Meningitis is an inflammation of the meninges.

Metabolism
The body's physical and chemical reactions. Any series of, or single, reactions may be described as metabolic.

Microbes
Minute *bacteria*, viruses or fungi invisible to the naked eye.

Mucous membrane
A *membrane* lining a part of the body, such as the mouth or vagina, which secretes a watery or slimy material.

Neuro-
Pertaining to the body's nervous system. For example, a neurosurgeon specializes in surgery of the nervous system.

Neurologist
A doctor who specializes in treating diseases of the brain and those related to the nervous system. Neurologists often work closely with neurosurgeons, who specialize in surgery of the nervous system, principally the brain and spinal cord.

Obstetrician
A doctor who specializes in looking after women during pregnancy and immediately after childbirth.

Oedema
A swelling of the body tissue caused by excess fluid content. The condition most commonly affects the ankles.

Ophthalmologist
A doctor who specializes in treating eye injury or disease. An optician, who may or may not be a doctor, detects eye defects and supplies corrective lenses, but does not treat injury or disease.

Ophthalmoscope
An instrument for examining the tissues of the interior of the eye, by shining a light through the pupil.

Orthodontist
A dentist who specializes in treating teeth abnormalities and jaw disorders.

Orthopaedics
The process of curing deformities arising from disease of, or injury to, bones and joints.

Otoscope
An instrument for examining the middle and inner ear, viewed through the semi-transparent eardrum, in order to diagnose disease.

Paediatrician
A doctor who specializes in treating children, usually until the age of puberty.

Paracetamol see *Analgesic*

Penicillin
The first *antibiotic* to be discovered, used in the treatment of many infections, including tonsillitis and otitis media. Penicillin may, however, provoke an allergic reaction (see *allergy*) such as asthma or a rash. If your child is allergic, ensure this is entered on his medical records and that he wears a

Glossary

medic-alert bracelet so that he isn't given the drug.

Physiotherapist
A person trained to give treatment through the use of physical exercise and manipulation. Physiotherapy is often used to help children suffering from arthritis, cerebral palsy, muscular dystrophy, and other neuro-muscular diseases.

Plasma
The liquid (as opposed to cellular) part of the blood, which can be used as replacement fluid in the treatment of shock and burns.

Possetting
In babies, the harmless habit of regurgitating milk soon after, or during, a feed.

Postnatal
Literally, after birth; refers to the health of the baby and its mother in the first weeks after birth.

Prophylactic
A substance or procedure that helps to prevent disease (immunization, for example).

Psychiatrist
A medically qualified specialist in mental illness.

Psychologist
A non-medically qualified person trained to assess behavioural problems, measure intelligence quotients (IQ) and develop-ment quotients (DQ).

Pus
A yellow/greenish semi-liquid substance, made up of decomposed tissue, *bacteria* and dead white blood cells; it is a sign of the body's fight against *infection*.

Sebum
An oily substance that is produced by the sebaceous glands just below the skin's surface. Sebum is the body's own skin moistener, spread-ing over the skin from the pores. Acne can be caused through a build-up of sebum under the skin's surface.

Secretion
The body's production of substances from special glands or cells. For instance, *sebum*.

Serum
The clear, liquid content of the blood when separated from other blood components, such as clotting substances, which are found in *plasma*. The term is sometimes used loosely as a synonym for *antiserum*.

Spasm
An involuntary and uncon-trollable contraction of one or more muscles.

Stools
The waste matter left over from food, expelled from the rectum.

Tinnitus
An intermittent or continuous ringing, buzzing or roaring sound in the ear, heard only by the sufferer.

Toxin
A poisonous substance pro-duced by *bacteria*, other *microbes*, and some plants and animals.

Tracheotomy
A surgical procedure to restore normal breathing when the throat or larynx is blocked. An incision is made in the neck and a tube inserted below the blockage.

Traction
Means "pulling apart" and is used as a treatment for broken bones, crushed vertebrae, and prolapsed discs. Damaged and com-pressed parts of the body are held apart and in the correct position (often for some time) until healed.

Tumour
A swelling; usually denotes one caused by abnormal cell-multiplication within the body.

Ulcer
An open sore affecting either an internal or external body surface.

Vaccination see *Immunization*

Vaccine
A solution made up of an altered, weakened or killed strain of a disease. Usually injected, a vaccine is designed to stimulate the body's resistance to the disease that has been introduced into it.

Vasoconstrictor
Any substance, whether a chemical produced by the body, or a drug, which causes blood vessels to narrow.

Vasodilator
Any substance, whether a chemical produced by the body, or a drug, which causes blood vessels to widen.

Virus
The smallest type of *microbe*, which invades the body's cells and multiplies inside them, giving rise to con-tagious viral infections such as influenza.

Index

Page numbers in *italic* refer to the illustrations and captions; * denotes a main reference

Index

Index

Index

Index

Index

throat, *20*
  examining, *55*
  foreign bodies in, 97,
    100, 284
  sore, 55, 73, 90, 114,
    142, 166, 215, 220*,
    241
  see also windpipe
thrush, 170, 180, 185-6,
  197, 238-9*
thyroid gland, *19*
tics, 97, 150, 240*
tinnitus, 316
toenails, ingrowing, 168*,
  175
tongue, 20, *20*
tonsillitis, *18*, 55, 97,
  114, 121, 133, 144, 172,
  187, 207, 211, 220, 241-2*
tonsils, 241
toothache, 121, 155
toothpaste, fluoride, 243,
  244
toxocariasis, 245*
travel sickness, 55, 246*,
  255, 256
tuberculosis, 213, 247-8*

U-V
ulcers,
  mouth, 87, 180-1*, *180-1*
umbilical cord, infection,
  249*
umbilical hernia, 161, *161*
unconsciousness, 153, 283-
  91*
urinary tract, 22*, *22*
  infections, 55, 63, 250*
urticaria, 162, *162*
vaccination, *see*
  immunization
vagina, *22*
  foreign bodies in, 251*
verrucae, 252*, 257
  infections, 90, 95
vision problems, 253-4*
  squints, 224*
vomiting, 36, 255-6*
  dehydration, 38, 108,
    112
  food poisoning, 136-7
  gastroenteritis, 139-40
  head injuries, 153
  migraine, 178
  projectile, 203

Reye's syndrome, 206
scarlet fever, 211
travel sickness, 246
when to call doctor, 25
whooping cough, 259-60

W
warts, 257*, *257*
  verrucae, 252*, 257
wasp stings, 227-8
wax, in ears, 195, 258*
weight, obesity, 191-2*
white blood cells, 18, 173
whooping cough, 97, 125,
  200, 259-60*
windpipe, 19, 20
  clearing the airway, 284*
  croup, 100*
  opening the airway, 283*
  see also throat
worms, 170, 245, 251,
  261-2*
wounds
  bleeding, 292*
  cuts and grazes, 103-4*
  foreign bodies in, 292

Acknowledgments
Dorling Kindersley would like to thank: Neville Graham for his skill in bringing both the design and project to a successful conclusion; Rachel Bateson, Jamie MacIntyre Buckingham, Thomas Brown, Isobel Bulat, Sophie Civardi, Aaron and Reuben Fleming, Nellie Frizzell, Nancy and Thomas Graham, Eliza Greig, Josh and Jake Jones, David Louden, JayJay Parkinson, Jack Thomson, (and all their parents) for help with referencing; Kathie Gill for proof-reading; Richard and Hilary Bird for indexing; Professor Iain MacIntyre and Dr Richard Coombs for medical advice; Donald Berwick, Steve Parker and James Allen for editorial

help; Julia Harris and Brian Swan for design help; Brian Retter and Chris Cope, and, finally, all the staff at Modern Text for their hard work and sense of humour.

Consultant paediatrician
Andrew Whitelaw MD MRCP

Author's acknowledgment
I am indebted once more to my editor, Charyn Jones, for her tolerance, clearness of vision and the inevitable improvement she makes to my work.

Illustrators
David Ashby
Karen Cochrane
Nicholas Hall
Andrew Popkiewicz
James Robins
Paul Saunders
Sue Smith
Photographers
Paul Fletcher Front jacket,
13, 15, 17, 18, 19
Nancy Durrell McKenna 6
Jennie Woodcock 23, 24, 27,
33, 37, 39
Tim Woodcock 265 (from
You and Your Baby)
Anthea Sieveking/Vision
International 2, 11, 49, 263,
281, 303
Typesetting
Modern Text Typesetting
Reproduction
Repro Color Llovet S.A.,
Barcelona